HEALTH
AND THE SUPERNATURAL
Disease and Cure in Tribal Societies

Important Books of Similar Interest Published Recently

Encyclopaedia of Tribal Religion,
in 12 Volumes
Edited by Dr. Subhadra Channa

International Encyclopaedia of Anthropology,
in 12 Volumes
Edited by Dr. Subhadra Channa

Landmarks in Indian Anthropology,
in 74 Volumes
Edited and Written by Several World Authrities

Encyclopaedia of Sociology of Religion,
in 3 Volumes
Edited by V.G.Nayar and M.G.Nayar

Encyclopaedia of Sociology of Politics,
in 3 Volumes
Edited by R.Motwani and R.D.Saksena

THE BUDDHISTS.
Encyclopaedia of Buddhism, in 5 Volumes
Edited by Subodh Kapoor

THE HINDUS.
Encyclopaedia of Hinduism, in 5 Volumes
Edited by Subodh Kapoor

Encyclopaedia of Ethics and Logic, in 10 Volumes
Edited by Piet and Prasad

HEALTH AND THE SUPERNATURAL

Disease and Cure in Tribal Societies

Edited by

DR. SUBHADRA CHANNA
President, Indian Anthropological Association

COSMO PUBLICATIONS
2002 INDIA

HEALTH AND THE SUPERNATURAL.
DISEASE AND CURE IN TRIBAL SOCIETIES

First Published 2002

ISBN 81-7755-195-7

Published by
MRS. RANI KAPOOR
for COSMO PUBLICATIONS Div. of
GENESIS PUBLISHING PVT. LTD.
24-B, Ansari Road, Darya Ganj,
New Delhi-110 002, INDIA

Composed at
Cosmo Publications

Printed at
Mehra Offset Press

Contents

Chapter-1

THE SPIRIT THEORY IN EARLY MEDICINE[1]

By John Lee Maddox

Chapter-1

QUICK to agree with Tennyson's hero that we "are heir of all the ages,"we "announce with confidence" or "point with pride" that in the twentieth century civilization has reached an enviable peak. How far this is from being universally true is apparent when we observe the medical practices of gullible and superstitious people, who in their search for a catholicon have not yet learned with Sir Thomas Browne that death alone is the cure of all diseases.Yet we need not look to the tropics or to the antipodes to find proofs of man's eagerness to be deceived. Radios and twelve-cylinder racers are no guarantee against over-credulity; superstition may go clad in plus-fours or opera hats in sables or glove silk. Neither Russia nor China is altogether unenlightened according to modern standards—witness the alacrity with which Oriental and Muscovite have adopted with dim perception of consequences, Western garb, machinery, political methods—yet in those countries people are still occasionally beaten to death or buried alive at the instigation of local spirit doctors. In Harlem, in the heart of New York city there are today according to credible authority, more than a score of voodoo doctors or negro shamans, reaping enormous yearly harvests from the purses of their infatuated brethren. A writer in central Pennsylvania, lamenting the benighted condition of that region, observes that:

> we consult "Powwow doctors"; we are "hexed"by those who have a grudge against us; we decorate our barns with odd designs to ward off the "evil eye"; we pass a baby three times around the leg of a table to cure the "liver groans!"

And in a circular, distributed from Atlantic City, a Brooklyn "doctor"announces, for cash or credit, with prices ranging from $15 to $1000, "Spells of all kinds broken or released. Love apples in all forms. Black Cat's Ankle Dust, and all kinds of highly appreciated roots and herbs."

All of which, not to multiply illustrations, may appear shocking and inexcusable to those of us who forget how slightly we are removed from the atavistic,how strong the primal ties between the aborigine and the elite. Yet it should not be difficult for us to trace back to the despised and ignorant medicine-man a far-reaching indebtedness. From the practices of the sometimes barbarous, sometimes ridiculous shaman have derived various of our most scientific and effective methods of treating disease; to say nothing of numerous and not altogether shadowy resemblances between religious ideas and civic institutions which heathen blindness and Christian progressiveness often possess in common.

The when of the primitive doctor's evolution is not ascertainable, the why is reasonably obvious. One day, in the Philippine islands, I observed several Visayan natives engaged in smearing something over the doors and windows of a hut. In the air hung the familiar but unpleasant odor of garlic. Wondering, I asked what was the idea. A spokesman replied that a child had just been born in the house which was being fumigated with garlic in order to keep out the asuangs-pernicious little sprites particularly fond of new-born children. When the malicious spirits smell the garlic, they take flight, for like some on us they cannot abide the pervasive and characteristic odor of the melting-pot.

Asuangs are not, of course, the only spirits supposed to work mischief. According to primitive notations there are ghosts, demons, spirits everywhere. The very air is filled with them. If a man falls ill, spirits are responsible. If he loses his knife, hatchet, head-ax, or spear, a spirit took it away. It he accidentally trips over a stone, a spirit placed it in his path. Why, we ask, should primitive peoples live a world so filled with baleful creatures? It is a not pleasant world in which to live. The answer is simple: evil spirits, according to the crude notions of the savage, are directly responsible for the presence of bad luck, sickness, disease, and death. In his crude gropings after a philosophy to explain his woes, the primitive man, passing over indifference and agnosticism, settles upon a third alternative, faith: there must be something in which to believe, so he manufactures for himself an unseen foe responsible for the falling tress which main his friends, for the beasts which devour them, and for the abysmal wickedness of human enemies.

Dreams are the storehouses from which the primitive man draws his illusory spirits. In dreams he sees once more his imperious and implacable ancestors, and concludes,therefore, that they must be alive; even though, waking, he remembers that he himself had helped to dispose of their bodies. He dreams of dead enemies, and in the morning imagines that he is surrounded by their ghosts. During their earthly existence, these ancestors had maltreated him and these enemies had worked against him. Since death has made them invisible and carried them beyond his reach, he thinks their power has been increased, and naturally he ascribes his woes to their ghosts and spirits. Sickness, especially, he finds hard to explain. Who is responsible for it? As evil spirit, he concludes, has gained an entrance into his body and is tormenting it by way of compensation for earlier deeds. Thus, the Finns believe that the souls of the dead feast on the hearts and entrails of the living. Spirits do not spare even a near relative, for these shades, being something like human, must eat and drink.[2] The Zulu of Africa offer the sacrifice of an ox to the dead ancestor whom a sick man dreams.[3] Australian tribes believe sickness is caused by a ghost eating the liver of the victim[4]. In Samoa illness and death are thought to be occasioned by the souls of the dead which have crept into the head and stomach of the living[5]. In cases of epilepsy, when the patient falls of the ground, foams at the mouth, his arms and legs torn by convulsions, the victim must be possessed by another spirit. Surely no man's own spirit would treat his body so.

Similarly, spirit activity is the cause of all bad luck, and death. When a savage falls ill, it is not of hostile germs or bacteria that he thinks. He calls in a doctor who knows how to deal with the malicious spirit responsible for his sickness and who, instead of administering ingredients to calm nerves and to kill germs, sets about soothing and banishing the possessing spirit.

The man who attends to the sick and demented is something more than a doctor. In the language of the North American

Indians he is called the Medicine Man, or the Mystery Man—for "medicine" is used by the aborigines of this country to describe anything sacred, mysterious, or of wonderful power or efficacy. Hence, the medicine-man is not only doctor, but diviner, rain-maker,soothsayer, prophet, priest, and sometimes chief or king as well. He is, in short, the great man of his tribe. Siting Bull, for example, the leader of the Custer massacre, was a medicine-man.

The medicine-man answers to many names, for he is called among various peoples, the shaman, the angakok, the voodoo-man, the obi-man, the conjuror, the magician, the wizard,and the sorcerer. But how does he rise to power? Sometimes he inherits the position from his father, but more often he has some unusual qualification that fits him especially for the post of mediator between the human and superhuman worlds.

A typical case was that of Enchong, whom I met while serving with my regiment in the Philippine islands, and who was one of the most famous "spit-doctors" of that archipelago. He told me, when I asked him, of how he became a doctor:

One day,as I was walking in the San-Mateo mountains, I became very tired. I lay down at the foot of a tree to rest and refresh myself. Sleep overtook me. I saw a wonderful being in my dream. This being had long, white whiskers, and made mysterious motions with his hands, arms, and legs. And, then, he talked with me. And this is what he said:

"Enchong, you are appointed chief doctor in these Islands. By virtue of this appointment you are empowered to heal all the sick that seek your aid. Spit upon them and you will receive their eternal gratitude."

When I returned to my barrio [native village] I told everybody about my dream, and soon the sick from far and near were coming to my door. I healed them all by rubbing them with my saliva.

Enchong, like quack doctors everywhere, was a great publicity seeker. His cures were notorious, and he was besieged by rich and poor alike for his miraculous saliva rubs. Civil authorities got word of his activities, however,declared him insane,and committed to an asylum. And that was the end of Enchong.

Other doctors' fame comes by different routes. A Pima Indian had only to recover from a rattlesnake bite upon the hand or near the heart, and he was elected chief wizard of the community[6]—rather a stiff entrance requirement, but then the position had its rewards. In Australia, again, a man was made a shaman as the reward of stupidly sitting upon the wrong end of the limb he was cutting from a tree, and climbing out unharmed when it fell to the ground.[7]

Spirits are responsible for the nomination and election of all medicine-men, and, naturally enough, insanity is an asset rather than a liability. The fact that an insane person is different from other people is proof positive that he has an indwelling spirit. Being, by virtue of his divinity, upon intimate terms with the gods, and possessing a knowledge of their nature and disposition, he is admirably equipped for devising ways and means of procuring celestial benefactions.

The thoroughfare of shamanic honors, of being initiated into the mysteries of the sacred calling and getting into the necessary inspired state is a hard road to travel. The medicine-man must often resort to sleeplessness, seclusion, and protracted brooding upon some morbid fancy in order to bring about hallucinations which prove his superior qualifications, both to himself and to his fellow-tribesmen. He is usually successful, for it is well known to medical science that the more frequently these diseased conditions of the mind are sought, the more readily they are found. The shaman tries repeatedly, until finally the nature he has tried so assiduously to induce by artificial means comes without seeking. He then, without effort, possesses hallucinations in all the garb of reality.

The horseplay initiation of college fraternities resembles somewhat the ordeal the shaman has to undergo when publicly inducted into office. Among the Dyak of Borneo the initiation ceremony is an elaborate process. The Menangs, or priests, lead the neophyte into a curtained apartment, while a medicine-man is posted on the outside to tell awestruck spectators what is taking place within. The officiating priests, the publicity man outside announces, cut open the young man's head and take out his brains, for, says he, the candidate's mind must be clean and clear to enable him to penetrate the mysteries of evil spirits and the intricacies of disease. After having carefully washed the brains, the operating priest surgeons replace them. The priests then inter gold dust into the eyes of the candidate in order to give him keenness and strength of sight that he may see the soul wherever it may wander. The Menangs then plant barbed hooks upon the neophyte's finger-tips, so that he may seize the soul and hold it fast, and, finally, they pierce his heart with arrow to make him tender-hearted. At last the new-fledged medicine-man emerges from the sanctuary looking fit and fine. We need hardly explain that all that was done to him behind the drawn curtains was a series of symbolic actions, representing the terrible things as they were described[8].

Initiation among the Tschi-speaking people of the west coast of Africa is a more serious matter. The candidate there must undergo a purity test. A circle, three feet in diameter, is formed by glowing embers, and the neophyte is made to step within its clear space. Rum, kerosene oil, and other inflammable liquids are thrown upon the embers, so that the flames leap high in the air, sometimes higher than a man's head. After an interval this process is repeated a second and a third time, and the ordeal is over. If the candidate survives all three trials without sustaining injury, he is thought to be pure—the gods have protected their favorite from the fire. If, however, the intense heat compels him to leap outside the circle, or if he receives a burn or other injury, he is believed to be impure. Only those candidates, whom the gods especially love, come through the fire unscathed, and, as a matter of course, become highly honored medicine-men[9].

Woman has her rights, too. Among the Karok of California, for instance, there are two classes of doctors: root doctors and barking doctors. The barking doctor is by far the more important person and is generally a woman. It is her office of diagnose sick cases. This she does by squatting upon her haunches, dog-fashion, and barking for hours. In addition to her diagnostic office, she doctors "poisoned" cases. This condition is very common among her people, for when sick they think they have fallen victims to withes who cause some noxious reptile or animal to grow through the skin into the viscera or intestines. When so attacked they apply to the barking doctor, who first locates the intruder and then sucks the "possessed" spot until the skin is broken and the blood flows. After having complete this part of the treatment, the shamaness takes an emetic and contrives to make it appear that she vomits up a frog or some other small animal which she pretends she sucked out of the patient.[10]

In east central Africa the medicine woman combines with her functions of healing and prophecy the office of witch-detective, and in this capacity is the most terrible character in village life. It is to her, supposedly, that the gods, through visions and dreams, make known their will. When she sees the spirits face to face—always in the deal hours of night—she begins her operations by raving by raving and screaming. She continues until the entire village is astir and she herself falls prostrate to the ground, where she reminds in a state of catalepsy while the awe-struck villagers gather around, awaiting her revelations. At last the beings to speak, and here words are accepted as commands of the gods. Even should she command human sacrifices she must be obeyed[11].

The position of medicine woman is no petty or despised office. In Borneo, as a matter or fact, the very notion of a medicine woman is so full of mystery and power that a male shamans deliberately assume to costumes and habits of women, and are treated l like women and do women's work. Such characters, known as manang bali, are most extraordinary persons, and in view of the enhanced prestige, which the idea of the feminine carries, go about their duties seemingly untroubled by the Nordic's masculine a version to effeminacy[12].

Medicine men and women are quick to appreciate the value of cooperation. They often work in associations, being banded together for their common interest. Among the Tschi-speaking peoples priests circulate bulletins of information conveying the intelligence of what persons are likely to seek advice, and upon what subject. A priest will sometimes frankly tell a client that his own god refuses to accord the assistance required, and pass him on to another shaman. The applicant, when he presents his cause to the second priest, learns to his amazement that the new doctor already knows the purpose of his visit[13].

The medicine-man is a wise individual; he understands his people, and knows how to deal with them. Realizing that fear and intimidation are powerful expedients, he makes good use of these means of offense and defense. Such a weapon is the detective function, referred to in connection with medicine women. It time of adversity and disaster, the savage asks: "Who prevailed upon the spirits to despoil the crops or slay the cattle? Who caused the unclean spirit to enter the patient, and bring about his sickness and death?" For "proper" answers, these questions are always submitted to the servant of the gods—the medicine-man. Woe, then, unto those individuals who are *persona non grata* with the shaman! Upon them will he throw the responsibility of the misfortune, and the end of the recalcitrants will not be peace.

Some of the ruder folk of Australia are unaware that death is ever owing to invisible causes. When, therefore, a man dies the belief prevails that it is only because some other person has killed him. The shaman is quick to turn this conviction to account. If murder actually has been committed, all is clear sailing, for in that case the medicine man is required merely to detect the criminal[14]. If there has been no homicide, however, of if nobody knows who gave the fatal blow, the shaman is not at a loss, for immediately after death has taken place he unhesitatingly asserts that he received the name of the murderer in the dying confession, and bluffingly points out the direction in which the criminal lives. It may take several years to track down the insubordinate, but sooner or later the resourceful medicine-man settles the score[15].

Among the Tschi-speaking peoples, priests are frequently

employed to prevail upon the spirits to send death to persons who have offended or injured the applicants. The individuals against who these priests work their evil magic sometimes die natural deaths, and in such coincidences the shamans take the credit, thus magnifying their office. In case the offender does not die from disease or accident, however, the priests, if they be sufficiently interested, cause poison to be administered secretly to the hap—less individual whose death is desired[16].

The medicine-man, therefore, by means of his detective function, his power of cunning, and his superior resourcefulness, can gratify his choicest malices, punish the recreant, whip the disobedient into line,and at the same time intensify to a superlative degree the superstition and awe which enshroud his own person. Because of the sentiments thus inspired he controls the savage tribe and moulds the community after his own desire.

It is plain, therefore, that an individual occupying an office so plenteous in possibility must, as already suggested, hold within his group a position of tremendous importance. The conviction of the shaman's supernatural origin, the effect of his adventitious aids, his superior mental and moral qualities in addition to the exhibition of truly wonderful powers, cause a feeling of awe which does not fail of assist in extending his spiritual sway over all classes. It is, accordingly, to the advantage of every tribal member to ingratiate himself with the medicine-man. If a person can so influence the spirits that they will do his behest, it is obvious that everybody will strive to the utmost to make friends with him. Even if he has no mystical power, since by reason of his detective function he can throw the blame of evil fortune upon the insubordinate, every person in the society will show him respect, reverence and even worship. The shaman is naturally keen in turning to advantage the unusual esteem and privilege which come to him by virtue of his office: and it is not surprising that he should use his power to elevate himself to the position of chief[17]. The medicine—man in some cases exercise not only kingly power pretends divinity.[18] He "goes from strength to strength."

The shaman even invades the realsm of the occult and takes unto himself the office of prophet. It is asserted that animals pigs, dogs, grouse, sheep, and the like—are sentient to atmospheric changes. When slug enter houses and cattle stand closely together , with their backs to the wind, a naturalist will conclude that a storm is at hand. As we go higher among the various forms of life, however, we find this atmospheric sensitivity becoming weaker and weaker, and when we arrive at civilization we discover that cultured man has, for the most part, lost power to forecast through feelings and sensations. But even in civilization some individuals through rheumatic pains or sense of oppression can foretell the approaching storm. Many medicine-men possess this meteorological sense, any, by predicting the approach of storm and calm, fair weather and foul, come to be regarded as possessing supernatural power.

Shamans do not confine their prophesying powers to the weather. They have a readiness at predicting other events with an accuracy which often seem uncanny. Some years ago, in northwestern California, a Kelta Indian murdered four persons, including Stockton, the India agent, and made good his escape. The murders created much excitement and speculation among the other Indians upon the reservation. A Kelta medicine-man, one day, suddenly cried out that he saw the fugitive at that moment with his spiritual eyes. He then proceeded to describe minutely the place where the criminal was concealed, told how long he had been there, and many other details. Subsequent events showed the spirit doctor to be substantially correct in everything he said[19].

The ability to ward off bad luck and to bring good luck is the medicine-man's chief claim to distinction. The worst luck possible to a pastoral or agricultural people is a season of drought; the best luck imaginable an abundance or rain. When vegetation is dying, when there is no water to drink, when man and beast have no nourishment, the individual, who can make the heavens open and give forth rain, is a person of importance. Rain-making is one of the great methods by which the shaman seeks to establish his reputation. If his power stands the test here, he can rest assured to going through life with fame untarnished and place secure. Now no man by any flash f genius or by any measure of effort has ever succeeded in bringing about the proper atmospheric conditions necessary to produce rain. But whether or not the medicine-man is conscious of his impotence, he never allows his people to doubt his ability to open the heavens, and in view of their belief in sympathetic magic he sets to work as a rain magician. One of the principles of sympathetic magic is that any effect can be caused by imitation. Thus,in Brazil, it is the custom of the rain-maker to mount the roof of his house, vigorously rattle a dried gourd containing pebbles, in representation of thunder, and scatter water upon the ground, to prevail upon the gods to send rain[20]. And whether rain falls sooner of later, the shaman need have no fear of losing casts; for when rain comes he takes the credit, and his people, since they are unable to appreciate evidence, allow one success to outweigh many failures.

Sometimes, however, the medicine-man is placed in embarrassing situations, from which he must use his wits to extricate himself. On one occasion, for example, an Australian rain-maker, after, calling upon the spirits, planted his rain-stick in the ground. When it rained it poured, and the country was flooded. Later, the shaman, in the presence of his constituents, boasted of his success to a white man. The white man retorted. "If you made the rain, cause it now to cease raining, for the crops are being ruined." Whereupon the rain-maker naively explained that such a feat was impossible, because the floods had covered the rain-stick so that he could not find and remove it. The child-like natives accepted this explanation without question[21].

It is evident, however, that this clever apologist is not always able to make his excuses tell. A plague, which killed many victims in a single day, once prevailed throughout Pima village. Three medicine-men, who were suspected of having caused the disease, were put to death, "and nobody was sick any more"[22]. Among the Bari of the upper Nile, the rain-maker, who does not succeed in bringing rain when it is needed, loses not only his reputation but his head[23].

During the British-Ashanti war of 1871—1874, a priest in the Ashanti camp was required to inform the public upon which day the English gun-boat, lying at anchor, would put out to sea. After making the proper conjuration he announced that the ship would depart upon the following day. The next day at sunrise, instead of the boat departing, two other enemy craft hove ominously upon the horizon. The priest was beheaded[24].

On the other hand, particularly is the practitioner has been successful, he is well paid for his services.

Here is a Sarawak doctor's price list: For getting back a human soul, six gallons of rice; for extracting an evil spirit, six gallons of race; for securing the soul of the rice at harvest festivals,three cups of rice from each family in the neighborhood[25].

The modern doctor's custom of making his fee proportional to the financial ability of the patient is, no doubt, the survival of a savage antecedent. The native doctor of the Makhelchel (Clear Lake Pomo) of north-eastern Calaifornia had a clever method of fixing his honorarium. He wrap ped the patient in blankets, and laid him upon the ground with his back to the fire. He next drove a stake into the ground near a the head of the sick man, and then bade family and friends of the invalid to stretch strings of shell beads (money) from the stake to ankles, knees, elbows, and wrists of the sufferer. When the medicine-man had "pow-wowed" sufficiently to make a well sick, he pocketed the money[26].

The Dakota often gave a horse in payment for medical services[27]. In Korea the sums demanded by the shamans were at one time estimated to aggregate annually two and one-half million dollars[28]. Sickness is so costly in Nias that persons often sell themselves into slavery to procure the funds necessary for medical aid[29].

Is the shaman sincere about his "pow-wowing" or is he an unprincipled charlatan and unmitigated knave? Is he a conscious impostor and contemptible quack or an honest man,doing his best according to the light given him? Candor leads to the assertion that this man is usually quite sincere and enters upon his profession in good faith. There are, of course, black sheep in every flock; but the majority of medicine-men honestly practice the principles of their art. In proof of this it is only necessary to observe that when a shaman becomes ill he calls in other shamans to treat him[30].

Does anything positive, however, come from this hocus pocus treatment? Again the answer must be in the affirmative. Even though the efforts of the medicine men may seem well nigh imbecile, amazing results have been achieved by them. The shamans of the Similkameen (Okanagan) of British Columbia are credited with curing persons apparently in the last stages of consumption[31]. In Liberia white people afflicted by certain kinds of tropical diseases have been cured by native doctors, after European medical men had confessed their inability to do anything for the patients[32]. Concerning the success of a native healer of West Africa, it is related, we met a woman lately who had come from Freetown with a dreadful disease in her face, and our doctors could do nothing for her and so her husband brought her right up here in the interior to one of these "medicine men" to be cured "country fashion," and she is getting better every day. Her suffering intense, but now she has absolutely no pain, and is evidently on the high road to recovery[33].

The way has now been cleared for an inquiry into the social significance of the shaman. Some writer assert that he is a parasite, that his influence has been altogether for bad,and that only after he has been routed from his entrenchments can civilization make any progress. It must be admitted that the medicine-man does no productive physical work, and that, therefore, he may technically be called a parasite. Granting this, however, he produces indirectly, and therefore, his efforts have not been in vain. He and his associates, supplied by other classes with bodily sustenance, constitute a leisure class. Without a leisure class it would seem impossible among savages as well as civilized peoples to attain any intellectual progress. For the leisure class the struggle for existence is eliminated, and these individuals of necessity have a surplus of mental energy to expend, and a large amount of leisure time to be consumed. That this energy and time have not been altogether wasted we have direct evidence. The priests of New Zealand, for example, turned to account their leisure time by acquiring skill in wood carving and in other arts; the shamans of the ancient Mexicans and Peruvians became adepts at mixing colors, at painting, at drawing hieroglyphics, at composing music and in reckoning time[34]. In Oceania and central California the religious leaders gave careful physical, mental, and moral instruction to the boys and young men of their people[35]. The observation of the heavenly bodies, the adjustment of the calendar, and the pseudo-science of astrology are indebted for their beginnings to the regulation by the priest class of religious festivals. From the study and practice of astrology came the real science of astronomy. Under primitive conditions the intelctual force of tribe and nation centers chiefly in the medicine-man class. The shamans hence become the preservers of the legends and traditions of the tribe and nation; and since they along of their people are acquainted with the art of writing, it is the members of this leisure class who compile these legends into history. The medicine-man, therefore, was the first musician, painter, teacher, writer, historian, reckoner of time, physician, priest, and astronomer.

The shamanistic class, furthermore, has aided social progress by enforcing an unbending, irresistible discipline upon wild and loosely governed tribes. The evil does much to restrain the savage from cutting and slashing his way through life to the confusion and detriment of the community in which he lives. The chief to a great extent keeps the commoner within bounds. If the individual does not comply with the chief's laws, he loses his head, and no longer makes himself obnoxious; he generally an may because he is afraid to disobey. Yet, law can be evaded; its guardian may be off the beat. The masters of the medicine-man, however, are omnipresent at all times and the fear of human vengeance is not a circumstance to the fear of the gods. The chief can lash a culprit or turn him out of his holding, but the goods can torment him both in this world and in the world to come. While the primitive man, therefore, might fail to conform with regulated conduct, he cannot forget that the gods and their representative are not mocked. As an illustration of the way in which fear of the supernatural works out in savage life, it is only necessary to say that among sundry peoples this fear is o intense that brave young men sometimes die of fright upon discovering that they have unwittingly violated one of the shaman's regulations36. Many of these priestly laws enforce labor, thrift, personal cleanliness, chastity, fidelity between husband and wife; they require obedience to the regulations of the cult; they demand self-sacrifice, restrict personal freedom, prescribe the renunciation of pleasure and property, and, in general, are quite, effective in disciplining savage peoples into an approximately fixed code of conduct. In view, therefore, of the shaman's service as a disciplinarian can it truthfully be affirmed that his presence in society has been a detriment?

The medicine-men, moreover, cooperate with the civil powers in enforcing submission to political authority as in a case which the writer observed at Bontoc,in mountain province of Northern Luzon, Philippine islands. A Bontoc Igorot was serving in the Philippine constabulary when he sickened and died from pneumonia. At the funeral his relatives, believing he had been murdered by Benguet Igorot, traditional enemies of their clan, nearly prevailed upon the Bontoc people to make a head-hunting raid upon the villages of Benguet for blood revenge. The United States authorities assembled the Bontoc priests and explained to them the real cause of the death. Those shamans then persuaded the angry relatives that their suspicions were unfounded, and the trouble was averted.

It is in the field of medicine, however, that the shaman's contribution to social culture is most apparent. When called to the bedside of a sufferer, the medicine-man, like any other practitioner, first diagnoses the case. The diagnosis consists in determining whether the sickness is due to the influence of a *friendly or unfriendly* spirit. If an unfriendly spirit is present, the doctor sets about casting it out.

One method of casting out spirits, of exorcism, is that os causing the patient's body to become such a disagreeable habita tion that the evil spirit will not remain in it. The shamans of Sumatra, for example, attempt to banish the evil spirit from an insane person by placing th unfortunate in a house and setting fire to the building, leaving the wretch of esape if he can[37]. In other tribes the sick person is fumigated, made to swallow narseous substances and drenched with foul concoctions which only the savage imagination could conceive—all for the distinct purpose of disgusting and driving out the unseen intruder. Absurd, says the modern man. And yet the administration of vile-tasting substanc for the purpos of routing evil spirits led to the discovery of drugs and medicines which have vomitory and cathartic effects—remedies indispensable in every modern medicine chest.

Physical force is frequently employed by the spirit doctor to expel the disease demon. Among the Columbian Indians in case of abdominal pains, the medicine-man pressed his clenched fists with great might into the center of the solar plexus.[38] The writer has known many innocent old men amd women of the Tagalog people, natives of the Philippine islands when they were thought to be possessed by vicious spirits, to be cruelly beaten and otherwise maltreated because the doctors believed that in this manner the evil spirit could exorcised

Navaho and Ojibwa medicine-men applied a bony tube similar to a European stethoscope to the part of the patient's body where the pain was most intence and sucked in order to give relief. The California Indian doctors had a tube called the "chacuaco,"made from a very hard black stone. This they used for sucking out the disease spirit.[40] Preposter ous, says the citizen of the twentieth century.The therapeutical expedient known as "cupping;"however, still in vogue, especially in country districts, had its beginning in this primitive, sucking method. The native doctor of Alaska uses the bone of an eagle's wing as a sucking instrument.[41] The transition from sucking with the mouth to a real cupping instrument is here seen. By use of a cupping glass, in case of a boil, for example, the blood is drawn to the surface of the body where the boil is located. The phagocytes, then, combat and destroy the cocci bacilli, which have gained entrance to the tissue spaces, and the patient is relieved. It is not interesting to know that the procedure of cupping, a real scientific measure, was unwittingly hit upon by the shaman, whose intention was not to bring the blood to the periphery but to abstract an evil spirit?

Another method of exorcism is by kneading and massaging the body. This process as practiced in central Australia has been described as follows by eye-witnesses:

A middle-aged man fell sick. His illness was at once ascribed to the fact that he had deliberately done what he perfectly well knew was contrary to the custom, and no one was in the least surprised. "Amongst the men in the camp were five doctors, and as the case, evidently a very serious one they were called into consultation. One of them a celebrated medicine-man from a neighboring........tribe gave it as his opinion that the bone of a dead man attracted by the camp-fire had entered the body of the patient and was causing all the trouble. The others agreed with this opinion but not to be outdone by a stranger the oldest [home doctor of the tribe] decided that in addition to the bone, an arabillia, or wart of the gum tree had some how got inside the man's body. The three less experienced doctors looked very grave, but said nothing beyond the fact that they fully concurred in the diagnosis of their elder colleagues. At all events it was decided that both the bone and the wart must be removed, and under the cover of darkness they were in part [supposed to be]removed after much sucking and rubbing of the patient's body.[42]

Cases of this kind might be multiplied, but one must suffice. The point in question is that the shaman, in spite of an untenable theory, lighted upon a modern method of treatment.For the practice of osteopathy is based upon massaging processes. The osteopath, be it understood, does not pretend to remove an evil spirit or other disturbing agents;his object is to restore dormant organs to normal action. Massaging is recognized by physicians of repute as a therapeutic agency in cases of sprains,bruises, indigestion,and many other complaints. Again our savage friends have anticipated a distinctly modern method.

Fire is regarded by the medicine-man as a powerful means of spirit expulsion. According to his theory fire is caused by spirit activity. Whence came fire? How did man first obtain possession of it? In volcanic regions its discovery is easily explained. It was belched up from the depths of the earth. To the savage mind there is but one explanation of volcanic eruption—it is mysterious and therefore due to spirit or is itself a spirit. In non—volcanic territories there is another explanation for the discovery of fire:electrical storms have always occurred over all the earth. Fire then must have come from the lightning's flash which ignited the trees of the forest and the grass of the steppes. Since, however, lightning comes from the skies, it must, in savage thought, be sent by the spirit, who abide in the heavenly regions.

Fire crackles, sputters, and inflicts pain. Primitive man ascribes these powers to a spirit in the fire or to the spirit which is the fire itself. Now, since fire either is, or contains a spirit, may it not be used to drive away infernal spirits? This the savage believes especially since he finds it useful in ridding himself of his mundane foes. Since, therefore, fire can vanquish earthly enemies, it can likewise drive away spirit adversaries. The reasoning is clear.

Thus, among the Yakut,

> a boy whose finger had become inflamed came to the conclusion that a "yor" or spirit, had established itself in the finger. This opinion was shared by a group of bystanders. Desiring to drive out the spirit, the boy took a burning coal and began to apply it around the place while blowing upon it. When the burned flesh began to blister, and then burst into a little crackle the curious group which had crowded, around him flew back with cries of horror. But the wounded boy with a smile of satisfaction said, "you saw how it *(the spirit),* jumped out."

Curiously the medicine-man by his crude employment of fire unconsciously initiated a scientific procedure. Fire is the only infallible germicide known to the scientific world. By it water is purified surgical instruments are sterilized, and by the cooking of food, germs of disease are destroyed and many a period of sickness thus prevented.

The invaluable process of cauterizing infected bites and wounds goes back to a cure by the Araucanians, by the Gilbert islanders and by the Indians of southern California.[44] When the shamans of those tribes applied the live coal to an infected wound it was of course for the purpose of driving out an evil spirit. What they really did however regardless of intentions was to cauterize the wound.

Water, too, in primitive thought, is believed to have a powerful influence over spirits. The sea rolls, the breakers roar, the waves lash the shore. Floods overwhelm men and beasts canoes are overturned and the occupants drown—all this calls for explanation. The savage reasons that water abounds in spirits who do these beautiful mysterious and terrible things. And so the shaman uses its occult powers. He observes that water can clean clothing weapons and the human body. Why then cannot water spirits clean and purify invisible stains? Here is an anticipation of our own baptismal rites and also of hydrotherapy—the cold bath the wet sheet packs the Russians bath, the Turkish bath-"water cures" which are recognized as treatments for various ailments.

If the primitive doctor thinks the disease spirit is friendly, his method changes from exorcism to propitiation. Among all primitive peoples the most unfailing means of appeasing the angry gods and of securing their favour, is thought, to be the offering of blood. The spirits as has been suggested, are anthropomorphic beings, and since, therefore they relished the taste of blood when in the flesh, they have not changed subsequently to their apotheosis. Thus, the rulers of the ancient Mexicans were the descendants of conquering cannibals. The idols, representing their gods, were fed with human hearts. When the priests represents to the chief, that the idols were starving war was waged and captives taken "because the gods demanded something to eat."

It is not always necessary that the priest kill a victim, however, in order to obtain sacrificial blood. He sometimes cuts the skin of the victim's head with a seal's tooth catches the blood, in rags and lays the bloody rags, beside a corpse as a substitute. In other instances he simply pierces the ears and shoulders of the victim, gathers the blood in a sponge, and squeezes it into a sacred vessel.[46]

The striking thing about sacrificial blood-letting is that the shaman in his zeal to propitiate the spirits by blood offerings, unconsciously and inadvertently initiated a therapeutic agency which has never been abandoned—that of venesection or the cutting of veins in order to draw away the patient's blood. In the seventeenth and early eighteenth centuries, blood-letting was applied by doctors in every kind of sickness. During the latter half of the eighteenth century, however, there was a reaction against its excessive use, and the practice was to a great extent discontinued. But within the last quarter of a century there has been a revival in its favour, and it has been employed by progressive physicians in cases of advanced mitral disease, pneumonia, and other complaints. Here again the twentieth century practitioner owes something to the medicine-man, and has been benefited by the pioneering work of his precursor.

Additional evidence that the shaman's contribution to the science of medicine has been most real and positive is forthcoming from the assertion that

> materia medica owes tobacco, gum-copal, liquid amber, sarsaparilla, resin of tecamaca, jalap, and huaca to (the medicine men of) the Aztecs;

and, again, that

> guiacum, ipecacuanha, and certain purgatives first became known through the Indian medicine men.

and from the fact that a painstaking personal comparison between the Cherokee pharmacopoeia and the United States

Dispensing reveals the fact that about twenty remedies examined were correctly used. I have in another place, traced scores of useful drugs back to the custom and practices of medicine-men.[48]

The shaman, therefore, adverse criticism to the contrary notwithstanding, is not a social octopus. Despite the strong conviction of many writers concerning the perniciousness of his influence,he and the principles for which he stand have always formed the conservative element in his group. Despite the selfish aims and ambitions of the medicine-man and his fellows,the growth of political institutions has been tremendously promoted by the activities of the priest class. Despite the parasitical imposition upon society of this "hanger-on"certain phases of history education literature and natural science have had their origin with him. Despite the shaman's oppression of the masses he has been instrumental in the enforcement upon men of a rigorous uncompromising discipline and for that reason alone he represents one of the most socially beneficent institutions, ever evolved. Despite the multitudinous faults and even crimes that have been laid to the charge of this personage, to him and his class must be credited the initiating, fathering, fostering, and for centuries of preserving the noble art of healing.

Upon this fragile foundation the science of medicine has built its imposing structure. Beginning with the blind gropings of the shaman in his efforts to expel or appease malicious or angry spirits, medical science left long ago the lap of its mother superstition,learning anatomy from Egyptian embalming, increasing its knowledge from the Greek study of living bodies, adding, as time went on, public hygiene from the Jews and the beginning of operative surgery from the Hindus. It acquired skill in sick nursing during the Middle Ages,and developed anatomy as a science during the Renaissance;it began the study of pathology and the practice of instrumental diagnosis during the eighteenth century. Nineteenth century practitioners brought the crude beginning of surgery well-nigh to a state of perfection and organized medicine into a science;while contemporary physicians have honored their profession by the introduction of antiseptic surgery serums and preventive medicine. A truly wonderful record! And the medical is one of those sciences which seems capable of boundless, measureless development;it is ever advancing, and showing the capacity for we know not what illimitable progress. "Thus far but no farther"is not written for it. Could any future be more alluring?

References

1. A lecture delivered before the Anthropological Society of Washington
2. J. Smirnov, Le Cannibalisme et les Sacrifices humaines chez les Ancetres des Finnois orientaux. Congres international d'Anthropologie et d'Archeologie prehistorique,11:316,1893.
3. *Encyclopaedia Britannica* ed. 9, 7:61.
4. E. B. Tylor, *Anthropology*, 354.
5. *Encyclopaedia Britannica*, ed. 9, 7:61.
6. Frank Russell, *Pima Indians*. Bureau of Ethnology, Annual Report 26:257.
7. R. Brough Smyth, The *Aborigines of Victoria*,465.
8. H. Ling Roth, *Natives of Sarawak and British North Borneo*, 280-281(quoting Archdcacon Perham). Journal of Straits Asiatic, no. 19,1887.
9. A.B. Ellis, *Tshi-Speaking Peoples*,138-139.
10. S.Powers,*The Tribes of California*.Contributions to North American Ethnology 3:26.
11. J.Macdoniald, *East Central Africal Customs*. Journ. Roy. Anth. Inst.,22:105-107.
12. H. Ling Roth, op.cit,. 270 quoting Brooke Low.
13. A.B. Ellis, op.cit.,128-129.
14. A. W. Howitt,*The Native Tribes of Southeastern Australia*, 357; On Australian Medicine-Men(Journ.Roy.Anth.Inst.,16:26);

Spencer and Gillen,*The Native Tribes of Central Australia*,46-48.

15. Spencer and Gillen,*The Native Tribes of Central Australia*,533.

16. A.B.Ellis, op.cit.,142-145.

17. A.S.Thompson,*The Story of New Zealand,Past and Present*, 114; H. R. School craft, Information Respecting the Indian Tribes of the United States,4:495;G.Turner, Samoa, A Hundred Years Ago and Long Before,278.

18. A. Bastian, *Der Mensch in der Geschichte*, 468.

19. S.Powers, op. cit., 91.

20. D.G. Brinton, *The Myths of the New World*, 184; Brinton, Religions of Primitive Peoples,174.

21. W. E. Roth, *Superstition, Magic, and Medicine*. North Queensland Ethnography Bull. 5:9-10,1903.

22. F. Russel, op.cit.,48, 59.

23. F. Ratzel, *History of Mankind*,3:26

24. A. B. Ellis, op. cit., 124.

25. H.L. Roth, op.cit., 267, note.

26. S.Powers, op. cit., 216—217.

27. Max Bartels, *Die Medicin Der Naturvolker*, 58—59.

28. Isabella B. Bishop, *Korea and her Neighbors*, 403.

29. Max Bartels, op. cit., 59.

30. E.M. Curr, *The Australian Race*,1:48,2:75; D. G. Brinton, Religions of Primitive Peoples, 58; Max Bartels, op.cit., 92.

31. Mrs. S. S. Allison, *An Account of the Similkameen Indians of British Columbia*. Journ. Roy. Anthro. Inst., 21:311, 1892.

32. Max Bartels, op. cit., 50.

33. Dorothy Cator, *Every-Day Life Among the Head-Hunters*,189.

34. J.G.Wood, *The Natural History of Man*,2:178;Ratzel, op.cit., 2:155.

35. Dixon, *Some Aspects of the Amercian Saman*. Journ. Am. Flok-Lore,10,1908.

36. A. G. Keller, *Social Science,* 138.

37. William Marasden,*The History of Sumatra,*156.

38. H.H. Bancroft,*The Native Races of the Pacific States of North America,*1:286.

39. Max Bartels, *op.cit.,* 270

40. M.Venegas, *Historie Naturelle et civile de la Californie,*1:126.

41. Max Bartels, *op.cit.,* 270.

42. W.B. Spencer and F.J.Gillen, *The Northern Tribes of Central Australia* 515-516

43. W.G. Sumner, *The Yakuts,* Journ Roy. Anthro. Inst., 31:105,1901(abridged from the Russian of Sieroshevski).

44. E.R. Smith,*The Araucanians,* 233;Max Bartels, *op.cit.,* 287.

45. Antonio de Herrera, *General History of the Vast Continent and Islands of America,* 3:206–213(translation by Stevens).

46. Julius Lippert, *Die Kulturgeschichte der Menscheit,* 2:32.

47. Lucien Biart, Lez Azteques, 285(translation).

48. John Lee Maddox, *The Medicine Man,* 217–282.

---

* *American Anthropologist.* Vol. 32. 1930.

Chapter-2

Spirits and the Healing of the Sick in Ontong Java[1]

By H. Ian. Hogbin

Chapter-2

Ontong Java is a coral atoll in the Western Pacific situated at approximately latitude 5° 30' south, and longitude 161° east. Politically it belongs to the British Solomon Islands Protectorate, though geographically it really does not form part of the group. It has also been called Lord Howe, and, incorrectly, Leuaniua. In the very meagre accounts that have been given of the natives they have been called Polynesians.[2] They do speak a Polynesian dialect, and some of them are not unlike the Samoans in appearance, but their culture is not typically Polynesian. The atoll is made up of about 100 small islands. Those to the north belong to the Pelau tribe, those to the south to the Luaniua tribe, these tribes being called from the two main villages, Pelau and Luaniua.

The tribes are further divided into totemic joint families. In general the descent of the joint family is patrilineal, but in certain cases a person may belong to the joint family of his mother's brother. Each of these joint families owns a strip of land in the village of Luaniua or Pelau, and some, in addition own one, two or even three of the smaller islands. This landed property is vested in the headman of the joint family who is always the eldest man in the group. At the head of each tribe is a king. Formerly there were also priests, but all of these are now dead.

I

The natives of Ontong Java believe that men are distinct from animals, birds and stones because these things do not have a spiritual part of their being. Man, on the other hand, has a spiritual entity, which is known as the *kipua*. So much is admitted by everybody, but the details of belief vary no only from person to person,but to a great extent in one person's mind. Thus, in working with the most reliable of informants it is possible to arrange his ideas on this matter and then to find him making a later statement that seems to contradict what he has already said. When this is pointed out he will admit the inconsistency, and perhaps again orient himself, only to go back again to his first point of view a week later. I noted down some of these differences, and, when a favourable opportunity offered, gathered four of my best informants together and had them sift out the matter. The final result may be called the orthodox view, but even this is in one or two places self contradictory.

When a person is born he automatically receives a shadow *(neina)*. This shadow is not a part of him, but a separate thing, although alone it can have no existênce. It is, however, a living thing, and is to some extent a protection to its owner, since it always follows him about. It is quite impossible to kill a person by destroying his shadow, though it dies soon after he does, surviving as a rule until the man is buried.

As soon as a baby can crawl about tit receives its *kipua* (spirit). It is a sort of double or airy body, which is invisible to ordinary eyes. In appearance it exactly resembles the person to whom it is attached, growing old with him and being subject to other changes also. Thus, if the person develops a limp, so will his *kipua*. These spirits are not closely attached to their owners, but move about more or less freely. They spend most of their time in the bush and only rarely enter the village. Normally they are invisible.The only direct knowledge a man can have of his *kipua* is by his echo *(ano)*, which is actually the voice of the *kipua*. This spirit, however, is not entirely free, for it follows its owner at a distance. Thus, when he goes to a nearby island, it is compelled to go too. A canoe is not necessary since neither distance nor time limit its movement. *Kipua* are able to talk to one another, but, provided their owners are still alive, they are not able to influence the destiny of human beings in the smallest degree.

Dreams are accounted for by the belief that *Kipua* speak to one another, and to the spirits of people who have died. This is not a dogmatic belief, but merely an opinion expressed after some thought when one enquires. Dreams, except those of the *koulaiku,* a person to be considered later, are not of great importance at Ontong Java; they play little part in the life of the people unless they are exceptionally vivid. In that case they are regarded as omens of approaching sickness.

It is not known how a person gets a *kipua* or how this is created—it just comes of itself. Moreover, a *kipua* cannot be destroyed by any means whatsoever.

As soon as a man dies his *kipua* is absolutely free, and it rejoices when this event takes place. Everything else connected with the man persishes at this time, or soon after,—his life, his being and his shadow; the *kipua* alone is immortal and lives on for ever. It is never reincarnated as another person nor may it become the *kipua* of another person. To the end of time it remains the spirit of the original man. The spirits of the dead, like the spirits of the living, are still known as *kipua.*

Death is not the result of a man's *kipua* leaving his body. The *kipua* has absolutely no control over a man, and death is actually due to the stoppage of the heart. The thing that maintains life is the pulsation within the body. Whether it is known that the heart actually causes this is not clear, but in native opinion the heart is certainly the center of the motion, and if it ceases so does the throbbing in the arteries. When that throbbing is no longer present the man is dead. With this, however, a man's own *kipua* has nothing to do.

Such is the orthodox view. Some people, however,will say that the echo and the shadow are one and the same thing, and that both are related to the *kipua.* Again, one of my committee of inquiry at first insisted that babies had a *kipua* as soon as they were born. He was finally convinced to the contrary though, as we shall see presently, one phase of the belief demands that this be so.

II

Normally it is believed that there is no land to which the *kipua* repair after their owners have died, but sometimes it is said that certain spots are especially dangerous because the *kipua* live there. These places are generally rather isolated reefs quite bare of vegetation, and may possibly have received this reputation because they are dangerous to navigation. Sometimes the island of Nguhakai, one of the most distant from Luaniua, is held to be their home, though why I was unable to discover. One reef, "Hakupa nga memea," is supposed to be the place where the *kipua* of all very young children go, including those who are still-born, while sometimes the fringing reef is regarded as the home of these *kipua.* For all practical purposes, however, people disregard this, and treat *kipua* as if they have no land of their own.

Some people will tell you that the *kipua* eat and drink like living men and women. if you ask where their gardens are you will be told that they are invisible to human eyes, but that they are none the less there, floating in the air round about the islands. Others, again, deny this altogether.

Once their owners are dead *kipua* are free to go about as they wish, and now for the first time they are able to exert their influence on the living, an influence which is profound, especially in the period following decease. In appearance they remain like the living man just before he died. I have also been told often enough that they become terrible to look at and grow and enormous mop of hair. They not only walk about in the bush,but come and sit in the houses and even listen to conversations that are not their concern.A great deal of their time is usually spent in sleeping in the graves where the men whose likeness they are lie buried, but they always have sufficient time to see what their relatives are doing and to find out all the open and the hidden motives of their conduct. They already possess all the knowledge of the man with whom they ware associated in life. It follows then that people do not willingly speak slightingly of the dead since their *kipua* now have such great powers.

Sometimes *kipua* change themselves into visible ghosts or *hamaka'u* in order to frighten people. These *hamaka'u* are most hideous but generally recognizable. The *hamaka'u* of a woman who had died in childbirth appeared while I was living at Luaniua.

It was a moonlight night and she was seen wrapped in grave-clothes with a dead child in her mouth. The spirits of women who die in childbirth, however, are no more liable to appear than those of anyone else.

Hamaka'u have never been known to kill people, but they give a severe fright, especially if they throw stones or drop coconuts in the path. On account of them no native will go about at night without a torch, and even then very rarely without a companion. Unless he is a mourner on no account will he go near a cemetery.

Hamaka'u, by the way, have shadows. They only appear at night, and, like *kipua,* are afraid of fire. *Kipua* are afraid of their reflections, which are also visible to human beings. A good safeguard against them is to put mirrors in front of the house-doors, or else bowls of water.

The spirits of men who knew the various formulas necessary for catching sharks, and who taught them to their brothers or sons, are sometimes knows as *akua.* Otherwise, despite the fact that they have so much more power, there is no distinction in terminology between the *kipua* of the living and of the dead.

There are a few spirits which were never at any time men; these are also known as *kipua.* Every island has at least one rock which is tapu, and which is a *kipua* of non-human origin. At the island of Kemalu, for instance, within the memory of two living men, a rock was seen to move and go across to another rock and the two had sexual intercourse together. Afterwards the rock returned to its place. Two or three people saw this, but others refused to believe them. The next night the whole village watched, and sure enough the same thing happened, whereupon everyone knew that these two rocks were *pkipua.* Almost every reef and nigger-head is regarded similarly, and although people will never sit down upon such rocks, they otherwise treat them with little respect. Occasionally, but very seldom, such *kipua* make people ill, but their chief sphere of interest is in folk-lore.

III

It is clear that we have to distinguish between *kipua* of men who are still living and those of men who are dead. The first play absolutely no part in the lives of the people. That may be why the opinions concerning them vary to such an extent. The *kipua* of the dead, however, influence the living in every way. They are not only responsible for nearly all illness and disease, but they also send death and are the cause of birth. Like so many natives, those of Luaniua formerly had no idea of physiological fatherhood. Continued sexual intercourse was necessary, they believed, for impregnation. Many applications of semen at last made a sort of stopper for the uterus, and behind this the menstrual blood was held back. Out of this impounded blood the *kipua,* if they were so minded, permitted the foetus to form.

Kipua are responsible for the weather, success in fishing, sorcery and a hundred other things which affect the everyday life of the people.

Apart from their interest in human beings the *kipua* of the dead lead a free life. They can go anywhere, though they are not omnipresent. Two of my friends told me that when they were dead their *kipua* would come looking for mine and we could again talk together. Their life is very like the life of human beings; they fight and they marry though they cannot beget children. On the whole, however, this life is very much to be preferred to their life. One hears of *kipua* who, they say, weep to be alive again. This is rather illogical since one is also told that the *kipua* were never actually any different from what they are now, except that after the death of their human owner they are more free. To regard *kipua* sometimes as separate entities and sometimes as an integral part of the living which survives the grave is but another of the contradictions of native belief.[4]

IV

The people of Ontong Java know nothing of the theory of medicine as we understand it. They realize that if they sit for several hours in the rain until they are cold they are likely to get an attack of malaria after wards, but that is almost as far as they are able to go. They believe that all illness is caused by supernatural means, and as a result of this belief, and of their ignorance of pathology, they have no medicines, as we comprehend the term. The treatment for disease is generally not an internal or even an external remedy , but consists of various ceremonies which are believed to operate upon supernatural forces. The only complaints which are treated by purely natural means are boils, contusions, ringworm, malaria, sprains and swelling of the limbs.

Boils are treated with preparations made from coconut oil and pounded leaves. The two favourite varieties of the latter are the *puakolo* (an unidentified creeper) and *valovalo* (a fragrant shrub). The leaves are pounded in a bowl and warmed oil is poured on top of them. Hot water is sometimes added to the mixture and at times crushed shells. The mixture is then rubbed on the affected part, which is bound up with a piece of mat or a leaf. If contusions are very painful a red-hot stick is applied to them. The patient is held down by a couple of people, and the stick thrust on the spot and held there for a few seconds. The burn is then smeared with oil and bound up.

Ringworm, as is usual in the Solomon Islands, is very common. it covers the whole body except the scalp, the palms of the hands and the soles of the feet. It is a great disfigurement, and the natives themselves dread it. A man who is stricken with it is not at all popular with the opposite sex, and is liable to have difficulty in securing a wife. besides, it is irritating and has an unpleasant smell. The natives have no cure of their own, and the only way to remove the ringworm is to burn away the affected part. This a great many have not the courage to do, and in any case can only be done while still a small area of the skin is diseased. In the past at an island group close by, the Tasmans, people with ringworm had to consent to this treatment or were put to death. My authority for this is not a Tasman Islander, but a man of Ontong Java.

Malaria is said to have been introduced to Ontong Java about forty of fifty years ago. If this is so we must lay the charge on the white man. It is probably the truth because there is still no malaria on Rennell Island, an uplifted coral atoll to the south of the Solomons which is infrequently visited by white men. Here the *Anopheles* have been found, but they are as yet uninfected. In slight attacks of this fever at Ontong Java the sick person lies near the fire, but this is only because he is cold, and such action is not regarded as a cure. There is no native word for malaria. The cold stage is described as *semalio,* the ordinary word for cold, and the hot stage by 'of, the word meaning hot.

Sprains are massaged in one direction with coconut oil. Swollen limbs are treated in the same way.If the swelling persists the skin is cut, to permit some of the surplus blood to flow away, it is said. Quite frequently two operation are combined—tattooing and blood-letting. The idea is that one might as well have some ornamentation to show for the incision since it has to be made.

V

The more serious diseases are classified as follows:— (i) heart failure, (ii) dysentery *(alualu),* (iii) chest complaints (*kale-mahana,* literally coughing sickness), including influenza, tuberculosis, pneumonia and the common cold, (iv) convulsions *(ke'i)*, (v) difficulty in breathing, choking, etc. (*manava),* (vi) paralysis (*nipui),* (vii) yaws (*loha)*, (viii) vomiting *(ua)*, (ix) excessive menstrual flow and (x) general malaise *(kino-haeo).* Of these two are regarded as incurable, *ki'i* and *nipui,* so that if a person is so affected nothing can be done. The latter seems to attack a number of people in the legs. Blindness is also found, chiefly due to cataract, which is also, of course, incurable. Blindness due to venereal disease does not exist.

There is a general remedy applied to all diseases, but in addition most of those mentioned above have specific modes of cure. These I shall consider first. The remedies are the property of certain joint families, and are transmitted from headman to headman. The chief accessory in most cases is the white cowrie shell, *pule (Ovula ovum).*

When a person is suffering from *alualu,* the specialist in doctoring that complaint is found. He takes a *pule* shell and ties white unbroken coconut leaf, dried pandanus leaf and a piece of his own hair to it. He then visits the sick man and rubs his stomach with oil. After he has done this for a few minutes he holds the shell over him and makes a prayer to the *kipua* of his own ancestors to make the man well. The *pule* is left with the patient, and if he recovers the specialist is paid with gifts of calico. In olden times mats would have been used instead. If the patient dies no payment is expected.

The other specific remedies are all similar, save one, that which is used for excessive menstrual flow, and sometimes for general malaise. With this remedy I shall deal later. The rest, however, all have as an essential factor a *pule* shell, in addition to unbroken coconut leaf plaited in various ways, pandanus leaf and hair. In each of these remedies, moreover, a special prayer is recited to the *kipua* of the ancestors. Those which I collected were perfectly straightforward in style except one. They all, save this single example, appeal to the spirits (i.e., *kipua)* of the ancestors of the specialist,the exception being characterized by an appeal to the totemic fish. I have recorded many prayers from other ceremonies, but this, is the only one which even brings in a reference to the totem. It is a prayer used for *kale-mahana* by one of the wealthy joint families of the group. It runs as follows:

kou kapule, kumai kapule,
kou kapule kiki kapule,
kapule laue,
ke mouli, kou kapule,
kumai kapule,
kiki kapule.

(Kapule is the totemic fish;[5] *kou kapule* = my *kapule; kumai* = come to me; *kiki* is dried pandanus leaf; *laue* = good; the *mouli* is the cricket, whose song is regarded as a good omen).

There is practically nosick room etiquettee except that one does not ask a comparative stranger what ails him. Sick people are sometimes painted with turmeric by their friends because that is a way of showing one's regard.

VI

It has been noted that all sickness is thought to be caused by supernatural means. It is visited on the living by the *kipua* of the dead, and generally by those of his own immediate dead relatives, father, father's brothers and sisters, and grandparents.[6] When a man is taken ill, therefore, before anything is done to relieve him it is necessary to find out exactly which of these *kipua* wish him to recover, and which, if any, wish him to die. There are three ways of doing this, two of which are very simple and can be carried out by any of a great number of people, and one which is more elaborate and demands as specialist. The first two methods are known as *lou niu. Lou niu* is the name of the unbroken coconut leaf, but in only one of the methods is this actually used. The man who understands how to perform the operation takes a bundle of the unbroken leaf to the house where the sick man lies. He seats himself close to the patient, but with his back to him. While he is carrying out the ceremony it is tapu to walk near him. He breaks a leaflet and spirits it in halves so that each is of exactly the same length. Then he mentally asks one of the *kipua* of the relatives of the sick man whether it has made him ill. Next he ties form three to five knots in the leaflets. If they are still equal in length the answer to his question is in the affirmative; if they are unequal it is negative. Other simple questions that can be answered with 'yes' or 'no', may also be asked. The result of this is always that some of the *kipua* say that they have sent the illness and that they wish the man to die, while others say that they wish him to live. The vital question of which are favourable and which are not is thus settled.

The other *lou niu* method is carried out with small stones. The man who is making the inquiry frames his question and then picks up at random a handful of pebbles from a heap. If the number is even the answer to his question is 'yes,' if it is odd the answer is 'no.' The odd stone is left to one side and not used again.

After both *lou niu* methods have been carried out the materials, leaf or stones, are sprinkled with water and thrown into the sea, as they are tapu.

The third method of finding out the wishes of the *kipua* is much more elaborate. For it the assistance of a person known as the *koulaiku*[7] is necessary. he is a medium by means of whom the *kipua* are able to speak to the living directly. They are able to possess his body and speak through his lips to the people.

If a man is sick and it is thought advisable to seek the aid of the *koulaiku,* a member of the family first makes him a present of eight coconuts. If these sick man is able to be moved, and it is very rare that someone is so ill that his relatives are afraid to carry him, he is now borne to the house of the *koulaiku* and laid upon the bed mats there. The interior of the house of this person is the same as that of any other house except that in one corner are the paraphernalia of his calling. These consist first of a white coconut leaf split down the middle and tied to a rafter. Underneath this is tied a bottle of coconut oil and a bundle of dried pandanus leaves. The latter are known as *henua,* and are the choicest leaves available, bleached white, split open and then smeared with orange-coloured turmeric. These *henua* represent *kipua* who are in the habit of using the *koulaiku* as a medium. As soon as a new one does so, which may be only a few hours after the death of the person to whom it originally belonged, the surviving relatives give the *koulaiku a henua* representing it to add to his bundle.

After nightfall the *koulaiku* prepares himself to be possessed. He smears himself with the oil and then lies down in the corner of the room under the *henua* bundle. The lights are extinguished, and all remains quiet for some minutes. Gathered round the sick man, of course, are his relatives and friends. Soon the *koulaiku* begins to writhe about, and may even become quite frantic and have to be pinned down by both arms and legs. Sometimes he screams and foams at the mouth, but at other times the possession is of a rather simple order, and all that passes over his body is a slight quiver. Then a low whistle is heard, the signal that a *kipua* has now dominated him. The assembled relatives of the sick man begin to ask questions, which it is believed that the *kipua* itself, and not the *koulaiku,* will answer. The questions are confined chiefly to encquiring which *kipua* is sending the disease, whether it wishes the man to die, and what are the reasons for the visitation. When it is desired that no more questions be asked of this spirit another whistle is heard, the signal that a new *kipua* is in possession of the *koulaiku.* These *kipua* are always dead relatives of the sick man. They do not speak in the natural voice of either the *koulaiku* or of any other living person, but in a shrill squeak.

After all the *kipua* concerned have used him as a medium there is a much longer whistle than any of the others, and the man returns to consciousness. He drinks copious draughts of water, but is otherwise unaffected by association with the forces which have been manifest in him. He is quite unaware of what has been going on, and has to ask in order to learn what words have passed his lips.

There are usually some half-dozen *kipua* concerned; those of the mother and father, mother's brother, father's brother and any other dead relatives who have stood in an important relation to the man, his headman perhaps, or his grandfather, or brother. Sometimes half of them say they want the man to die, and the other half say they want him to live. The *kipua* of the mother and the mother's brother are nearly always favourable to the patient, while the members of the man's own joint family, his father and father's brother, usually wish him to die.

VII

Koulaiku may be either men or women. The two who have the largest clientele at the present time are women. Both of these I found quite satisfactory informants. In addition, there are two other women and two or three men who are *koulaiku.* The histories of a couple of these are interesting.

Let us take the most famous one of all, Pipia'a. While she was a young girl she fell down in the street, and when picked up she was foaming at the mouth and all her limbs were twitching. She was carried home, and it would seem that for two days she was delirious. This was regarded as nothing more than a severe illness by both herself and other people. Then almost the same thing happened again—a fit and delirium. When she regained consciousness she announced that she had been possessed by the spirits of the dead, and that henceforth she was a *koulaiku.* The extraordinary symptoms of her disease seem to have been accepted as proof without question, and ever since she has practised this calling. Not only does she become a medium in the normal way, but at times she is possessed when she is doing her ordinary work or even talking to people in the street.

Pipia'a wields considerable power. She is to some extent feared by the other women, though on one occasion during my stay she took part in quite a serious squirrel and fought with another women. It was the latter who began the quarrel. I had, however, one clear indication of her power. It was not till my second visit that I took any physical measurements. Notwithstanding that by this time I knew many of them well, I had a certain amount of trouble with some of the women. Then I measured Pipia'a, and after that most of them made scarcely any protest. If they did they were generally silenced by a remark from some bystander that Pipia'a had already been measured.

This woman reports her dreams whenever they concern the living, and they are accepted as the commands of the *kipua* and nearly always obeyed. There was one dramatic instance of this. It concerned the fate of one of the wealthiest joint families. The headman, Kakasoe, died and there was no member of the group old enough to succeed. The king put the property in charge of another man, Kilamu, the headman of a quite unrelated joint family, an action contrary to all law and custom. The following morning Pipia'a announced that during the night the *kipua* of the joint family concerned had appeared to her and said that they had persuaded those of the king to kill him unless he revoked his order. Kilamu, they said, had no right whatever to the position.The result of this was that before ten o'clock that morning the king had changed his mind and deprived Kilamu of what he had given him the day before. I might add, incidentally, that it was not his to give in the first place.

Another *koulaiku* is Ke Ahua. She married Ke Ho, who was one of the most famous *koulaiku* at the time. When he died his *kipua* possessed her and taught the other *kipua* to do the same.

Malehu is a male *koulaiku.* He suddenly announced two or three years ago that he was able to see *kipua,* and now he has a large clientele. It seems that such a statement is generally accepted at once because people think that no one would dare to lie about such a tapu thing as *kipua.* But if a new *koulaiku* made several announcements which were contradicted by subsequent events there is a possibility that he would soon be called a fraud. Just before I left, a youh, Pakilau, announced that he could see *kipua* People were, however, sceptical about him, because he was known to be a shiftless person, and altogether not a worthy member of the community. Doubtless though, if the meets with no direct contraditions he will time be accepted. At Pelau some years ago a man told people that he was a *koulaiku* and a couple of men determined, unknown to him, to test his statement. They decided that when a *koulaiku* was possessed his body should have no feeling; he said he did not know what his lips were saying, and he therefore should not be able to tell what was happening to his body. These two men agreed to stick a pin in him while a *kipua* was speaking. If the man made any response he must obviously be a fraud. The upshot was that the man called out, was denounced, and then committed suicide in shame.[8]

People never consult two *koulaiku,* so that there is little chance of a quarrel between them. Occasionally, however, it does happen. Malehu was consulted about a sick man and the *kipua,* through him, answered questions in a certain way. Some time later Ke Ahua dreamed that the *kipua* told her something else.

She told the relatives this, and as a result she and Malehu had a quarrel. The estrangement was not of long standing, and after a couple of days they exchanged gifts and were good friends again.

It is almost impossible for people to imagine that well established *koulaiku* may be frauds. They are able to cite dozens of cases of what they have said coming true. They pass over the numerous times that wrong predictions have been made with the excuse that the *kipua* must have changed their minds. As a matter of fact, speaking for the two I know best, Pipia'a and Ke Ahua, I am quite sure that they are genuine and really do believe that they are from time to time mediums of the spirits. I am also prepared to believe that they do not know what they are saying while they are possessed.

There is little point in fraudulently becoming a *koulaiku,* for if there are advantages to be gained, there are equally inconveniences to be borne. In the first place the payment is quite small, a few coconuts and a yard of calico. True, when the *henua* are worn out and have to be changed, the *koulaiku* is given a pudding by the descendants of each *kipua* represented. They are changed only once or at most twice a year, so that the puddings are not a serious consideration. These *henua,* I should mention, are supplied by the descendants themselves, not by the *koulaiku.* He merely oils them and hangs them up. The chief inconvenience is that the house of the *koulaiku* becomes a sort of hospital. The seance must, save in most exceptional circumstances, take place there, and the sick man must be in the room at the time. It is thought beneficial for him to remain there even when the seaance is not taking place. It is regarded as a specially tapu spot, not only on account of what occurs there, but also because of the bundle of *henua* representing the *kipua,* their ever in the conditon of the sick man,the *benua* bundle is placed right over his face or heart. Now no native on Ontong Java likes to have his house molested. People do not go into each other's houses unless they are friends or receive a direct invitation to do so. I have seen folks refrain from issuing such an invitation even to allow passers-by to shelter from a sudden shower.[9]

Koulaiku, on the other hand, have to welcome all the sick even if they are their enemies,[10] and, what is worse, all the patients's friends and relatives as well. At times, especially if someone is likely to die, there are far more people within the dwelling than is comfortable for its normal occupants.

VIII

When it is quite definitely settled which of the *kipua* are exerting their evil influence on the sick man, a ceremony has to be performed to counteract it, or else to mamke them give up their designs on his life. This ceremony is the *sau.* Sick people are said to be in the *umu* (oven) of the *kipua,* and the ceremony is to take away the earth and stones front he *umu* to allow the person to escape. This is also performed by the *koulaiku,* and is covered by the first free of eight coconuts.

If the *kipua* concerned have been dead a long time the *sau* ceremony generally takes place on the shore. One favourite place is the reef to the sourt-east of the village, and another is the beach near one of the cemeteries. If the *kipua* who is sending the illness is that of a person recently dead, then the ceremony is more usually performed over the top of the grave. Should the patient be very ill, he has to be carried there on a mat.

The *koulaiku* provides himself with a coconut, several *benua* and strips of white coconut leaf plaited in certain ways. The patient merely takes four coconuts to use as a seat. He sits down on these in a place indicated by the *koulaiku,* either on the shore or in the cemetery. The *koumalo,* or plaited coconut leaves, are spread about, one on either side of the patient, one to the rear and one to the front. Some *koulaiku* place them two hundred yards away, some a hundred yards distant and some quite close. The practitioner then takes a *benua* intertwined with coconut leaf an places these on the patient's head. He recites a prayer to the *kipua* who are sending the illness, asking them to give good things in place of evil ones; then he imitates the action of sweeping and goes of to one side. When he reaches the *koumalo* he kneels with one hand upon it and repeats the prayer again.

He picks it up when he has finished, runs forward with it, and places it on the patient's head, recites the prayer again, and then repeats the rite with the *koumalo* on the other side. After he has finished, he sprinkles the sick man with the fluid of the coconut. The *henua* and *koumalo* are also sprinkled and then thrown into the sea because they are tapu. The patient then returns to his house.

There are individual variations in this ceremony, but I have described its essentials. Malehu, for instance, puts oil on his shoulders before he performs it, Ke Ahua runs all the time instead of walking, and so on.

The *sau* may be repeated if the patient does not recover, but generally in that event only the last part of it, the sprinkling, is performed.Should the man grow worse he is taken to another house, or, more rarely, another *koulaiku* may be tried. It is thought that the change of house may be beneficial because new *kipua,* the *kipua* of the inmates of this dwelling, may persuade the harmful ones to abandon the idea of killing him. Ashes, too, are sometimes thrown over the house, after which it is sprinkled with fresh water. Another device is to put bowls of water or mirrors before the doors so that the image of anyone entering falls into them. This is done to keep out the *kipua,* which, as already mentioned, are said to be afraid of their own images.

Sau is carried out not only if a man is sick. The *koulaiku* sometimes see *kipua* while they are walking about the streets. The *kipua* are invisible to all other people, but they can see them uite clearly. If these *kipua* make grimaces at their living relatives the *koulaiku* inform them and *sau* is performed to counteract any evil influence. One day Ke Ahua, another friend of mine, Ma'o and I were walking through one of the cemeteries. Suddenly Ke Ahua stopped and pointed to a newly-made grave, that of a young girl who had died a few days before. She told us that the *kipua* of the girl was sitting on top of the grave weeping because she had died and left all her friends.[11] Two or three seconds afterwards Ma'o slipped and almost fell. Ke Ahua assured us that she had seen this same *kipua* come up behind and push him. The girl had been a relative of Ma'o, and now was envious of him. No time was wasted, and an hour or so later Ma'o was the subject of a *sau*. He paid Ke Ahua a small present of coconuts, half a dozen or so. She gave him a *henua* tied up with strands of her hair as a protection against the machinations of the *kipua* of this girl.

IX

There is one series of complaints which cannot be cured under any circumstances by the *sau* of *A koulaiku*. This series comprises the following diseases:— excessive menstrual flow, which has always been common, they say; a swelling of the abdomen (dropsy) in men, a very rare affection; and sores on the feet. These are all caused by a god Ke Ui.

This god, who was once a man, still exists as a spirit unseen by mortal eyes. His favourite practice is to rape women in their sleep. After he has committed the outrage the woman will bleed to death unless a preventive ceremony is carried out. Another trick of his is to change into a woman and lie with men while they are asleep. The men then conceive and become pregnant by Ke Ui. They swell as the foetus grows and eventually die unless something is done. The entire bush of the island of Luaniua belongs to Ke Ui. He takes it as a personal insult if anyone trips or falls on his property, and to punish him he causes sores to appear on his feet.

The remedy for all three of these misfortunes is to have *sau* performed by the headman of the joint family founded by Ke Ui. This *sau* presents some differences from the ordinary ceremony. To begin with it is performed several times, once in Ke Lahu, the temple of Ke Ui, once before the image of Ke Ui, once on the path running down near the beach to the garden, and once actually on the beach itself. The intertwined leaf and *henua* have added to them *vapulu*, a creeper which grows along the ground, and *valavalo*, a much prized fragrant herb.

The headman anoints his patient with oil on the breast and shoulders and sprinkles lime over his head with a sweeping motion from which the ceremony derives its name of *sau.* The prayer is made direct to Ke Ui, and also mentions his descendants, asking them to influence Ke Ui and make him undo the wrong he has done.

The interesting point about sickness is that although it is all caused by the spirits of the dead, the gods,[12] with the single exception of Ke Ui do not under ordinary circumstances appear. They do not reveal themselves to the *koulaiku* in the normal way, nor do they make use of mediums.

There is one exceptional sickness which is held to be caused by the gods, and that is a universal plague of a very serious nature. In the past it is said that the gods sent these pestilences which wiped out many people. The present depopulation is said to be caused not by the gods but by their representatives and priests, the *maakua* or *ali'i,* as they are called. The *maakua,* or rather their *kipua* , are said to be taking vengeance because some of the people of Ontong Java forsook their gods and became Christians. There was a very serious epidemic in 1925, and the remedy which was carried out was not to restore the ceremonies in full—indeed that would have been quite impossible for many reasons—but to carry the images of the gods out of the temples and turn them face downwards in the mud, to rot in ignominy.

This was to some extent the extension of a quite common custom which has been forbidden now by the government, but which nevertheless was performed as late as 1927. When several people from the same family or joint family all die within a few months and all,according to the *koulaiku,* because of the action of one *kipua,* then the body of the erstwhile owner of that *kipua* is disinterred and burnt. This, it is admitted, will not kill the *kipua,* and might even make it more angry still, but it is to show the spirit just exactly what the living think of it—at the gods were shows by having their images defiled.

X

Fainting, as in some other primitive societies, is regarded as temporary death. If a woman faints she is sprinkled ritually with coconut fluid or water and rubbed with *henua* and white coconut leaf. When it is quite certain that she has not fainted but is dead, a female relative is summoned, and the body is put in a sitting position. This woman calls her name in the dead woman's ear three times, and if there is no response, it is accepted that she is dead, and the relatives begin to weep. Fainting is not common, but heart failure seems to have been so. One girl died very suddenly during my stay, and from the symptoms I gathered that heart failure was the cause.

Death by drowning is be lieved to be caused by the *kipua* also. It is said that people drown not from lack of air, but from drinking too much salt water—the possibility of anyone drowning in fresh water at Ontong Java is so remote that it has probably never occurred. As one would expect, there is no system of artificial respiration for the apparently drowned. The only means employed are simply, as usual, prayers to the *kipua*. These prayers may only be used for women and children. There is probably a good reason for this. If men are drowned it is in deep water when the body cannot be recovered for some time—perhaps a few days. Women and children are drowned only in the shallow water of the reef unless their canoe founders on a long voyage. Their bodies are fairly easily recovered, therefore, and there is some possibility of restoring them.[13]

These prayers for restoring the apparently drowned, as all other special prayers, are the property of certain headmen of joint families, and are passed on by them to their descendants. The ritual for one of those which I recorded was as follows:—

The body was taken by the specialist and laid face upwards across his knees. He took white coconut leaf, and waving it over the face prayed:

> *"melili mai kai,*
> *a na pu i mouli,*
> *maki mouli.*
> *a aale a hale ke laue,*
> *a aale ke lama i 'anua"*

(May the water for me run out at the anus,
completely from the anus.
May it leave a sound body behind it,
and may the deed bring me fame).

This was said to the *kipua* of his ancestors.

The leaf was sometimes inserted in the anus or in the mouth, but there was no massage or manipulation. Cases of recovery from insensibility caused by drowning are therefore very rare indeed.

Battle wounds were thought to be really caused by the *kipua* since they permitted the receiver of them to by vulnerable. The only cure was a *Sausths* ceremony. Spearpoints were pulled out with the fingers or else cut out, but the results were nearly always fatal.

People who died a sudden death, either through heart failure, drowning, being wounded in battle, or on account of some other accident, such as falling from a coconut palm, were not buried with full honours. Instead of being painted with turmeric, their bodies were smeared with ashes. They were mourned in the usual way. As well as a tombstone each person who died in this manner had a memorial placed outside his house. This took the form of a stick, a manne in figure or else a stone. It was painted from time to time and tied up with leaves during festivals. The *kipua* of such people were not especially feared nor did they have more or less power than their fellow *kipua*. They were, in fact, unique in no particular.

XI

Men sometimes fell from coconut palms, and if they were not killed, they frequently had a bone or two broken. The secret of bone-setting was confined to two joint families, one of which has now died out completely. The founder of the other group was a man whose name was 'Alehu. The ritual carried out by the headman of this group is as follows:

He approaches the injured man, who must not be disturbed

at all. He puts oil on the shoulders of the patient and on his own, and leaf on his own wrists, meantime his son has walked behind a bush or palm trunk a few yards of. All the bystanders, of whom by this time there are a great number, cut a coconut leaf. Four times the headman calls upon' Alehu, his ancestor, to help him make the man well again. Each time the hidden man answers "O-o-o." As the last note of this dies away for the fourth time all the people bring their leaves down on the ground with a swish and a thud. The injured man is then picked up and carried on a mat to the house of the specialist. He manipulates the limbs and finds out where the breaks, if any, are. He has two of his kinsmen stand at the head of the man and two at the end of the broken limb, and among them these four pull the bone back into place. It is afterwards bound between splints made of pads of dried pandanus leaf tied together. These are made firm with sinnet and leaves. The patient is finally sprinkled with coconut fluid and carried off to his own house. The specialist is paid for this with coconuts, but not for some time after the recovery of his patient. If the latter dies no payment is expected.

XII

Though the point is not stressed here it will be apparent from certain indications I have given that there is a very intimate connection between illness and punishment. The people of Ontong Java do believe that most of their illnesses are sent to them by the spirits as a punishment for having committed actions which are wrong. This matter is not discussed more fully here because I hope to follow it up later in another context. The supernatural punishment of sin is but one aspect of a more complex problem which, for a complete understanding, has to be taken as a whole.

H. Ian Hogbin.

REFERENCES

1. This paper contains results of field research carried out as Science Research Scholar of the University of Sydney and with the aid of a grant from the Australian National Research Council.

2. Brown : *Melanesians and Polynesians* and *George Brown, pioneer Missionary and Explorer..*

   Parkinson: *Dreissig Jabre in der Sudsee.*

   Vide also *Journal of the Polynesian Society,* 1917, p. 98.

3. The word for this pulsation is u'a, which is also the word for blood-Vaessel and sinew, from which it is probably derived.

4. The *kipua* of the living do not interest the natives very greatly. I did not hear them speak of the subject unless I mentioned it. On the other hand the *kipua* of the dead are probably the most common subject of conversation.

5. Unidenitified.

6. It is noteworthy that all these people are on the father's side of the family.

7. Literally "spirit-anchor." Compare the Samoan and Niue terms.

8. Unfortunately these are all the details I was able to obtain.

9. Of course a person caught in a shower will have no compunction about sheltering in the house of a relative or friend.

10. Shortly after the quarrel I mentioned above, between Pipia'a and another woman, the latter had to be received into her house as a patinet although the two had by no means made up their difference.

11. This statement contradicts the general native view already given,but the contradition in itself illustrates the fact that the beliefs about *kipua* vary from individual to individual.

12. The gods are the *kipua* of the people who founded the settlement at Ontong Java. They may be described as culture heroes. Certain ceremonies are carried out in their honour and offerings of food are made to them daily.

13. On re-reading this statement some months after it was written I am inclined to reject my explanation as unsound. I witnessed no

drownings so had no opportunity of testing the statements. Although they were corroborated by several informants I cannot help but think that there is more in the matter than I have stated. What it is I am not able to say.

* *Oceaina.* 1930-31. Vol-1.

Chapter-3

Medicine as an Ethnographic Category: The Gimi of the New Guinea Highlands

By Leonard B. Glick

Chapter-3

This paper proposes a method for the ethnography of medical systems and illustrates it with a description of medicine among the Gimi, a people of the New Guinea Highlands.'

The introduction such a term as "medicine" into an ethnography entails certain important methodological considerations. First,there is the question of whether one has arrived at a definition of "medicine," and an ethnographic method corresponding to that definition, applicable not only to the data at hand but perhaps to a number of other medical systems as well. Second, and closely tied to the preceding, there is the larger question of whether the assumptions underlying any such definition are still acceptable in anthropology—in other words, whether it is still feasible to try to establish ethnographic categories for which one claims even partial cross-cultural validity.

The second question may be answered immediately. Although this paper is confined to a single cultural domain, it is predicated on what would seem to be the truism that generalizations in any ethnographic domain are impossible unless one ventures definitions comprehensive enough to apply to a number of individual situations. This is not to deny the principle that one should present a people's world as nearly as possible in their own terms, even though it seems plain that any attempt to formulate cross-cultural categories must begin by compromising that principle. In brief, it must be made clear from the start that the paper attempts to find a middle road between the requirements of ethology and the structures of the ethnoscience approach to ethnography. It aims to achieve, for a single ethnographic domain, a method offering a measure of ethnological promise with minimal ethnographic (i.e., "ethnoscientific") fidelity. Put simply, the question it seeks ultimately to answer is: In an ethnography, what should be the subject of a chapter entitled "Medicine"?

In many ethnographic "medicine" is implicitly defined according to Western criteria, with the result that all sorts seemingly irrelevant, contradictory, and paradoxical observations intrude. One is, for example, confronted with so-called medicines that have nothing to do with illness, that may in fact be used to cause illness (cf. Nadel 1954: 132 ff).[2] One reads of curers who cause illness as often as they cure it (hence the term "witch-doctor"); indeed at times a man may cure the very illness he has caused. One finds only occasional associations of particular illnesses and; and treatments, the more common premise being that whatever cures everything. And so on, until the paucity of meaningful correspondences is so obvious that the ethnographer is reduced to placing many of his key terms that medicine, treatment, doctor, diagnosis—in quotation marks. Related to this is the frequent practice of collecting medicinal substances for pharmacological analysis, to ascertain whether or not their use passes inspection before the court of Western rationalism.

Moreover, although it seems reasonable to expect that responses to illness (treatments) world be the logical outcome of ideas about illness (diagnoses), seldom does one find this relation spelled out; it is not made apparent that ideas and actions are complementary facets of a cultural system. Treatments in particular are often presented as though they were a phenomenon unto themselves. This failure to think about medicine as a coherent cultural system is related to uncertainty about its onto logical status, hence about its place in an enthnography. I have in mind especially the relationship between medicine and religion; one appears to be part of the other (cf., for example, Nadel 1954: ch. v; Murphy 1958: ch. iii), or closely related to the other (Field 1937), although everyone knows that whereas some treatments are plainly associated with supernatural causes and magical cures, others seem incontestably empirical and down-to-earth.

Medicine, Religion, and the Idea of Power

As a start toward resolution of these problems, I suggest that we abandon conventional ideas about "medicine"and phrase our initial question as: What is a medical system? And for the time being I would answer this with a simple working definition:A medical system is a patterned set of ideas and practices having to do with illness. If this sounds so straightforward as to be disappointing, it should be noted that its validity hinges on how one defines "illness," on whether one can demonstrate patterned relationships,and on whether one can isolate a system or subsystem having to do with illness and with nothing else.

To employ the definition only as an opening wedge, it is common knowledge, that, in many cultures,ideas and practices relating to illness are for the most part inseparable from the domain of religious beliefs and practices. Illnesses are said to be caused by gods, ghosts, angry ancestors, demons, spirits,and other so-called supernatural beings; or they may be attributed to human beings who are in some way able to mobilize unusual powers—witches,sorcerers,evil shamans. Likewise,curing may involve visions, guardian spirits, invocations, sacrifices, manipulation of sacred objects,and so on. The association is by no means alien to our society; Christian Science and the many forms of faith healing are all predicated on the essential interdependence of medical practice and religious belief. It would appear,then,that we must think about how and where "medicine"fits into "religion." To reduce the question to practical terms: In an ethnography of a religious system,where does the description of the medical system belong; and how does it relate to the remainder?

The answer as I see it depends on whether one can single out some aspect of the total domain of religious ideas as crucial to that lesser domain comprising ideas about illness. What we require, in other words is an idea around which a specific kind of ethnographic information can be organized—an idea more comprehensive and less culture-bound than say, "the supernatural," one that will make it possible to meet standards of ethnographic fidelity without sacrificing all possibility of ethnological comparison.

I suggest that these requirements are most adequately met by the idea of *power*—not diffuse unattached power but power existing as a manifest attribute of persons and of objects in their environment. I am aware that in an imprecise sense this concept has been part of anthropology since at least the time of Codrington (1891),but I am proposing that we reassess it. First of all, there is no need, it seems to me, for becoming entangled in arguments about what particular words—Polynesian *mana* or Algonkian *manitu* "really mean." Recently, both Hallowell 1960:44-45 supporting Radian (1957:12-13) and Evans-Pritchard (1965:110), citing Firth (1940) and others, have reasserted that, however these terms are translated, it is fallacious to equate them with ideas of diffuse power. We may accept this particular argument as settled:indeed if this has any consequences for the present discussion it is supportive of the point of view I am developing. In any event attempts at ethnological comparison of ideas must begin with the premise that particular words in particular places cannot serve as more than guides or clues:whatever ideas an ethnologist compares must transcend definitions of individual words. Second we need not become involved in discourses on religious ontology: we need not be concerned with whether power or any other idea is the "essence"of religion (cf.Van der Leeuw 1938), at the "threshold"of religion (cf. Wax and Wax 1964) I am willing that it be considered simply as a heuristic device that may advance our ability to generalize about "medicine"with minimal distortion of ethnographic detail.

Where power resides in a particular socio-cultural system is a question for the ethnographer to answer. Obviously the answers will not be the same everywhere, but that is where comparison enters in. Likewise, how power is controlled—how it may be mobilized counteracted, neutralized, or otherwise resisted—will also vary cross-culturally, again, that is what one compares. But these unavoidable (indeed, from the ethnologist's viewpoint, indispensable) variations in belief and practice must be organized at a level of generality sufficient to make comparison feasible. As I shall eventually try to demonstrate in this paper fitting specific ethnographic information into a framework centered on the idea of power makes it possible to present potentially comparable data without submerging ethnographic detail or violating the canons of the culture in question. Even where people have no word for power or do not discuss events in this frame of reference, the ethnographer is not precluded from using the concept as a means to ordering information and relating theory and practice. Here I am thinking of power as an ethnographic category comprising more than just medical beliefs and practices;but for the ethnography of medical systems in particular this approach would I believe represent an advance on the great bulk of studies which beg the question altogether by implicitly equating "medicine"with what Western physicians do.

How does this work out in practice? To begin, the ethnographer, whether or not the medical system is his main concern, will be interested, on the one hand, in people's ideas about loci of power and, on the other, in their ways of controlling it. Specifically, he will need to answer the following questions. In this particular society, who or what is said to be powerful—potentially either beneficial or harmful, or both? How is this power controlled? Can one, for instance, mobilize nonhuman sources of power to serve human purposes? Can harmful sources be effectively resisted or overcome? Further specific question come to mind but all of them can be subsumed under two fundamental headings:locus and control. One must learn where people be live power to reside or inhere:and one must learn how they endeavor to put it to their own uses. Note that this information will not necessarily relate only to illness or the medical system;it may have to do with agriculture aspects of social control and so on. But if, for the time being, we concentrate on the possibilities of such, approach for the study of the medical system alone we find that answers to questions about locus and control correspond to what are ordinarily signified by the terms diagnosis and treatment. A diagnosis involves ideas about sources of disease-causing power, and treatment involves attempts to overcome that power.

Diagnosis: Ideas About Causes of Illness

A diagnosis is a kind of classification:a diagnostic statement about a condition declares it to be an illness and assigns it to a particular category of illnesses. Since diagnoses are classification, we may expect to find diagnostic systems differing in two respects. First, they may comprehend different categories; they may recognize different kinds of illness and may group them in a variety of ways. Second, they may not all employ the same criteria: that is to say from the total array of signs and symptoms that might be taken as evidence for significant illness (with some emphasis on "significant"), people may differ in what they select for attention and in how much weight they assign to one kind of evidence as against another. Therefore one must keep several questions in mind. First, in this culture what constitutes an illness? Second, what kind, of illness are recognized? And, finally, what criteria underlie diagnosis?

In answer to the first question, an illness is any situation evoking a response that can be identified as part or the medical system. A fuller definition of "medical system" must be developed as we go along; here it will suffice to note than an ethnographer who concentrates exclusively on what he considers to be illness may emerge thoroughly confused if (as is likely to be the case) his subject's ideas differ sharply from his own. Subtle considerations enter here. Thus apparent agreement or disagreement about whether something is an illness may have to be rephrased as agreement or disagreement about whether it is a significant illness, for people often distinguish plainly between illnesses having significant causes and demanding co-operative responses from the sick individual's social group and what might better be labeled "ailments"—conditions having no significant cause and requiring no treatment other than what might be called "remedies"(cf.Nadel 1954:145—146). Once ailments have been identified in a particular culture,I would exclude them and their remedies from consideration as part of the medical system proper. If, for example, an infected insect bite is looked upon as purely the concern of the individual, as having no socially significant cause and as requiring no treatment other than a leaf plaster or perhaps just patience, I would not call it illness and would not include matters relating to it in a chapter on medicine. This argument should become cleaner as we proceed.

The second and third questions must be answered together because, in contrast to Western medical thought, the most important fact about an illness in most medical systems is not the underlyings pathological process but the underlying cause. This is such a central consideration that most diagnoses prove to be statements about causation and most treatments, responses directed against particular causal agents. To be more explicit any diagnostic statement about illness may take into consideration three dimension which I call evidence process and cause. Each dimension may support a system or part of system of diagnostic terms. I would argue that the third is always present as a critical consideration and moreover is of central importance to comparative studies.

Evidence is whatever is taken as empirical indication of the existence of an illness. It is what our physicians call "signs and symptoms";but in Western medicine signs and symptoms are never in themselves diagnoses, they are only clues to diagnosis. Lung cancer or lobar pneumonia, for example, may both cause coughing, but they are not formally grouped together, at least by physicians, as "coughing illnesses."

Process or what is actually happening to produce evidence of illness is the focal concern in Western medicine. Pathology the study of disease processes is the foundation of our system of medical classification: illnesses are grouped together because they are understood to represent related pathological processes. Identification of these processes is for the most part dependent, of course, on the technology, investigative capacities, and, most important, cognitive oreiention characteristic of modern medical science. To our way of thinking then pathological process is the fundamental dimension of illness; but it is often precisely this dimension that other medical systems bypass altogether.

Cause the third dimension in diagnosis, is the one to which I want to draw particular attention. When a Western physician establishes a cause for an illness this becomes part of his diagnosis supplementary (although not necessarily secondary) to the statement about process e.g.,lobar pneumonia (process) due to *Diplococcus pneumoniae* (a bacterial cause), or cerebro-vascular hemorrhage (process)due to hypertensive cardiovascular disease (a physiological cause but itself a process with determinable causes). Other cultures also have ideas about the causes of illness but they bear no resemblance to these. The ethnographer who asks what causes illness is not likely to here about bacteria or disordered physiology:instead he hearts about competition jealously greed and lust; withes sorcerers and demons;mothers brothers and grandfathers recently deceased. In brief whereas in Western medicine causation has no essential relationship to socio-cultural context in most other medical systems causation and context are so intimately linked as to be the ethnographer's principal concern. Moreover in the absence of understanding of disease processes diagnosis may resolve into conclusions about causation inferred from evidence; that is the dimension of process may be overlooked altogether or it may be relegated to strictly secondary significance. In any event in contrast to our own medical system, in such systems as we are now discussing a statement about process can never be more than a partial diagnosis, whereas a statement about causation may stand alone.

Thus the ultimate significance of illness in folk medical systems is so much a part of the victim's socio-cultural identity and experience that a diagnosis cannot be made or understood in any other terms. Causes may turn out to be as invisible as viruses, but never as impersonal. Instead, illness, are caused by *agents* who in some way bring their powers to bear against their victims. Such agents may be human, "superhuman" (Spiro 1966:91) or nonhuman; but always they are conceived as willful beings who act not indifferently but in response to consciously perceived personal motives. For this reason it is misleading to cite "disease object intrusion"as a cause of illness on a par with "sorcery" (Clements 1932;cf.Caudill 1953:772). Sorcerers are *efficient* causes of disease—agents whose action are explainable. Disease objects are *instrumental* causes; sorcerers may employ them in producing illness but it is sorcerers and their motives not the objects they insert that require ethnographic explanation (cf.Hallowell 1935).

In line with our theme, it may be noted now that power may also reside in plants, artifacts, or objects of any sort (again it is for the ethnographer to discover specific loci), and that when a sorcerer uses such objects e.g., a "poisonous" packet combining plant and animal materials with human exuviae he is tapping this power.The distinction drawn by Evans-Pritchard (1937:21,387) between witchcraft and sorcery calls attention to the difference between persons possessing inherent power to harm—witches—and those who harm by tapping outside power—sorcerers.

Soul loss (another of Clements "disease concepts"),whether spontaneous or attributable to an agent involves loss of vital internal power; but the result is the same and as will be seen the same concepts of treatment apply.

An instrumental cause is what is done or what is used; an efficient cause who does it or uses it. The latter the agents of illness are with a few arguable exceptions, persons; they are part of the same socio-cultural system as the sick individual and they demand consideration in this wider context. Gaining an understanding of why they act of what induces them to bring on illness, leads the ethnographer beyond the medical system proper and into the realm of ultimate causes-kinship and political relations, property and inheritance disputes, jealousy 'envy' rancor, and spite.

Treatment: Responses to Illness

It will be apparent to anyone who reads ethnographies that the number of treatments people employ is virtually infinite, so that unless one imposes some form of organization on the plain ethnographic facts the ethnology of system of treatment resolves into little more than "comparative" lists of potions and ointments. But there are more appealing possibilities. As a first step, I suggest that we put aside for a moment the tabulation of botanical remedies and ask whether people's responses to illness everywhere are perhaps formally, even though not substantively, comparable.I think it can be shown that treatments are formally comparable, by continuing along the line of thought we have now established. Treatments are responses to illness reflecting ideas expressed in diagnostic statements about illness. If diagnoses are statement, about malevolent sources of power, we may expect that treatments will be designed in some way to restore the "balance of power"between antagonist and victim. This presents two possibilities:either one tries to weaken the antagonist, or one tries to strengthen the victim. (Often of course, people try both.)

First, we may consider attempts to weaken (neutralize), or eliminate malevolent sources of power. These might be called "negatively directed" in that they are intended to negate the powers of antagonists or of the objects and substances they control. The patient may not even be present, for treatment is here conceived as essentially a struggle on his behalf against external forces. For example, a curer may magically retrieve and destroy a packet in which a sorcerer has combined poisons with his victim's refuse. Or he may remove from his patient's body a poisonous object which a sorcerer has inserted. The sufferer's kinsmen and friends may perform rituals of invocation, perhaps accompanied by sacrifice asking or ordering a ghost, a god, or a demon to cease torturing its victim. Homeopathic principles may be employed:the Gimi sometimes leave tasty food parcels where vicious disease-causing forest trolls are likely to nibble them; the sick individual then eats the remains of the parcel and is thereby "immunized" against the powers of his antagonist. The list might be extended but the same point would remain:such treatments are ways of opposing harmful sources of power.

In contrast, a second class of treatments is "positively directed"in that it comprises attempts to augment or restore the personal power of the victim himself. The foremost representative of this kind of treatment is the consumption of medicines.

Ethnographers seem uncomfortable with this word;often they enclose it in quotes,apparently to indicate that what is being called "medicine"is not really medicine (cf.Middleton and Winter 1963:3). In this paper the term means any substance used as part of a response to illness in the expectation that some of its power will augment that of the patient. Note that this definition restricts medicine to the medical system but does not remove the possibility that the same or similar substances may at other times be applied to any number of situations having something to do with power but not with illness e.g., improving an arrow's effectiveness or stimulating the growth of crops.

Medicines are often plants or parts of plants. but by now it should be evident that efforts to link up particular plants with particular illness may prove futile for people are not unlikely to take the common-sense view that if a substance is therapeutic for one illness it is probably therapeutic for another. (Think of our ideas about vitamins, tonics, chicken broth and tea.) An adequate ethnographic statements on this point might resolve them into the simple assertion that many plants are potential source of therapeutic power. The plants should of course be identified by native names and taxonomic domains (Conklin 1962), and also botanically identified if possible, but it is essential to add that there may not be a finite number of items to be discovered and that a complete record of the native "pharmacopoeia"may be misleading if people are using plants with uninhibited catholicity and have only vague notions about the value of particular plants for particular illnesses.

Plants are, of course, not the only sources of medicine. Flesh, blood, fat, pigments, fumes, and ritually empowered substances or objects of any sort may all be eaten, drunk, inhaied, rubbed, or blown into and onto the body in the quest for restored health. An important source of power is the shaman or curer himself. He may rub or message his patient, blow breath or smoke on him or manipulate his body—all practices designed to impart power. These same persons, as is well known, may become sorcerers when offended. This is not a reversal of role; it is simply another way of using power.

In summary, the second class of treatments includes all procedures designed to strengthen the victim and increase his personal capacity to resist whatever or whoever is afflicting him. Just as diagnosis is understandable as a people's ideas about malevolent sources of power and how they make men ill,treatment is understandable as a reflection of their ideas about how benevolent sources can be mobilized to make them well again.

The gimi Medical System

To illustrate how all this works out in practice, I shall now describe in some detail a medical system known to me at first hand, that of the Gimi, of the Eastern Highlands of New Guinea. The Gimi are horticulturalists and pig raisers living in the relatively isolated Labogai subdistrict south and southwest of Mount Michael (see map in Watson 1964:307).They reside in villages and hamlets loosely grouped into communities but essentially autonomous, strung out along the ridges and sides of the steep mountains which dominate the environment .Village are ideally the homes of patrilineal patrilocal descent groups but in fact there is considerable moving about and as elsewhere in the Highland residence emerges as the key to social organization (Langness 1964) .Relations among villages, comprise all there is of political organization;from the viewpoint of any one village other villages are the home, of either consanguineal kin, affinal and avuncular kin or enemies. These relations shift over time so that today's enemies may be tomorrow's affines. But the day-to-day life of a Gimi man is predicated on the assumption that social identity and social relations are timeless and ineradicable; he himself is loyal to his home village to the point of fierce chauvinism and is ready to believe anything about men in other villages.

Prior to the imposition of Australian control less than fifteen years ago, intervillage fighting was endemic and seems to have been heartily enjoyed. Now everyone is formally at peace, but basic attitudes have not changed, men still look upon the residents of other villages, including their distant or putative consanguines affines and matrilateral kin as people to be manipulated exploited when possible and actively opposed whenever the home villages interests are in the balance (cf.Read 1954:22; Berndt 1964).These elementary aspects of Gimi social life are the essential background to Gimi medicine (cf.Glick 1963).

Gimi Diagnosis

How do the Gimi diagnose illness? First, it must be noted that many afflections that seem on first consideration to belong in this discussion are what I prefer to call ailments, and are thus not part of the medical system as defined in this paper. For example, sprains, fractures, minor, burns, skin ulcers, rashes, infected insect bites, and so on, all elicit some response among the Gimi at least some of the time; they may have names denoting what I have called evidence and perhaps in a limited sense process; but nothing that is said or done about such conditions suggest that people attribute them to identifiable causes. "Chance"or "accident" are the only causes I could cite in this connection but these are not Gimi concepts and have no place in a Gimi ethnography. I conclude, therefore, that ailments—relatively minor and temporary afflictions lacking significant sociocultural antecedents or consequences—are a separate category of experience in Gimi life, standing in contrast to true illnesses, which have named socio-culturally relevant causes and require culturally defined and socially mediated responses. The descriptive account that follows is concerned only with illness in this strict sense.

Gimi diagnostic statements center on the premise (so integral to their world view as not to receive overt expression) that what matters most about an illness is its cause. Although one encounters names for some illnesses that seem to refer principally to evidence or perhaps, in a loose sense, to processes, the foremost consideration in any illness, named or not, is always the same: Who or what brought this on? In trying to answer this question, the Gimi make an implicit distinction between sever (*adabu)* illness and those marked by an element of the weird or peculiar (*neki*). The great majority of severe illnesses are attributed to sorcerers (of whom there are two kinds, "poison sorcerers," *rubeseke bana*, and " assault sorcerers," *rukabi bana)*, while the great majority of peculiar illness are attributed to vicious little troll-like creatures called *Nekina,* "weird beings."

Two infrequently encountered exceptions are convulsive illnesses and insanity. The former are caused by creatures called *amora bana*, "demonic beings." The word *bana*, which it will be noted also appears in the terms for sorcerers, is most simply translated "man" (or "men"), and for this reason I include convulsive illness with sorcery-caused illnesses in the category of severe illnesses attributable to human (*bana*) or human-like antagonists. Conversely, insanity fits appropriately into the category of peculiar (*neki*) illnesses. A mentally disturbed or psychotic person is called *neki bana* and is said to be ill because a ghost (kore) has entered his body and interfered with his capacity to behave sensibly and respond appropriately. Figure I summarizes the above information in the form of a simple paradigm for Gimi diagnosis.

FIGURE I: PARADIGM FOR GIMI DIAGNOSIS

EVIDENCE	CAUSE (AGENTS)
Severe Illness	*Human Antagonists*
Insidious and tenacious	"Poison sorcery"
Violent and bizarre	"Assault sorcery"
Convulsions	"Demonic beings"
Peculiar Illness	*Nonhuman Antagonists*
Deformity, destructive lesions, severe illness in children	"Weird beings"
Insanity	"Ghosts"

Severe lingering illness: *poison sorcery*. Most severe illness are attributed to sorcery. In this domain, however, there are two possibilities; some illnesses are due to "poison sorcery" (*rubesekena*), others to "assault sorcery" (*rukabina*). Poison sorcery is associated with illnesses, that are marked by an insidious onset, perhaps seeming even trival at first but then proving to be tenacious, progressive, and eventually crippling or fatal. Such illness are called *kio*, "lingering illness." There are special names for its more noteworthy varieties, not necessarily mutually exclusive since they refer to both causes and evidence. Examples include *asakikina kio*, literally "rubbish lingering illness," referring to the sorcerer's having cooked his victim's offal with poisons; *sokere kio*, "pocking lingering illness," characterized by destruction of flesh, as in leprosy or yaws; *amusa kio,* "pregnant lingering illness," marked by extreme abdominal distention; and *forebare kio*, "repulsive lingering illness," a simple reflection of people's reactions to sorcery and its effects. It must be emphasized that all kinds of *kio* have but one kind of cause, namely poison sorcery; people do not try to equate particular forms of *kio* with particular forms of poison sorcery. Sorcerers may, as a matter of fact, achieve essentially the same effects through a variety of procedures. Most often they employ exuvial magic, combining an intended victim's discarded hair, nail parings, feces, or food scraps with poisonous substances *(anarisa)* in a packet, which is then cooked over a slow fire; at other times they may turn to disease object propulsion, food poisoning, or soul stealing.

What a sorcerer is believed to have done bears, of course, on how his victim is treated, but a more important consideration, especially if the latter dies, is placing blame for the deed. It is always assumed that the sorcerer is a resident of some other village, usually one in a state of chronic enmity with that of the victim. He is seldom if ever identified by name, and indeed people disagree as to what kind of man is most likely to be responsible; some maintain that only puny second-rate men *(foipa bana,* "worthless men"; *aru bana* "shabby men") would ever stoop to sorcery, while others say that it is the most forceful and impressive men *(fakeke bana*, "competent men") who know best how to kill other men[6]. But the sorcerer's individual identity hardly matters anyway; what matters is the identity of the village, his own or another, that induced him to carry out the act. The Gimi seldom if ever conceive of sorcery as an act of personal vengeance; rather it is planned aggression by one village against another, sometimes for revenge, sometimes simply to weaken the opposition by eliminating a valued man or woman.

(It may be noted here that, with a very few questionable exceptions, sorcerers are always males, and that there are no witches of either sex. I think this is because women are for the most part believed to be too ignorant, erratic, and irresponsible to control forces as momentous as those involved in sorcery. They may, however, be sorcerers' victims, for as workers and bearers of children they are by no means without value to their husbands and the men of their husbands' villages.)

Violent illness: assault sorcery. The term *rukabina*, literally translatable as "violence," may refer to nothing more serious than a family squabble; indeed any man who enjoys fighting may be called a *rukabni bana*[7]. But in the particular sense intended here, open assault is combined with magical actions to leave a victim both mutilated and poisoned. Because it demands boldness and aggressiveness, rukabina is not work for a weakling. In fact, it is said that in former times one way for young men to demonstrate their virility was by participating in these assaults, which once again took the form of aggression by one village against another. Typically, three or four men, their faces masked with soot, station themselves along a remote path where members of another village are likely to appear. When an unwitting victim passes the ambush point, they leap out, grasp him, by the head and neck, and hold on while one of their number jabs a poisoned needle into his chest. Stunned and bewildered, the man is unable to resist or even cry out. His assailants test his state of consciousness: "Where does the sun come form," they ask, "from above or below?" (There are no terms for or categories of direction except above or below.) If he answers correctly—that it rises from below—they stab him further, but if he mumbles that the sun comes down from above they realize that job is completed. They plaster bits of frog skin over his wounds (frogs are considered particularly ugly and repulsive) and leave him to stumble home, dazed and befuddled, unable to remember who or what injured him, or even to recognize that he is ill. His Kinsmen interrogate him anxiously but he insists that nothing has happened. He sits along, poking about in the dust, groaning or weeping to himself. Eventually, unless treatment proves unexpectedly successful, he dies, for sorcery of this kind is said seldom to fail in its purpose.

Convulsions: demonic beings. Despite their name, *amora bana,* the "demonic beings" who control storms and lightning, are aloof from the realm of human relationships. People express only vague ideas about their appearance but seem to conceive them as creatures monstrous in size and capacity, indifferently destructive, and utterly unapproachable. They are said to strike their victims during lightning storms, leaving them dying or else subject to repeated convulsions thereafter. With all this power they are still mortal, for, although their bodies are never seen, in certain locations high up on mountainsides men sometimes encounter their bones. These bones (called *amora adapu*) are so potent that not every man is willing to risk taking them, but they are valuable therapeutic aids, particularly in the treatment of convulsions. Sorcerers may also use them to induce convulsions or, worse, to cause lightning to strike a victim.

Peculiar illnesses: weird beings: The word *neki* stands for whatever is weird, peculiar, irregular, or unnatural in the Gimi world. The term *neki bana* (or *neki bada* for a woman) may refer to anyone who is unable to perceive *(fe-)* and respond adequately to speech (*kaina*). The phrase *neki bana miri kaina kafei,* "he is a *neki man,* he doesn't perceive [understand] speech," may refer to someone whom we would identity as either deaf, mentally defective, psychotic, or perhaps just plain foolish. In the Gimi view, all such people are in some way peculiar; normal persons are social beings, but *neki* people are in some way crippled for social roles. Animals, places, and things may also bear *neki* qualities. Frogs and lizards, for instance, are considered so ugly and disgusting as to be the model for people's ideas of what *nekina,* "weird beings," are like.

It will be remembered that *nekina* are the troll-like creatures that cause certain kinds of peculiar illnesses. Few people claim to have seen them. The evidence for their existence lies in the illnesses they cause when offended, illnesses marked by a *neki* quality that betrays their origin. Wherever land is distinguished by some topographical or vegetational peculiarity, and particularly wherever ponds and swamps are found (for in this mountainous environment, with its rushing streams and treacherous whirlpools, still waters are, in a sense, peculiar phenomenon), *nekina* congregate and claim the location as their own. Such a place is a *neki maa*, "weird land", and everything it contains—not only the *nekina* but all other plants and animals living there, even the very soil-bears a *neki* quality spelling danger for human intruders. Trouble comes whenever someone behaves disrespectfully or arrogantly in *neki* territory e.g., chops down a tree, pulls out a plant, kills an animal, or—even more foolishly—urinates, defecates, spits, or tosses away food scraps. If the *nekina* can get hold of some such refuse *(asaki-kina),* through exuvial magic. Serious childhood illnesses, especially in previously healthy children, are often explained this way; a child falls ill, for instance, and its father recalls that he recently urinated in a *neki maa.*

Diseases leading to destruction or distortion of body parts are similarly explained. The story was told of a pregnant woman who chopped up and ate á snake in a *neki* place with the result that her son was born with a stump in place of one arm. Another woman removed taro from a plot of *neki* land; later some of the taro rotted; and her infant son developed a destructive disease of the genitals. A boy cut a vine growing near a pond in a *neki* locale, and as the vine grew again, the flesh over his left eye grew until it was little more than scar tissue. Children are the most frequent victims of encounters with *nekina* and *neki maa*, but adults are not altogether immune. Young men who copulate in such places, for instance, and leave behind, may develop fatal illnesses.

Psychotic behavior: ghosts. Men or women who are *neki* in the sense of being deaf, mentally defective, or somewhat silly are not usually considered ill, although such an affliction suddenly befalling a previously vigorous man would no doubt be looked upon as an illness with a significant cause. A *neki* person who is unquestionably ill, however, is the one who is acutely psychotic. Psychotic behavior is attributed to possession by a ghost, which enters the body and sets up a whirring or buzzing noise in the victim's head so that he cannot "hear" properly *(kania kafei)*. For a few days after a death the ghost *(kore)* of the deceased wanders about in search of a weak victim, perhaps a child, whom it can carry off as company. Occasionally an adult is accosted by a ghost who flaps about and tries to carry him away, but without success. One such episode, as related to me soon afterward, was rather ludicrous and ended with the intended victim, a youth of seventeen or so, batting off his oppressor and running away. After a few days of this sort of behavior, the ghost sinks into the grave to join its corporeal counterpart, and there it remains, unable to participate in the affairs of men unless someone is unfortunate enough to be possessed.

In one instance which I witnessed a young man suffered a sudden full-blown *neki* episode as a result of having thoughtlessly wandered too near the grave of a man who had died several years before. He raced about aimlessly, decked out in a bizarre costume, brandishing a bow and a large clutch of arrows, and threatening to shoot all and sundry[8]. People responded with calm indulgence and a touch of amusement. He was not considered responsible for his own behavior of a *neki bana* very much like that of ghosts themselves? An attempt was made to feed him therapeutic leaves, but he refused to co-operate, and as it turned out his principal "treatment" was the patience of his fellow villagers and the quiet insistence of several older men that he behave more appropriately lest everyone in the village suffer. After two days of *neki* behavior he recovered spontaneously.

Illness as sanction. A number of taboos, prohibitions, and injunctions are sanctioned by the expectation that violation will lead to illness. Boys may be told, for example, that eating certain foods in the years between initiation and adulthood will cause stunted growth, weakness, or the like. Prohibitions against contact with woman are a more important case in point. *Gimi men* take every opportunity to express distaste for females and things feminine. There can be little question that their reactions to women are grounded in fear of contamination from menstruation, which they do not every superficially understand but associate only with a female essence, called *araka*, believed to be "in the air" when a woman menstruates. Young men and boys are warned to avoid women, especially menstruating women, lest they become scrawny, sickly, and pimply-faced. The point to be noted here is that, when illnesses actually occur, the Gimi do not turn to such explanations but think rather of causes beyond personal control—of sorcerers, *nekina*, *amora bana*, and *ghosts*. Diagnosis is a retrospective judgment. Breaches of taboo and contamination lead only to hypothetical illnesses, by what might be called prospective diagnosis; they do not explain real illnesses.

Gimi Treatment

Gimi diagnoses are statements about causative agents based on kinds of evidence associated with each agent. In the Gimi environment these agents, and the substances they sometimes use, are loci or sources of power, in this case power applied to malevolent ends. How to resist such power—how to neutralize or destroy it, how to strengthen its victims—is the problem to which treatment must be directed. Gimi treatment techniques are ways of mobilizing, negating, or otherwise controlling power.

Medicines. We may begin with the "positive" aspects of treatment, with ways of strengthening sick person, increasing their powers of resistance, through the use of medicines. The Gimi attribute therapeutic potential to many more substances than we would ordinarily call medicines—not only expectable items like leaves, barks, and other parts of plants, but also meat, blood, fat, salt, tobacco smoke, pandanus oil, human bones, and more. With a few exceptions these are not categorically related to particular illnesses, and never are they said to be cures for specific disease processes; they are substances with the power to strengthen and renew anyone who is ill. The curative properties of most plants, for instance, are so nonspecific, and so much a matter of individual judgment, that it would be quite impossible to compile a finite list of Gimi "medicinal plants." Some plants, e.g., *abakikira,* a wild raspberry (*Rubus moluccanus*), *mane doni*, a club moss (*Lyopodium*), and *rakuri ,a rhododendron*, stand out as popular favorites, and some are more or less closely associated with particular illnesses; for example, the bulbous "belly-like" stem of *amukotiba*, an orchid (*Coelogye*), is said to be good for abdominal illnesses. But to continue listing such plants would be gratuitous, for what we are concerned with is how the Gimi perceive and utilize them; and from this point of view there can be no question that most plants are used because they are there and because it is believed implicitly that some measure of power potentially beneficial to man inheres in them. To try to explain their use by pharmacological analysis—to determine whether or not they are "really" therapeutic—would be to leave the principles of Gimi medicine far behind.

The same can be said for all other medicines. Although leaves and bark may be consumed along, they more often form part of a therapeutic meal (very likely to be shared by the patient's kinsmen and friends) consisting also of pork, edible greens, salt, and ginger, all of which (with the probable exception of the greens) are credited with therapeutic properties of their own. Pork and pig blood, for instance, are full of the power of pigs, which are said to have *iuna*, "vital powers", similar to those of men (see *aona* below).

Any substance suitable for consumption is suitable for external application as well. A victim of assault sorcery (*rukabina*) may be offered a meal of pork and therapeutic plants, after which his kinsmen may smear the same plants, mixed with pork grease and blood, over his wounds. Tobacco smoke is widely credited with beneficial qualities, whether inhaled or blown onto the body, and this is sometimes part of a curer's activities.

Counteracting malevolent power. In addition to treatments designed to strengthen an individual's capacity to resist illness, a considerable proportion of Gimi treatments are primarily intended to weaken whoever or whatever is causing the illness. In this class of treatments we encounter four kinds of activity: ritual retrieval and destruction of exuvial sorcery packets, disease object extraction, procedures employing homeopathic principles to neutralize the power of "demonic beings" *(amora bana)* and "weird beings" *(nekina),* and ritual injunction to combat unidentified agents causing individual or epidemic illnesses.

Although no one among the Gimi is a full-time specialist in curing, and although curing is in a sense the province of every mature person, when someone fall seriously ill and sorcery seems the most likely diagnosis, people turn for help to certain specially endowed men called *anona bana,* "men of power," who are credited with curative abilities considerably beyond the ordinary. The word *aona* might be translated "soul," "shadow", "vital force," or "familiar spirit," for it has each of these meanings depending on content. But *aona* is not exclusively the property of men, for animals, plants, rocks, whirlpools, lightning, and a host of other phenomena are at times credited with a vital component. When someone dreams of an animal or object in the natural environment, it is an *aona* that has become manifest. Having once experienced such encounters, individuals anticipate repeated contact, in dreams, throughout life. Mystical bonds are thereby established between the *iuna* (plural of *aona* of humans and those of their nonhuman familiars, such that the qualities of one are transmitted to the other. A man who has encountered the *aona* of a wild pig, of example, can be identified (for he would not announce this himself) by his physical endurance and by his speed and elusiveness in battle.

Men turn to their *iuna* for information about puzzling situations of forthcoming events, working themselves into a trance-like state by smoking quantities of tobacco or chewing a special bark *(Himantandra blgraeveana).* An occasional individual has an *aona* of power sufficiently beyond the ordinary to enable him to combat sorcerers and other agents of disease, and in recognition of this special capacity such men are singled out as *aona bana.* This term might be translated "man with a powerful familiar spirit" or "man with superior vital force," but I think it is not a distortion to translate *aona* simple as "power" and to call the man who cures a "man of power".

The *aona bana* whom I knew best was Robako, a middle-aged man in the village of Kora. According to his wife's brother, Robako's familiar spirit was a wild black pig that had made him a ferocious warrior in the old days. His twelve-year-old-son, on the other hand, was convinced that when Robako engaged in curing his *aona* took the form the insects, for once a grasshopper had appeared at a critical moment in a curing ritual, and another time a fly was heard buzzing overhead. Robako himself never spoke of his *aona*, and indeed did not like to discuss his curing powers at all.

A typical ritual takes place at night, but the light of a low-burning fire, with the patient and a few kinsmen in attendance. To summon his spirit, Robako smokes tobacco and a favorite bark, kikisira *(Bubbia sp.),* until he passes into a dreamlike state. In time his *aona* appears to him, reveals what he already suspects—that the illness is due to sorcery—and flies away. Robako quietly smokes on. Suddenly something drops at his side; it is the sorcerer's packet of poisons and exuviae, which has been cooking over a slow fire in some hidden spot. Robako opens the packet and places it outside to cool in the night air. With the cause of his illness thus dramatically displayed and the sorcerer's power crushed by that of the *aona bana*, the patient may look forward to recovery.

Disease object extraction is an infrequent mode of treatment, applied mostly to illnesses of questionable severity and not necessarily requiring an *aona bana*. Attention seems to be directed entirely to the object itself, and only in a limited sense can the procedure be interpreted as a contest between rival powers. In the community where I worked, in fact, the man who was said to be especially talented at disease object extraction was a mild ineffectual soul who would certainly not be considered an *aona bana*, and I doubt that anyone would have turned to him for treatment of a serious illness.

A number of interesting treatment procedures employ homeopathic principles in attempts to neutralize the neutralize the malevolent power of "demonic beings" (*amora bana*), "weird beings" (*nekina*), and "weird places" (*neki maa*). Lightning is demonic power in its extreme from and is said to be under the control of the *amora bana*. The association between lightning and *amora bana* on the one hand, and convulsions on the other, is not clearly formulated, but, as noted earlier, the general belief seems to be that conclusive episodes are evidence that the victim has been stuck *(fa-*, to strike or kill) by a demonic being. The treatment for convulsions is thus aimed at neutralizing *amora bana* power through homeopathic principles, by feeding a patient, or applying to his body, substances bearing some relationship to *amora bana* themselves. The most valuable items in this regard are their "bones," the aforementioned *amora adapa*. In appearance these are not unlike the bones of ordinary men, but they contain vestiges of the power of their demonic owners. In the past a man could increase his fighting abilities by tying an *amora bone* to his war shield, but nowadays the bones are valued principally for their medicinal properties. Bits of the bone may be added to a therapeutic meal (pork, medicinal plants, etc.), or the bone may be immersed in water which is then drunk by the victim or (if he is unable to drink) poured over him.

Other items that may be combined with *amora* bones in the treatment of convulsions all have *amora* (which bears a connotation of lightning-like redness) as part of their names: *amora dasi*, leaves (*dasi*) that have turned reddish-brown: two plants, *amora nora* (? *Commelina*) and *amora rakari (Pipturus)*; and a red insect called *amora kaba*. In contrast to my earlier statement about Gimi medicines, we have here substances with very specific uses. But they are neutralizing medicines, not strengthening medicines, and the principle underlying their use is rather comparable to that of immunization, namely, that a small dose increases resistance to much larger doses. Moreover, and a most important point, they are chosen not because of any manifest relation to the illness proper but because of their relation to *amora bana* the causative agents of that illness.

Similar principles emerge in the treatment of illnesses caused by trespassing or misbehaving in a "weird place" (*neki maa*). The patient's kinsmen bind bits of meat or sugar cane and some therapeutic leaves into a small packet (called *mutana*, "detoxifier") designed to seduce the *nekina* into participating in the cure of its own victim. They take the packet to the *neki maa* near where the violation occurred, and lay it at the edge of a pond in the hope that the *nekina* will encounter it. If the venture is successful, they return later to find their bait partly nibbled away; the *nekina* has in effect left behind his own refuse and with it some of his own essence. The men blow smoke over the bait, presumably to lessen the danger of contact with something now so intimately connected with an agent of illness. Then it is brought to the victim, to be eaten or rubbed over his body, thereby enabling him partly to incorporate the very power that made him ill.

A *neki* plot of land is itself credited with power to cause illness, as is evidenced by treatment procedures aimed at neutralizing the actual site of a violation. One such procedure consists simply of pouring pig blood over the site. An elderly village headman was said to have shot an arrow into a tree in a *neki maa* when he was a young man, and to have fallen ill soon thereafter. His father poured blood of a freshly killed pig over the tree, and the victim recovered. (Note that the young man sat off to the side, so to speak, while his father and a pig fought the battle for him).

A related technique combines the principles of homeopthic counteraction and positive therapy: water collected from a *neki* maa pond is placed in a ceremonial flute and poured over the sick individual. Flutes are objects of central importance in Gimi ritual; they symbolize all that Gimi men hold dear: continuity, social solidarity, male dominance (Glick 1963: 81-86; cf. Read 1952). Used in a medical context, they transmit some of their own therapeutic power along with that of the homeopathic pond water.

To warn away trespassers from privately owned land, Gimi men sometimes drape pieces of a fern called *fuba* in the branches of trees. The name of the fern and the term for a trespass warning are the same; one says, *fuba arome arai*, "he cut and placed a warning." The same phrase appears in reference to certain kinds of treatments designed to combat unknown agents of illness by ritual warnings and injunctions to release their victims. Thus on one occasion I saw a chronically ill girl, about six or seven years old, treated by her elder brother, her mother's brother, and the headman (*luluai*) of her village. They cooked for the child a preparation of dog meat and assorted therapeutic leaves. But before she ate, her mother's brother took a bit of the food in his fingers, stepped over to a nearby fence, and turned away from the others; he waved the food several times over his shoulder, mumbled a few words, then returned, and fed it to his niece. There is no set formula for this rite, and I did not hear what the man said, but later an informant ventured the following (freely translated) soliloquy as an example of what might have been said: "Listen, you men everwhere: men of Kora, men of Ise, men of Fokuru, men of Ukai, men of Raro, men of Mekino, whoever poisoned this girl; she shall eat this medicine, and she shall not die!" In explaining the rationale of this procedure, my informant said, "He cut the *fuba* and gave it to her" *(fuba arome amei);* the medicinal food was, in short, a tangible expression of the spoked warning or spell. Here again we encounter a medicine that both strengthens the sick individual and counteracts the power of her antagonist. The informant's meticulous listing of village did not, of course, include the girl's own.

A similar procedure was said to be suitable for someone presumed to have been attacked by an unidentified *nekina.* The victim himself, I was told, might hold out his medicine and say something like this: "Listen, you who poisoned me. I looked everywhere for you and now I've found you. I went to Noberai, but they (i.e., the *nekina* there) said, 'We didn't poison you....' I went to Menebi, but they said,'We didn't poison you'.... (other places named). Then I came to Rabokai and found you! But now I will eat this medicine, and you'll have to release me!" The tour (imaginary, of course) of places known to contain *nekina* finally arrives at the place suspected.

During May, 1962, several children died in an epidemic in the Gimi community of Mekino (Mingino). To combat this visitation the people erected a barrier, again called *fuba*, across the main path leading into the community. This was plainly a symbolic device: three poles entwined with leaves (unfortunately not identified) and tied to form a ricketysquared arch. People expalined: "We made and placed a warning" (*fuba ome maraune*).

Blood and Self-purification

Mention must be made of a set of interrelated ideas and practices that lie on the borders of the medical system as I am defining it, yet play an important role in the efforts of men to maintain health and vigor. These have to do with the belief that blood—particularly that of women, but all blood, human and animal—is a powerful and at time dangerous substance. There is evidence for this throughout Gimi culture, but here I shall confine the discussion to two practices that bear sufficiently on the medical system to require attention.

First, men afflicted with the aches and pains of advancing age, or with vague symptoms of malaise and lethargy, may attribute their disabilities to accumulation of excessive blood in the body: *naupi kuri obai,* literally, "in my skin heaviness afflicts," which is to say that the aching and lethargy are due to the skin's being congested with blood. To gain relief they employ a kind of venesection. This is performed with a miniature bow and arrow, the bow only about twelve inches in length, the arrow some nine or ten inches long and tipped with a sharp chip of stone or, nowadays, a sliver of glass. Anyone may perform the operation. Cords are bound around the arms at biceps level and left in place for several minutes until the veins bulge. Then the operator places a leaf rolled into a tube against a prominent vein as a guide for the arrow, which is now fitted to the bow, inserted into the tube, and snapped into the forearm. If and when the arrow pierces a vein, the stream of blood is directed into a bowl or a large *banana* leaf until perhaps a half pint has been collected. The blood must be buried or tossed into a river to prevent its falling into the hands of a sorcerer. Although this may seem to be a treatment like any other, it is in fact not an adequate procedure for a severe illness. That is, if a man feels achy and lethargic he may turn first to venesction to improve his general state of health; but should this progress to serious illness, the diagnosis will most likely be that a sorcerer has attacked him, and different, strictly medical, procedures will be warranted.

The second practice, though seldom if ever observed today, was formerly one of the most dramatic events in the lives of the Gimi and most other Eastern Highlands peoples. As one of the first steps in boys' initiations, and also whenever it was known that a newly married woman in a village was menstruating, the men withdrew in a group to the nearest river, where in vivid rites is of self-purification, they jabbed and twirled sharp blades of bush grass within their nostrils until blood flowed vigorously. The operation took place at the water's edge, so that the blood would be washed away from the reach of sorcerers. Boys were taught that this procedure was an essential step in their transition to manhood, and indeed men had recourse to it whenever they felt a need to reinforce their virility and to guarantee that the general vigor of the male community would be preserved.

Are venesection and nose—bleeding to be included as medical practices? Strictly speaking, I would say not. For one thing, they are confined to men, whereas treatments for illness ordinarily apply to everyone. For another, neither of these procedures actually treats illness; what they do is to insure or restore masculine vigor. The association between blood and woman is pervasive in Gimi thought; to bleed is to expel female essence from one's body—and not merely in a metaphorical sense. Gimi men do not understand menstruation or its relation to women's capacity to bear children, but they value that capacity highly, and they do know that blood has something to do with it. I venture to postulate that the detestation with which Gimi men regard women is at least partly explainable with reference to their poorly repressed fears of female powers and capacities that can be neither understood nor controlled. In drawing blood from their noses and forearms, men somewhat pathetically imitate women, paradoxically transcending their maleness and at the same time guaranteeing its perpetuation.

Responses to Death: Divination and Revenge

An illness ending in death, particularly that of an able adult male, is a genuine blow to his village. The survivors, convinced that only a sorcerer could have brought on such a catastrophe, and that ultimate responsibility rests, therefore, with the men who instigated the sorcery, feel it incumbent on themselves to identify the guilty party and gain revenge. Prior to Australian hegemony this meant warfare—killing in return, at times to the point of massacre. Now warfare is no longer possible, but there remain subtler ways of gaining satisfaction.

First, however, we need to consider the matter of identifying the responsible agents. People's thoughts turn first to their traditional enemies, and what follows is more often than not an attempt to verify suspicions that are already firmly rooted. Identification procedures are predicated on the expectation that the ghost *(kore)* of the deceased will disclose to his kinsmen the identity of his murderers, either by revealing their names, leading, searchers to their village, or singling them out in groups of visitors who are invited for just that purpose. To illustrate the first possibility, I present below a brief account of a divination rite, witnessed in 1961, in which people tried unsuccessfully to obtain information directly from a kinsman immediately after his death.

After a prolonged illness manifested by abdominal distention and wasting (diagnosed as *amuse kio),*a man named Tene died one evening in the home of his wife, where a number of his kinsmen and neighbors had gathered in anticipation of what was clearly imminent. Within an hour after his death several men began a deviation ritual to identify his killers. To the top of a long bamboo tube they tied several varieties of leaves, ferns, and shrubs; although none were popular therapeutic plants, they were undoubtedly there to augment the ritual powers of the tube. A tuft of hair pulled from the dead man's head was fastened an inch or two from the tip of a war arrow, which was then placed point down in the tube. The principal performer was Reba, an affinal Kinsman from a neighboring village who had settled in Tene's village. While he rested the tube in the palm of one hand, two assistants inhaled deeply on a special pipe mixture of tobacco and selected leaves *(Eleagnus, Amaracarpus),* then blew draughts of smoke onto the tube, beginning at the base and in one rapid motion shooting a stream of smoke up the side. This they repeated several times, following which one pipe was passed to Reba. He inhaled deep and rapidly until he appeared to pass into a trance-like state, but without losing command of his faculties. His eyelids fluttered, then closed; his head tilted; then his hands began to tremble, first gently, then vigorously, until the arrow was rattling violently in the tube.

The onlookers, who until this point had chatted and paid little attention to the proceedings, now fell silent and stared at the arrow. Meanwhile, a young man named Famuti, Tene's wife's brother's son, who all this time had sat quietly and familiarly next to the corpse (munching a sweet potato at one point), turned toward it and softly asked that it reveal the killer's identity. As he whispered the names of those he suspected, the arrow rattled even more violently, indicating that the ghost was indeed present and willing to participate. Had Famuti lighted on the correct name, the arrow would have leaped from its container. But on this occasion they were not to succeed. Their failure cannot be attributed to lack of enthusiasm, for one man smoked so vigorously that he was forced to race out of the hut to vomit.

As far as I know, Tene's killer was never detected, and the matter was dropped. Although in this day of imposed fraternity there is little point in pushing divination to its conclusion, in the recent past men would probably have turned to other procedures to identify their antagonists. I did not witness any other divination or detection procedures, but several were described to me. In one, a kinsman ties to his finger a tuft of the deceased's hair, then smokes until he enters a trance-like state similar to that described for Reba; but this time his arm extends and the marked finger points the way to the killer's home. Accompanied by other men of the village, he goes from one community to the next until eventually the group are led to the home of the sorcerer, whom they may attack and kill on the spot.

Failure to visit an ostensibly friendly villages after a death has occurred their is itself suggestive of guilt, so that men make a practice of appearing before suspicions have time to mature. Again this probably seldom holds true now, but in the recent past they came prepared to submit to guilt detection tests. For example, each visitor might be expected to touch the corpse's toe; should the guilty man do so, the body would twitch. (One man remarked that it might also defecate.) Or a cord might be tied from the corpse's finger to a house rafter, and each visitor expected either to loop his thumb and index finger around it or to place an extended hand just beneath it; if the cord vibrated, the jittery, and thus presumably guilty, individual might be attacked.

A recently deceased man's kinsmen might also visit all village in their area and obtain from each a bit of potato or taro. They then returned home and cooked all the food together in an oven; a contribution from a guilty village would remain uncooked. Alternatively, a portion of sweet potato might be placed before an opossum and the names of suspects recited to the animal, who, upon hearing the correct name, would grunt and gobble down the food.

If a sorcerer and, most important, those who encouraged him to act could be identified, the obvious response was overt counteraggression. But for those who were perhaps uncertain or not strong enough to risk open attack, and nowadays for anyone who fears administrative reprisals, there are counterattack techniques that operate at long range and entail no risk. First, the sorcerer himself can be made to suffer and die by a procedure known as *kapari funa*, "stinger blowing." The *kapari* is an unidentified bush or tree bearing barbs on its stems. In *kapari funa* the barbs are burned on a low fire, then one blows the ashes into the air, whereupon they magically seek out the sorcerer and fly up into his anus. Although he may realize nothing at the time, he is from then on a stricken man; soon some form of disaster—severe injury of illness, death in a quarrel—overtakes and destroys him. Second, it was said that those who sought vengeance against all of a sorcerer's kinsmen and cohorts might shoot flaming arrows, with tufts of the dead man's hair attached, in the direction of suspected village. Apparently the intent was not to burn a village at once but to induce to guilty village to burn in the future.

Summary of the Gimi Medical System

The Gimi medical system has essentially nothing to do with medicine as we ordinarily understand this term, for the Gimi do not share our understanding of disease processes. When a Gimi individual falls seriously ill, people deduce from the signs and symptoms of his illness—the evidence—a probable cause, and this constitutes their diagnosis. But causation has several dimensions, not all of equal importance. First, there is the relatively minor question of how an illness was brought about (what I call the instrumental cause); then there is the much more compelling question of who was the responsible agent (the efficient cause); and finally one encounters more extensive explanations for why agents act as they do (ultimate causes), at which point one has moved beyond the realm of the medical system and into such considerations as social and political competition, intra-familial disputes, quarrels, conflicts, and crimes.

The diagnostic paradigm (Figure I) stresses efficient causes because that is what concerns the Gimi. This principle, insofar as I can judge, would also apply to the medical concepts of many or most of the people whom anthropologists study. Instrumental causes are of the relatively little importance because as explanations for illness they are incomplete; they tell nothing about who acted or why. It might be added that, taken out of context and considered as "culture traits," they are entirely inadequate for ethnological purposes, because they are so widespread and nonspecific as to be useless for characterizing a particular medical system or comparing it with others.

Causative agents, human or nonhuman, bring alien power to bear against their victims. Gimi treatments can all be understood as attempts to resist such power, either by tapping additional power for the victim or by neutralizing or destroying the power of his antagonist. Like most people, the Gimi look to plants especially for therapeutic help, but they depend also on substances whose potential is fully understandable only in the context if Gimi culture: the flesh, blood, and a fat of pigs; water and blood poured from ceremonial flutes.

Finally, it must be emphasized that the Gimi do not face illness alone or respond to illness as a phenomenon independent of the personal identity of its victim. An illness has meaning for a community, not just for an individual, and this is what is expressed each time a man or woman's kinsmen and friends gather to establish a diagnosis or to co-operate in a treatment procedure. But the most striking social response follows death, when the survivors must decide who is ultimately responsible so that they can gain revenge. The conviction that most severe illnesses are ultimately attributable to aggression on the part of other village is perhaps the most distinctive feature of the Gimi theory of illness, but idea that causative agents are the central consideration in diagnosis and treatment is something that Gimi culture shares with many others.

Conclusion

Although the idea of "universal categories" of culture has held little currency in anthropology in recent years, there is lately discernible some reawakening of interest in what looks very much like universal categories, albeit not under that label. For example, the introduction by Burling (1962) of the idea of maximization into economic anthropology is grounded in the conviction that one can isolate universal principles of human behavior. A parallel example is the recent definition of religion advanced by Geertz (1966; 4): "a system of symbols which acts to establish powerful, pervasive, and long-lasting moods and motivations in men by formulating conceptions of a general order of existence. . . ."

Work of this kind represents movement in two directions. First, long entrenched ethnographic categories are being subjected to critical examination and redefinition. The question is whether or not such categories, as conventionally defined, belong in ethnographies, and, if so, what they should contain. Second, these authors have ventured definitions that are more comprehensive, more abstract, and at the same time less rooted in Western conceptions and biases. With the accumulated wisdom of some fifty years of detailed ethnographic work by their predecessors at their command, quite a few anthropologists seem not so sensitive to the possibility of being labeled "Frazerian." Their work reveals a shift in emphasis not only toward rather bold generalizations of the kind just cited, but also toward more intensive attention to the ideas, principles, and symbolic correspondences underlying the concrete actions and behavior to which we have for a long time been adjured to confine ourselves (cf. Leach 1961: Turner 1964, 1966).

In opposition to this point of view, although seldom explicitly, anthropologists engaged in what has been called "the new ethnography" (Sturtevant 1964) have advanced the argument that ethnographic categories must be indigenously derived, that they reflect without distortion the categories of the people whom that particular ethnography is about. These workers seem unprepared to admit compromises; there can be no misunderstanding the firm insistence of such a statement as the following by Conklin (1964: 25):

> An adequate ethnography is here considered to include the culturally significant arrangement of productive statements about the relevant relationships obtaining among locally defined categories and contexts (of objects and events) within a given social matrix.

Although it is unfashionable to dispute this position[10] it seems to me that unqualified adoption of such a course would steer us still farther from all possibility of significant accomplishments in ethnology. On one level, therefore, this paper may be read as an attempt to achieve, within the context of a single ethnographic category, a course somewhere between those associated with ethnoscience and ethnology. For the particular problem set here, I have suggested that the idea of intrinsic power—where it is found, how it is controlled—offers a focal point around which certain ethnographic materials can be organized so as to be potentially comparable. It would appear that similar themes or concepts can and should be isolated and tested for other categories.

But first and foremost this paper is intended to be read as a contribution to the ethnography of medical beliefs and practices. Compared to the sophistication and organization of ethnographic account of social and political systems, even of religious systems, descriptions of that body of beliefs and practices called "medicine" lag far behind. I have tried to demonstrate that by approaching this subject as system, in which behavior reflects belief, we may be able to put ideas in order, present comparable materials, and show how a people's medicine relates to other dimensions of their experience.

How then do I suggest that we proceed in the ethnography of medical systems? By beginning with the idea of power and asking: Where in this culture are the loci for power? How is it mobilized, resisted, and otherwise controlled? How does it enter into the various domains of a people's experience,such as subsistence practices, social control, and religious,belief? Finally, how do ideas about the loci and control of power relate to ideas about illness and responses to illness? The answers to this final question rightly constitute the subject matter of a chapter on "Medicine."

Bibliography

Berndt, R. M. 1964. Warfare in the New Guinea Highlands. American Anthropologist 66: iv, pt. 2, 183-203.

Berreman, G. D. 1966. Anemic and Emetic Analyses in Social Anthropology. American Anthropologist 68: 346-354.

Burling, R. 1962. Maximization Theories and the study of Economic anthropology. American Anthropologist 64: 802-821.

Caudill, W. 1953. Applied Anthropology in Medicine. Anthropology Today, ed. A. L. Kroeber, pp. 771-806. Chicago.

Clements, F. E. 1932. Primitive Concepts of Disease. University of

California Publications in American Archaeology and Ethnology 32: 185-22.

Codrington, R. H. 1891. The Melanesians. Oxford.

Conklin, H. C. 1962. Lexicographical Treatment of Folk Taxonomies. Problems in Lexicography, ed. F. W. Householder and S. Saporta, pp. 119-141. Indiana University Research Center in Anthropology, Folklore, and Linguistics, Publication 21. Bloomington.

1964. Ethnogenealogical Method. Emplorations in Cultural Anthropology, ed. W. H. Goodenough, pp. 25-55 New York.

Evans-Pritchard, E.E. 1937. Witchcraft, Oracles, and Magic Among the Azande. Oxford.

1965. Theories of Primitive Religion. Oxford.

Field, M.J. 1937. Religion and Medicine of the Ga People London.

Firth, R. 1940. The Analysis of Manā: An Empirical Approach. Journal of the Polynesian Society 49: 483-510.

Frake, C. O. 1961. The Diagnosis of Disease Among the Subanun of Mindanao. American Anthropologist 63: 113-132.

1962. The Ethnographic Study of Cognitive Systems. (With Comment by H. C. Conklin.) Anthropology and Human Behavior, ed. T. Gladwin and W. Sturtevant, pp. 72-93. Washington.

Geertz, C. 1966. Religion as a Cultural system. Anthropological Approaches to the Study of Religion, ed. M. Benton pp. 1-46. London.

Glick, L. B. 1963. Foundations of a Primitive Medical System: The Gimi of the New Guinea Highlands. Unpublished doctoral dissertation, University of Pennsylvania.

Hallowell, A. I. 1935. Primitive Concepts of Disease. American Anthropologist 37: 365-368.

1960. Ojibwa Ontology, Behavior, and World View. Culture in History, ed. S. Diamond. pp. 19-52. New York.

Langness, L. L. 1964. Some Problems in the Conceptualization of Highlands Social Structures. American Anthropologist 66: iv, pt. 2, 162-182.

1965. Hysterical Psychosis in the New Guinea Highlands: a Bena Bena Example, Psychiatry 28: 258-277.

Leach, E. R. 1961. Golden Bough or Gilded Twig? Daedalus 90: 371-387.

Marett, R. R. 1914. The Threshold of Religion. 2nd edit. London.

Middleton, J., and E. H. Winter, eds. 1963. Witchraft and Sorcery in East Africa. London.

Murphy, R. F. 1958. Mundurucu Religion. University of California Publications in American Archaeology and Ethnology 49: 1-154.

Nadel, S. F. 1954. Nupe Religion. London.

Newman, P. 1964. "Wild Man" Behavior in a new Guinea Highlands Community. American Anthropologist 66: 1-19.

Radin, P. 1957. Primitive Religion. New York.

Read, K. E. 1952. Nama Cult of the Central Highland, New Guinea. Oceania 23: 1-25.

1954. Cultures of the Central Highlands, New Guinea. Southwestern Journal of Anthropology 10: 1-43.

Spiro, M. E. 1966. Religion: Problems of Definition and Explanation. Anthropological Approaches to the Study of Religion, ed. M. Banton, pp. 85-126. London.

Steiner, F. 1956. Taboo. London.

Sturtevant, W.C. 1964. Studies in Ethnoscience. American Anthropologist 66: iii, pt. 2, 99-131.

Turner, V. W. 1964. Betwixt and Between: The Liminal Period in Rites de Passage. Symposium on New Approaches to the Study of Religion, ed. J. Helm, pp. 4-20. Seattle.

1966. Colour Classification in Ndembu Ritual. Anthropological Approaches Van der Leeuw, G. 1938. Religion in Essence and Manifestation. New York.

Watson, J. B., ed. 1964. New Guinea: The Central Highlands. American Anthropologist 66: iv, pt. 2.

Wax, M., and R. Wax, 1964. Magic and Monotheism. Symposium on New Approaches t the Study of Religion, ed. J. Helm, pp. 50-60. Seattle. Webster,, H. 1942. Taboo. Stanford.

NOTES

1. An earlier and briefer vision of this paper was read as part of symposium on "Ethnoscience" at the annual meeting of the Central States Anthropological society, St. Louis, April 29, 1966. I am indebted to the organizer of that symposium, Oswald Werner, for the opportunity and stimulus this provided. The paper incorporates materials first presented in a dissertation (Glick 1963) prepared at the University of Pennsylvania under the guidance of Ward Goodenough.

2. This entire chapter, which is entitled "Medicine," may be read as an illustration of most of the points being made here. Nadel's failure to follow out the implications of his own insight into the meaning of the Nepe word *cigbe* led him to a number of unfortunate interpretations.

3. My emphasis thereby differs from that of Frake (1961), who concentrates on evidence and process. Frake may have included more than would be acceptable as medically significant according to the criteria established in the present paper. (He would reply that his only criteria are those of the Subanun.)

4. In some cultures "tabooed" objects, places, words, or thoughts may cause illness reflexively (fc. Webster 1942: 22-26). Obviously they are not persons, but they as loci of power whose actions or effects are socio-culturally relevant. Just an individual may bring on his own illness by offending a shaman, so he may bring it on by defying a culturally recognized source of danger. Steiner (1956: 146-147) concludes that the taboo concept enables people to exercise control over otherwise frightening powers by the "narrowing down and localization of danger."

5. Field work was conducted by my wife and myself in the Gimi community of Hegeturu for seventeen months between September, 1960, and June, 1962. The National Institute of Mental Health furnished generous support during and after this work through grants MF-11, 680 and M-4025.

6. This apparent paradox resolves into whether one is thinking about sorcery aimed at the home village or at that of an enemy, for controlled, socially beneficial aggression is highly valued.

7. Native police are also called *rukabki bana,* not because they control violence but because they themselves are violent.

8. As with every illness discussed here, there are of course other

possible explanations for why this young man behaved this way. He had a disturbed family history, had achieved only a borderline adjustment to his role,and probably responded in this culturally expectable manner to the pressures of approaching marriage and adult responsibilities. The episode and its dynamics are discussed in more detail in Glick 1963: 127-129, 172-173. For a detailed analysis of a similar episode among a nearby people, so Langness 1965; also Newman 1964.

9. Leach's paper is programmatic. "although in any one context manifest customs reflect only a local system of ideas and beliefs, there is still certain level at which one can legitimately think of ideas and beliefs as cross-cultural phenomena. It is surely fair to assert that `the same'belief may appear in different cultures yet be reflected in quite different forms of manifest custom. If this is so, then it is the task of contemporary anthropology to re-esablish a science of cross-culural compassion by devising some kind of synthesis between Frazerian and functionalist techniques. But where Frazer concentrated on the assembling of similar ideas" (Leach 1961: 382). Turner's papers are brilliant demonstrations of how this can work out in practice. See also the observations by Spiro (1966:90) on definitions and generalization.

10. But see Berreman 1966.

---

* *Ethnology*- 1967. Vol vi. No. 1

Chapter-4

The Hot-Cold Syndrome and Symbolic Balance in Mexican and Spanish-American Folk Medicine

By Richard L. Currier

Chapter-4

In contemporary Mexico (and,Spanish America as well), one important aspect of folk medical belief and practice is a simplified form of Greek humoral pathology, which was elaborated in the Arab world, brought to Spain as scientific medicine during the period of Moslem domination, and transmitted to America at the time of the Conquest (Foster 1953: 202-204). According to this classical pathology, the basic functions of the body were regulated by four bodily fluids or "humors," each of which was characterized by a combination of heat or cold with wetness or dryness (blood—hot and wet; yellow bile—hot and dry; phlegm—cold and wet; black bile—cold and dry). Proper balance of these humors was considered necessary for good health, and any imbalance resulted in illness. Curing of disease consisted of correcting such imbalances by the addition or subtraction of heat, cold, dryness, or wetness (Taylor 1063: 15).

In Latin America today, most foods beverages, herbs, and medicines (and some other substances as well) are classified as "hot" *(caliente)* or "cold" *(fresco or frio).* This classification is usually independent of such observable characteristics as form, color, texture, and physical temperature, and it is descriptive only of the effects which a substance is thought to have upon the human body. As in classical humoral pathology, illness is often attributed to imbalance between heat and cold in the body, and curing is likewise accomplished by the restoration of proper balance. On the other hand, there is no corresponding classification of substances as "wet" or "dry", nor do the concepts of wetness and dryness appear in folk medical belief and practice. Why has the hot-cold syndrome persisted for centuries as the basis of folk medical beliefs, while the wet-dry syndrome, equally important in classical theory, has long since been lost? The following functional hypothesis is offered as an explanation of this phenomenon.

In the process of weaning, the Mexican child is subjected to a prolonged period of acute rejection. As a result of this experience he forms strong subconscious associations between warmth and acceptance or intimacy on the one hand and between cold and rejection or withdrawal, on the other. In adult life these associations appear in those beliefs intimately concerned with the problem of personal security theories about nourishment and about the prevention and cure of disease and injury. On a conscious level, then, the hot-cold syndrome is a basic principle of human physiology, and it functions as a logical system for dealing with the problems of disorder and disease. On a subconscious level, however, the hot-cold syndrome is a model of social relations. In this case, disease theory constitutes a symbolic system upon which social anxieties are projected, and it functions as a means of symbolically manipulating social relationships which are too difficult and oo dangerous to manipulate on a conscious level in the real social universe. In this latter sense the hot-cold syndrome is the kind of secondary institution which Kardiner (1945:39) called a projective system. Finally, the nature of Mexican peasant society is such that each individual must continuously attempt to achieve a balance between two opposing social forces: the tendency toward intimacy and that toward withdrawal. I propose, therefore, that the individual's continuous preoccupation with achieving a balance between "heat" and "cold" is a way of reenacting, in symbolic terms, a fundamental activity in social relations.

Unless otherwise indicated, the data on Mexican folk medicine presented in this paper were gathered in Erongaricuaro, Michoacan, during the summers of 1963 and 1954.[1] Erongaricuaro is a peasant village on the southwestern shores of Lake Patzcuaro in the central Mexican Highlands; it has a population of about 3,000. Although it is surrounded by several smaller villages in which Tarascan is still the principal language spoken, Erongaricuaro is a mestizo village. All my informants were Spanish speaking Mexican peasants.

The Hot-Cold Syndrome as Medical Belief

The hot-cold syndrome in Latin America has been reported for Mexico (Beals 1946; Foster 1948; Lewis 1960; Redfield 1934), for Mexican-American communities (Saunders 1954; Clark 1959; McFeeley 1949; Rubel 1960), for the Gautemalan Highlands (Gillin 1951; Adams 1952), for coastal Colombia (Reichel-Dolmatoff 1958; Velasquex 1957), for the Colombian Highlands (Reichel-Dolmatoff 2902), and for coastal Peru and coastal Chile (Simmons 1955). It appears in a discussion of Inca medical practices at the time of the Spanish conquest (D'Harcourt 1939). A more thorough investigation would doubtless reveal its presence elsewhere, but for the purposes of this paper the above references suffice to establish that the syndrome is widespread among the Latin American peasantry. That, in addition, it often forms the basic theoretical foundation of indigenous folk medicine is illustrated by the following sample quotations:

> [T]here is one important concept which enters into the ideas of disease and its treatment...[and] constitutes a sort of physiological principle of the folk. This concept is the distinction between things "cold" and things "hot" (Redfield 1934:161).
>
> A strict observation of the rules imposed by these categories of "cold" and "hot" is imperative in the treatment of all illness (Reichel-Dolmatoff 1958: 236; my translation). The single common thread that runs through all popular medicine is the distinction between "hot" and "cold" (Simmons 1955:61).

Any cultural institution which survives with such vitality for so many centuries can hardly be a relic, stubbornly but uselessly buried in the matrix of a traditional culture. The concept of hot and cold qualities in Latin American folk medicine must have functional significance in peasant culture, or it would have suffered the same fate as its counterpart, the concept of wet and dry qualities.

Although to the casual observer the hot-cold syndrome is most conspicuous in the classification of foodstuffs, several facts point to the conclusion that it derives its ultimate importance from the problem of disease and injury. First, its historical roots are in medicine, not in the culinary or agricultural arts. Second, the "temperature' (henceforth I will use the Mexican term *calidad,* literally "quality") of a foodstuff is relevant only to its effect on the human body, and then only because it might have an adverse effect on health. Third, the qualities of heat and cold play an important role in numerous situations that have nothing whatever to do with food (for example, it is considered dangerous to expose oneself to the night air when one's body is warm).Fourth, the only way of determining the *calidad* of a food or other substance is by observing the effect it has on an illness known to be hot or cold. Finally, there is relatively little agreement as to which foods are hot and which are cold, not only between one geographical area and another but even among the members of a single community. In a study of Mexicans living in the United States, McFeeley (1949:41-53) prepared a list of plants and foodstuffs and asked several informants to identify *calidad* of each. Of the first 52 items which more than one informant identified, the informants agreed on the *calidad* of 25 and disagreed on 27. Foster (1948: 51), Saunders (1954: 147), and Lewis (1960: 12), each reporting from a different Mexican community, found substantial disagreement among the members of each community as to the *calidad* of various items. This evidence suggests that what is important is only that foodstuffs be assigned a *calidad,* and that, ultimately, it makes little difference which particular substances are classified as hot and which as cold.

Although these qualities affect the body only through the agency of the substances in which they reside, the people blame the damage on the qualities themselves and not on the substances involved. If, for instance, a person eats green peaches and develops stomach cramps, he does not complain that "those green peaches made me sick" but that "the cold of the peaches has gotten me in the stomach."

Some of the illnesses believed in Erongaricuaro to be caused by cold entering the body are listed below:

Chest cramp Cold air enters the chest when a person is overheated.

Earache. A cold draft of air enters the ear canal.

Headache. The coolness of mist or of the night air, called *aigre* (a localism corrupted from Spanish *aire,* "air"), penetrates the head.

Paralysis. A part of the body is "struck" by *aigre.* Sniffiness, considered a partial, temporary paralysis, is ascribed to the same cause.

Pain due to sprains. Such "cold pains" are the result of cold entering the damaged part.

Stomach cramp. When the body is warm, and not adequately covered, cold can enter from the air or from a body of water.

Rheumatism. Cold from some outside source lodges in the afflicted bones.

Teething. The pain of teething is a "cold pain," originating in the coldness of the white new teeth that are growing in.

Tuberculosis. Cold enters the body from water or carbonated beverages, especially when the body is overheated from work or travel.

The following are some of the illnesses believed to be caused by an overabundance of heat in the body:

Algodonciloo. Heat rises from the çenter of the body to the mouth, causing the gums, tongue, and lips to turn white.

Disipela. Overexposure to the sun can cause the sun's heat to collect in the skin, resulting in an outbreak of red spots on the hands, arms or less commonly the feet.

Dysentery. Since it is accompanied by bloody stool, and since blood is intensely hot, dysentery is classed as a hot disease, and may be caused by consuming too much hot food.

Sore eyes. A person may overstrain his eyes, causing them to "work hard' and thus to heat up, or, alternatively, cold wet feet can cause the body heat to rise to the ahead, overheating the eyes.

Fogazo. Heat rising from the center of the body causes the mouth and tongue to break out in tiny red spots. In contrast to *algodoncillo,* this is not a serious disease.

Kindney ailments. Any pain in the kidneys is a hot pain; most kidney ailments are accompanied by itching feet or ankles, a reddening of the palms of the hands, and fever.

Postemilla. An abcessed tooth results from heat concentrating in the root, evidenced by the fact that when the abcess bursts it releases blood.

Sore throat. Wet feet cause sore throat by driving the body heat up into the throat.

Warts and rashes. Whatever their cause (a subject upon which my informants refused to speculate), these ailments are the results of heat. This is a conclusion from the fact that warts and rashes are irritating,and irritation is always ascribed to heat and never to cold.

Another group of illnesses may be caused by either heat or cold. In other words, each has a hot and a cold form, to which, of course, different remedies must be applied. The following are examples:

Diarrhea. Diarrhea is usually cold—caused by "cold in the stomach"— but it may also be hot. In the former case the feces are merely loose; in the latter they are green, and steam when fresh.

Enteritis. A case of diarrhea, if not checked, may develop into a case of *torzon* or enteritis, a more serious ailment. *Torzon* may be of either the hot or the cold variety, and these types are again distinguished by the appearance of the feces—hot if these are streaked with blood, cold if they are white and covered with mucous (the cold wet humor of classical theory).

Toothache. Pains in the molar teeth are hot caused by improper diet. Those in other teeth are usually cold, in which case they are allegedly caused by a draft of air.

Cold maladies are principally phenomena of disablement, in which sensory and motor functions of the body are disrupted or entirely stopped. In almost every case the illness is caused by the intrusion of a quantity of coldness into a part of the body; in many cases this intrusion is made possible by the fact that the body, or a particular part of it, is more than usually warm. To be warm in any excess at all is to be vulnerable to attacks of cold which may come suddenly and unexpectedly, leaving the individual in crippling pain. For this reason, the people of Erongaricuaro are constantly on guard against the threat of cold and are unusually sensitive to the possibility that a given activity will produce warmth and, with it, vulnerability.

Maladies which are the direct result of recessive heat are, in contrast to cold maladies, often generated from within the body itself. Heat which resides in the outside world is never unpredictably threatening; illness caused by overexposure to the sun or overconsumption of hot foods is, in some ways, perfectly predictable and easily avoidable. The most dangerous aspect of the quality of heat is its ability to be displaced upward in the body. Normally, the stomach is the focus of warmth in the body, the head and extremities being relatively cool. When, however, the feet and legs come into excessive contact with coldness, either by being we or by being too long in contact with the cold ground, body heat withdraws from them and begins to extend upward into the throat and head, destroying the balance of various temperature within the body and prejudicing the eyes and mouth.

While sensations of pain are usually cold, sensations of irritation are hot. All skin ailments I know of are caused by excess heat on the surfaces of the body. It is thus a general principle of this system of pathology that cold harms the individual by invading his body from without, while heat harms the individual by expanding (or being displaced) from the center of the body outward to its surfaces. Finally, hot illnesses are not only visible but conspicuous to the outside world, taking the form of skin eruptions, fever, coatings, and hoarseness. Cold illnesses, on the other hand, are often not at all visible to the outside world; their principal symptoms are pain and immobility.

Digestive disorders account for virtually all of those illness which may be due either to hot or to cold.[2] This makes perfect sense, since inherent in the notion of achieving a balance between hot and cold foods is the premise that an excess of either quality will be damaging. The words for diarrhea, enteritities, and dysentery seem to connote the intensity of an intestinal disorder rather than its specific variety. The fact that these illnesses are defined broadly enough to include hot and cold varieties makes it possible to express the degree of imbalance without having to specify its nature. This implies that both heat and cold must be taken into the body to insure good health.

I will not burden the reader with long lists of foodstuffs and their corresponding *calidades,* at least partly because such information adds little to an understanding of the problem to which this paper is addressed. There are, however, some generalizations which it is possible to make about the classification of foodstuffs in Erongaricuaro. Bearing in mind that there is substantial disagreement among villagers as to the exact classification of the available foodstuffs, the following characteristics are generally true.

Cold foods include most fresh vegetables, the ancient Indian staples (maize, beans, and squash), most tropical fruits (including citrus fruits), dairy products, and low-prestige meats such as goat, fish, and chicken. Hot foods include most (but not all) chile peppers, most temperate-zone fruits, goat's milk, cereal grains, high-prestige meats such as beef, water fowl, and mutton, most oils, hard liquor, and aromatic beverages. A given foodstuff is often both hot an cold, depending upon whether and how it is cooked. Examples of foods that can be either hot or cold are beans, rice, wheat, pork, and peaches.

Warm foods are believed to be more easily digested than cold foods. Other things being equal, a person will often identify a food as warm simply because it is easily digested, and *vice versa.* Villagers explain this fact by pointing out that, since the stomach is warm, all foods must become warm in the body before they can be digested. Warm foods are, therefore, ready to be digested as soon as they reach the stomach. Cold foods, on the other hand, must first be warmed in the stomach, a process requiring more effort on heart of that organ. It would seem logical to conclude that if a person ate nothing but warm foods he would have no digestive problems, but, in fact, this is not the case. A partial answer to this paradox is that a diet consisting largely of warm foods will not necessarily make a healthy person sick, whereas a diet consisting largely of cold foods would sicken even the most healthy individual in a few days. Tepoztecans also believe that cold foods are less easily digested than warm foods (Lewis 1960:12).

The qualities of hot and cold are related to aspects of life other than those of nutrition and disease. It is in these other contexts that the symbolic meanings of warmth and cold are most clearly revealed: cold is associated with threatening aspects of existence, while warmth is associated with reassurance.

The two main sources of cold in Erongaricuaro are air and water, and both are threatening elements. Air can physically enter the human body, causing the same kind of damage as the attacks of cold described above.[3] Night air is especially threatening, and almost every man who ventures outside the house after dark keeps a corner of his blanket or serape pulled up over his nose and mouth, to prevent the night air from entering his body. A virtually identical belief and preoccupation has been described by Simmons (1956:62) for Peru and Chile. Water is approached with great circumspection, for it is the most intensely cold substance in the natural world. No one will approach the shore of Lake Patzcuaro, venture out in the rain, or take a bath when his body is warm from working, traveling, eating, or sleeping. Most people will not wash their hands immediately after they have handled physically or qualitatively hot substances. One villager, after having gotten oil of eucalyptus (a "hot" substance) on his hand, lost an entire night's fishing, being convinced that his hand would be paralyzed if he went out on the lake before an entire day had passed. Finally, villagers associate water with death, believing that when a person dies his blood turns to water. Adams (1952:49) reports that in Guatemala coldness is a more threatening quality than warmth. Rubel (1960:799, 807) describes the use of a remedy among Mexican-Americans, the toxicity of which is associated with its coldness.

Warmth, on the other hand, is closely associated with some of life's most reassuring activities; the human body is believed to grow warmer during work, digestion, sleep, and travel. Blood is both the primary source of life in the body and the primary agency of warmth. The presence of blood in any of the symptoms of an illness is usually sufficient to identify it as a hot illness. Blood can become weak by becoming watery, but strengthening foods and fresh blood itself (drunk at the slaughtering yard) can usually remedy this condition.[4]

The symbolic significance of heat and cold is most obvious in their effects upon the processes of reproduction and in the role they play in folk theories about the nature of these processes. In this realm, warmth most clearly assumes the symbolic significance of support and affection, while coldness most clearly symbolizes rejection and withdrawal.

In Erongaricuaro, a woman believes herself to be unusually warm during menstruation. For this reason, most women avoid cold foods until menstruation has ceased. Many women will not bath during menstruation, for fear that they will be harmed by the coldness of the water. In Colombia, Velasquez (1957: 227) reports that menstruating women should eat hot foods in preference to cold ones, and in Yucatan a cold wind is believed to halt menstruation (Redfield 1934: 162).

Notions about fertility are equally bound up with the hot-cold syndrome. Redfield (1934: 161) reports that cold foods are said to cause sterility in Yucatan. In the valley of Mexico sterile women are thought to have cold bodies, and "bad airs" can sterilize a woman (Madsen 1962:117). Clark (1959:170) discovered that Mexican-American women in California attribute barrenness to a "cold womb." In this connection, there is almost complete correspondence between fertility and warmth on the one hand and barrenness and coldness on the other.

A pregnant woman has an unusually warm body during the entire course of her pregnancy. This makes it necessary for her to avoid cold foods, a fact noted also by Velasquez (1957:228), Gillin (1951:32), and Madsen (1962:120:121). People in Erongaricuaro believe that pregnant women should take slow walks and bath often, in order to dissipate the large amounts of heat which they accumulate in their bodies. If a mother fails to do this, a fatty membrane will form on the baby's back, cementing him to the inside of the womb, with the result that the mother will experience a long and difficult delivery. In a curious way this belief is a small drama, for it symbolizes the mother's experience of relinquishing her child to the world later in life.

Let me now suggest that the intimate association of warmth with the reproductive cycle, fertility, and pregnancy is due to unconscious associations between the idea of warmth on the one hand and the notion of intimacy, epitomized in the relationship between mother and fetus, on the other. The drama can then be interpreted as follows. A mother must periodically slough off the natural feelings of protective intimacy generated by her relationship to her child, because there will come a time when she must give up the child to the world. If she fails to take such precautions, she will be virtually incapable of breaking the strong attachment she has allowed to form, and relinquishing her child will be a far more difficult, dangerous, and traumatic experience.

On the other hand, it is always possible that a pregnant women will so strongly resent the dangers and difficulties involved in the birth of a child that she will want to reject this new burden on her life. In fact, there are indications (such as the reluctance of many women to nurse their children adequately) that women in Erongaricuaro have strongly ambivalent feelings about their children; they are often both overly possessive of their children and, at the same time, resentful of the burdens which their children impose. For this reason, a pregnant woman is unusually susceptible to the emotionally based illness called *bills,* a cold disease (normally a person afflicted with *bills* is immediately wrapped in several layers of blankets) characterized by symptoms of physical and psychological withdrawal. Although in all other case *bilis* is a dangerous and harmful disease, it is harmless to a pregnant woman herself; instead, the child will be permanently injured and will suffer from chronic headaches throughout his life. Headaches are cold maladies, and they are often attributed to insufficient sleep and, especially, to insufficient nourishment. If we consider cold to be symbolic of withdrawal and rejection, we can easily interpret this kind of *bilis* as the expression of the rejection of the fetus by its mother. Hence there is nothing strange about the fact than as attack of *bilis* harms, not the woman afflicted with it, but rather the child whom she rejected. It is reasonable that such a child should grow up to display symptoms of chronic malnourishment, since the nourishment of a child by its mother is one of the primary human acts of affection and support.

Nursing, one of the most expressive symbols of intimacy and support in human life, is also closely bound up with the qualities of heat and cold. Exposure to cold diminishes the flow of milk, while warmth increases it. On the other hand, too much warmth within the mother may cause the child to become *enlechado,* a condition in which milk curdles inside the child and cannot be digested. Normally a baby will drink no more milk than it can assimilate, but if the mother is especially warm, e.g., from sitting near the fire, the baby will accept all the milk that she can give it and not reject any excess by vomiting. The remedy for this affliction involves treating the baby with cold substances, the purpose of which is to reject the excess milk.

Women in Erongaricuaro believe that it is dangerous and harmful to continue nursing a child after the onset of the next pregnancy. They say that the mother's milk becomes "weak" and "watery" and will sicken the nursing child. This implies that a woman should nourish only one child at a time, and that when it comes to a choice between a nursing child and a developing infant the former must be rejected in favor of the latter. Hence, as soon as a woman knows herself to be pregnant, she weans her nursing child abruptly and completely. At this point a child is expected to develop a children's disease called *chipil.* Villagers explain that the child is jealousof the unborn sibling and needs a great deal of affection from the other members of the family, who should hug him and sleep with him. *Chipil* is a hot disease, and, since a woman's body is believed to be especially warm during pregnancy, the pregnant mother must not hug him, pick him up, or sleep in the same bed with him. This is, of course, the moment when the child experiences the most traumatic rejection of his life. In the space of a few days he is deprived of a constant source of nourishment, security, and affection. The intimate ties that bound him to his mother have been shattered, and he is forced to turn to a host of poor substitutes in his search for the security he has lost. Mexicans interpret this increased need for affection as a disease of heat recess, and treat it with heat-diminishing remedies.

The Hot-Cold Syndrome as a Protective System

From birth until weaning Mexican babies are in continuous contact with another human body, usually that of the mother. In Erongaricuaro, a baby is usually wrapped up in his mother's *rebozo* (a long, wide shawl worn over the upper body) during most of the day. At night he sleeps in bed next to his mother. Consequently, every Mexican peasant spends that first year or two of his life in close contact with a warm human body, during which time he never experiences physical abandonment, isolation, or lack of warmth. Lewis (1960:73), Clark (1959:134), and Redfield (1943:188-189) have all commented on this fact. Nevertheless, at about the age when he begins to walk the child is both weaned and deprived of all but the most perfunctory physical contact with his mother. He is rarely carried or held, and he no longer sleeps with his mother. Instead, he is left to crawl or walk on the earth floor of the house, protected only by a layer of reed-mats. Undoubtedly one of the most novel experiences of his life is the discovery, after weaning, of the strong sensation of physical cold. To make matters worse, he had little previous experience in coping with this situation.

The period immediately after weaning is usually characterized by rage, acute depression, and psychological withdrawal on the child's, part, and he usually displays severe symptoms of protein malnutrition (no doubt owning to the almost complete absence of milk in his diet). Villagers identify this behavioral syndrome as *chipil,* a disease from which all children are expected to suffer immediately after weaning. Some children display the symptoms of *chipil* for as long as a year before recovering; many never recover, but sicken and die. This is evidence enough that weaning is a traumatic experience of some duration in the lives of the villagers. It is therefore difficult to see how most children could fail to make an intense and indelible association between the unanticipated and concurrent experience of rejection and deprivation of physical warmth. It is to be expected that such an association be carried into adult life by almost every member of Mexican peasant society; it is further to be expected that this association become institutionalized in cultural mechanisms for the protection and support of the individual in daily life.

Recent work in Latin American ethnography indicates that peasant life if characterized by lack of social cohesion, by distrust of social bonds, by instability in social relationships, by anxiety over intimacy, and by fear of abandonment (Guiteras-Holmes 1961; Lewis 1960; Paz 1961; Reichel-Dolmatoff 1961). In a series of articles, Foster (1961, 1963, 1964) has emphasized the importance of informal contractual relations between individuals in Mexican peasant society. Since these contracts are easily terminated, and are maintained only with deliberate effort, a number of social forms have arisen which stress social engagement and protect the individual against rejection (Foster 1961: 1186-1187; 1964:110) Yet at the same time there exists a fear of intimacy, lest it render the individual socially and psychologically vulnerable to those who might use him (Foster 1964: 115). Foster (1963:1280) notes that individuals hope to avoid social entanglements but that such entanglements are essential to both social and economic security. In such a world the individual survives by virtue of his ability to manipulate his social relationships so that he is rendered neither vulnerable because of over-involvement with others nor insecure because of lack of involvement with others. This encourages the attitude that social relations are means to an end and must be capable of rapid adjustments in strength or, if necessary, of abrupt termination. When all the members of a society are trying to manipulate their social ties in this manner, some people end up as losers while most others live in fear of losing. The two principal ways of losing are (1) being rejected and left without the security of friends and (2) being taken advantage of through too great a commitment to another.

We recall that cold in the outside world poses a threat to individual well-being as a result of its ability to pass through the skin into the body. I submit that in this case cold symbolizes rejection from without. Like rejection, it is an ever-present danger, and, since peasants are especially sensitive to rejection, it may cause great psychological pain to the individual by penetrating his psychological defenses. Cold is harmless to the individual when directed outward, for rejection directed outward merely reflects the necessary capacity to reject others for one's own benefit.

We may further recall that heat in the outside world posses no such threat, but that heat moving outward from the center of the body to its extremities is harmful. I further submit that this internal heat is a symbol of the need for intimacy, affection, and support, but that when this need comes so imperative as to show itself in a conspicuous way the individual jeopardizes his position is society. Advances made by others, represented by heat directed toward an individual from outside, do not normally constitute a threat since they can usually be parried or turned to personal advantage. Finally, the increased vulnerability of the body, when warm, to attacks of cold seems symbolic of the increased vulnerability of the individual, when unusually intimate with another, to the misfortune of rejection.

CONCLUSION

The biological relationship between man and his environment, and the threat of disease (which is a part of that environment), are reflected in a set of beliefs which also functions as a model of the individual's relationship to his social environment. This model serves as a symbolic system onto which social anxieties can be projected and within which social desires can be fulfilled. In other words, while it may be difficult or impossible, for example, to protect oneself against social rejection, it is usually easy and possible to protect oneself against the "cold" forces in one's diet or environment. In Erongaricuaro, as in most of peasant Mexico, one of the primary needs which society generates in the individual is the need for balance in his social relations. Lacking the luck, initiative, intelligence, or wealth to achieve this, an individual is still free to seek a balance in the world of nature, where it is always easier to find. Burgess and Dean (1962:68), speaking of food habits general, make the following observation:

> Other ways of attempting to deal with the internal stress of threats to life or to emotional security are to over-estimate external dangers, or to attribute internal treats almost entirely to external influence of various kinds; and, with this, to attempt magically to evade or appease an apparently external threat, or to balance one type of threat against another. *The practice of giving "heating" or "cooling" foods in particular kinds of clinical conditions may be a form of this kind of balancing technique for evading what are regarded as threatening influences—not of a nutritional kind* (emphasis mine).

We make a similar association in English when we identify a "warm" person as affectionate and intimate and a "cold" person as distant and withdrawn. It is possible that this association is similarly a manifestation in adult life of association we made as children, though in a manner less traumatic and less emotionally intense? The researches of clinical psychologists may some day provide an answer.

Finally, I do not wish to imply that the hot-cold syndrome can have no other meanings in Mexican peasant culture than the particular symbolic ones to which I have referred in this paper. Like any symbolic system, its use can easily be extended to other aspects of human existence, in which it may acquire additional symbolic significance. I do feel, however, that its primary importance is along the lines I have indicated, and that its ultimate origin is to be found in the unique combination of the historical background, the child-rearing practices, and the social relationships characteristic of Latin American culture in general and of Mexican peasant culture in particular.

Bibliography

Adams, R.N. 1952. Un analisis de las creencias y practices medicas en un pueblo indigena de Guatemala. Publicaciones Especiales del Instituto Indigenista Nacional 17: 1-105. Guatemala.

—— 1955. A Nutritional Research Program in Guatemala. Health, Culture, and Community, ed. B.D. Paul, pp. 435-458. New York.

Beals, R.L. 1946. Cheran: A Sierra Tarascan Village. Publications of the Institute of Social Anthropology, Smithsonian Institution 2: 1-225.

Burgess, A., and R. F.A. Dean. 1962. Malnutrition and Food Habits. London. Clark, M. 1959. Health in the Mexican-American Culture. Berkeley and Los Angeles. D'Harcourt, R. 1939. La medecine dans l'ancient Perou. Paris.

Foster, G.M. 1948. Empire's Children: The People of Tzintzuntzan. Publications of the Institute of Social Anthropology, Smithsonian Institution 6: 1—297.

—— 1953. Relationship between Spanish and Spanish-American Folk Medicine. Journal of American Folklore 66:201-217.

—— 1961. The Dyadic Contract: A Model for the Social Structure of a Mexican Peasant Village. American Anthropologist 63: 1172-1192.

—— 1963. The Dyadic Contract in Tzintzuntzan, II: Patron-Client

Relationship. American Anthropologist 65: 1280-1294.

—— 1964. Speech Forms and Perception of Social Distance in a Spanish-speaking Mexican Village. Southwestern Journal of Anthropology 20:107-122.

Guiteras-Holmes, C. 1961. Perils of the Soul: The World View of a Tzotzil Indian. Glencoe.

Kardiner, A. 1945. The Psychological Frontiers of Society. New York.Lewis, O. 1960. Tepoztlan: Village in Mexico. New York.

Madsen, C. 1962. A Study of Change in Mexican Folk Medicine. M.A. thesis, University of California at Berkeley.

McFeeley, F. 1949. Some Aspects of Folk Curing in the American Southwest. M.A. thesis, University of California at Berkeley.

Paz, O. 1961. The Labyrinth of Solitude: Like and Thought in Mexico. Transl. L. kemp. New York.

Redfield, R. 1934. Chan Kom: A Maya Village. Washington.

Reichel-Dolmatoff, G., and A. Reichel-Dolmatoff. 1958. Nevel de salud Y medicina popular en una aldea mestiza colombiana Revista Colombiana de Antropologia 7: 199-249.

—— 1961. The People of Aritama: The cultural Personality of a Colombian Mestizo Village. Chicago.

Rubel, A. J. 1960. Concepts of Disease in Mexican-American Culture. American Anthropologist 62:795-814.

Immons, O. 1956. Popular and Modern Medicine in Mestizo Communities of Coastal Peru and Chile. Journal of American Folklore 68:57-71.

Taylor, H.O. 1963. Greek Biology and Medicine, New York.

Saunders, L. 1954. Cultural Difference and Medical Care, New York.

Velasque, R. 1957. La medicina popular en la costa colombiana del Pacifico. Revista Colombiana de Antropologia 6: 193-241.

NOTES

1. I undertook field work during the summer of 1963 as research assistant to Professor George M. Foster, who supported the work from the Research Committee of the University of California at

Berkeley and by the National Science Foundation (Grant No. G7064). Field work during the summer of 1964 was supported by the National Institutes of Health (Training Grant GM-1229). I would like gratefully to acknowledge my debt to Susan K. Currier, who assisted me in both the original field research and the preparation of this paper, and to Professor Foster, without whose advice, encouragement, and support this paper would never have been written. I wish also to wish also to thank the Instituto National de Anthropologia e Historia of mexico, and its Director, Dr. Eusebio Davalos Hurtado, for permission to do ethnological field work in Mexico.

2. Dysentery, which I have listed as a hot illness, may more properly belong to the hot-or-cold category. A "cold dysentery" is recognized in Mexico (Madsen 1962: 106), but I did not encounter it in Erongaricuaro.

3. In fact, there is good reason to believe that villagers do not clearly distinguish between are and coldness. The word for the kind of cold which enters one's body is *aigre,* and some substances are *aigrios,* rather, than *frios* or *frescos.* This word is sometimes used interchangeably with the word *frio,* and it is also used interchangeably with standard Spanish *aire,* "air". Reichel-Dolmatoff (1961: 283) reports that in Colombia "winds' are always associated with `cold,' and often the two terms are interchangeable." Foster (personal communication) points out that *aigre,* is, in fact, a corruption of the word *aire,*.

4. Also associated with the notion that blood and heat are sources of life is the concept of bodily strength, which is thought to depend primarily on the quantity of blood in a person's body. Foremost among strengthening foods is beef, which is hotter than almost any other food. Adams (1955:446) found that the Guatemalan Indians conceive of blood as a non-renewable source of strength and life, and look upon the loss of blood as a permanently debilitating experience. My own experience in Erongaricuaro confirms the widespread existence of this belief in Michoacan.

* *Ethnology,* 1966. No. 3.

Chapter-5

The Maya Bonesetter as Sacred Specialist

By Benjamin D. Paul

Chapter-5

Among the dozen Maya communities that ring the shores of Lake Atitlan in the northwestern highlands of Guatemala, the town of San Pedro la Laguna is perhaps the most enterprising and progressive. A few decades ago the Pedranos, with their own labor and initiative, built a road around the steep sides of a huge volcanic mountain, and by now Pedranos own and operate two large buses and a dozen trucks, each representing a capital investment of over $10,000. These vehicles serve San Pedro and the surrounding region by providing efficient transportation to the coastal lowlands and to the capital of Guatemala. For reasons of history and ecology each village in the area has developed distinctive specialities (Tax 1937), and it can be said that in recent years modern transport service has become one of San Pedro's specialties.

Another Pedrano specialty of greater antiquity and of quite a different order is the traditional art of bone setting. In 1941, when we first began fieldwork, a healer named Ventura successfully treated a severe incapacitating ankle sprain sustained by my wife on a rocky San Pedro path. Ventura was then 77, and since the turn of the century had been setting broken bones not only for Pedranos but also for accident victims from many other parts of the republic and even from across the borders in El Salvador and Mexico. A decade later Ventura died, and a few years after that his daughter Rosario rather unexpectedly assumed the burden of repairing bone injuries. Because of her good results and widespread reputation, the town of San Pedro continued to attract sufferers from distant places. Rosario still practices today, but she is old and lacks the physical strength to mend some of the more severe fractures. But she is now only one of five or six bone setters practicing in San Pedro. This is quite a change from the time old Ventura was the lone expert in a town of 2,000 people. The population of San Pedro now approaches 5,000 but the number of native bonesetters has increased disproportionately.

From the outsider's point of view, the healer resets bones by means of adroit manipulation, massaging the area with marrow extracted from beef bones, placing heated tobacco leaves against the bare skin, and applying a tight bandage. A splint of cardboard or slats may be used to immobilize the injured ares. But the bonesetters and their clients see the process differently. In their view the work is not done by the human practitioner but by a special little bone concealed in the hand of the healer, who locates the precise point of the break by passing the bone back and forth over the general area of the injury. When the traveling bone finds the critical juncture it comes to a halt and stays clamped to the spot long enough to correct the break or dislocation. In describing the behavior of the searching bone, informants say it generates a force like an electric current that jumps in intensity when it reaches the injury, where it takes hold "like a magnet."

Any citizen of San Pedro can decide to become a carpenter or aspire to own a truck, but no one can simply choose to be a shaman, a bonesetter, or a midwife (Paul and Paul 1975). To enter one of these sacred professions the individual must receive a supernatural call. To act on one's own initiative would be both ineffective and unsafe; the presumptuous individual would be stricken with death or misfortune. And so would the person who receives the summons and refuses to heed the mandate. The channels for communicating the divine will are multiple and marvelous. In his old age, Ventura recalled how he was induced to be a bonesetter. His story illustrates the complex process of persuasion.

The Call of the Bone

Not long after marrying at age 20, Ventura had a strange dream. A bone was hopping about. He woke up worried and went off early as usual to work in his distant cornfield. As he neared his destination he saw a curious object in the distance which turned out on closer inspection to be very shiny bone. The bright object leapt toward him. He drew back in fright, but it jumped in his direction again, and then again. Fearful, and finding his way blocked, Ventura returned home, disguising the cause of his embarrassing retreat by feigning illness and going to bed.

During the night he had another curious dream. This time the visitor was a dwarf who asked Ventura "Why didn't you pick me up? If you go on refusing you will die." In the morning he arose determined. On the way to work the bone reappeared. Again it jumped. This time Ventura was not afraid. He picked up the object, which measured an inch in diameter, wrapped it in his kerchief, and tucked it into his sash. On the way back he felt it move about. At home he put it in a shoulder bag and hung it in a corner. He did not know the bone's purpose, but instructional dreams followed. The same little man told Ventura that he was destined to aid humanity by caring for the afflicted, "because they are our children." The dwarf taught him a secret song, and at night Ventura would sing it.

In a dream one night the dwarf appeared with a skeleton. He handed Ventura a whip and told him to strike it down. Ventura obeyed and the skeleton collapsed into a heap of bones. Then the dwarf ordered him to put the skeleton back together, threatening to whip him if he failed. Ventura protested, "Señor, I cannot." the dwarf then said, "Where is the bone I gave you?" Ventura fetched the bone he had found on the path. With its help he began to recognize the different parts and to rebuild the skeleton, starting with little toe bones and proceeding to the bigger bones. When Ventura had reconstructed the entire skeleton under the guidance of his magic bone, the dwarf said, " With this bone you will cure our children." Ventura still did not know just what he was to do, but he kept receiving instructions.

Ventura treated his bone with respect, placing it in a box of its own. When he closed the box he got on his knees and could hear the object making sounds as of people talking inside. He took it out, wrapped it in as silken cloth, blew on it repeatedly, and replaced it carefully. He was told never to let anyone touch the bone or else he or his children would die. The bone told him to guard it well because "I have work to do".

The bone announced that Ventura's young wife would give birth to a boy who would die. A boy was born and lived only a short while. Ventura experienced other misfortunes. He fell to quarreling with his wife, who expressed fear that because of his "*fortuna*" all their babies were destined to die. He replied that his call came from no human source but from God, that its true purpose was to give life, that they would live better and live longer on earth. But he made no use of the bone for a year. Meanwhile he got sick; his head and his heart began to ache, and he was on the point of death. Only by becoming a healer did he regain his health.

A boy he knew had broken a leg. In a dream the dwarf directed Ventura to use the bone. He complied; the break was mended and in three days the boy was able to walk again. Ventura told no one what he had done, but word spread and his practice grew. He never charged for his services, leaving it up to his patients to donate what they wished or to give nothing at all.

Some of the details of Ventura's experience are unique, but a comparison of his story and those of the other San Pedro bonesetters discloses a common pattern. The candidate encounters a small bone-like object that moves and he is instructed in his dreams to pick it up. He puts it away, and for a period of time, which may be short or last many years, he fails to act on any cryptic message he receives. He usually suffers for this in some way until he begins to exercise his calling. He is trained by no one, only in dreams is he told how to cure, and in any case it is the secret bone that does the work. Since bonesetting is a hallowed duty the practitioner must not charge for his service.

Bonesetters earn little income from their part-time curing speciality in this money-conscious community. Sometimes they are called to attend an accident victim in another town, staying with the patient for several days or weeks in Chimaltenango or

Antigua or wherever it may be. They receive meals and transportation costs and perhaps "*unos centavitos*", but it is difficult to see what they gain for their time and labor beyond the satisfaction of knowing that they are carrying out God's humanitarian purpose and perhaps gaining a certain amount of immunity from accidents themselves. One bonesetter, who also heads a marimba band that travels to many towns, remarked significantly that he was in four road accidents without ever being injured.

Another bonesetter, who is also a leading midwife in San Pedro, had just been incapacitated with two injured ankles when word arrived that one of her patients was about to give birth. Despite her husband's protests she insisted on going out, and was able to walk after hastily doctoring her own ankles with the aid of a curing bone she had found long ago and had stored away without realizing its significance. The success of this emergency action launched her practice as a bonesetter and changed her luck. Previously prone to slipping and spraining her ankles, she now became nimble and sure-footed.

While all healers claim they acquired their special knowledge in dreams, their dream experiences differ in content and degree of specificity. Ventura had rebuilt the skeleton from the feet up; one of the newer bonesetters recalls beginning with the cranium and ending with the legs and feet. Others do not mention such a dream test at all. The man in Venture's dreams was a dwarf. In another case he was a very large *ladino* with a beard, dressed completely in white from head to shoes. In the neighboring town of San Juan, which is nearly a suburb of San Pedro, a man destined to be a boesetter was visited by someone he described as "a dwarf dressed in white like a doctor and with a suitcase" (Rodeiguez Rouanet 1969:68). One Pedrano bonesetter described the visitor as a boy dressed in *ladino* clothes. Still another received his message from one of the two angels that guard Jesucristo. This same informant said that when he sets bones he begs forgiveness (*pedir un perdon*) just as Jesus did when he stumbled under the weight of the cross he was carrying.

The Zutuhil phrase describing a curer with supernatural connections is *k'orxin,* meaning he or she has the gift, and the gift is understood as referring equally to the charismatic quality of the object that embodies his power. In Spanish reference the power object, the bone in the case of bonesetter, is variously called the healer's *suerte, fortuna or virtud.* Bonesetters sometimes refer to the object as their instrument (*apart to, material*), although in their conception the mystic bone is the healer and its possessor the instrument.

The bone can alert its owner by moving or making a sound when a serious fracture occurs somewhere. Unaided, it can hop out of its box into the curer's shoulder bag or the folds of his sash when he leaves the houses to travel or work in the field. If the owner drops the bone while mending a fracture, it can bring death to the patient. It can make itself invisible; a stranger might be looking directly at it and yet not see it. It can assume the guise of a man. It can disappear, as Ventura's bone did after that celebrated bonesetter died.

Normally the special objects belonging to sacred curers—shamans, midwives, bonesetters—accompany them in their coffins when they die. But according to Rosario, Ventura had a vision before dying that Rosario one day would become a bonesetter and that the bone should be kept in its usual box. Somehow it came into the possession of a man in San Juan who used it to cure his son's fractured limb, proclaiming that he had found his magic bone. He attracted patients and charged very high fees. This displeased the bone and in a few weeks it came to Rosario in dream. The bone told her it had returned because it was displeased by the Juanero's unconscionable behavior and would now remain with Rosario all her life. It said she was to become a bonesetter like her dead father and never charge for the services. In the middle of the night Rosario heard a noise and thought someone was tampering with the box that had belonged to her father. When she examined the box, she found the bone back in its usual place. She burned incense and two candles. Later, she had dreams and eventually, despite delay and reluctance, became a bonesetter, but only after a series of increasingly severe illnesses.

The bonesetter's bone is a sacred object, surrounded by taboos and credited with miraculous abilities. It is a repository of supernatural power, a potent cultural symbol binding patient and practitioner in a bond of faith and assurance. It partakes of the same mystique that draws pilgrims to the site of an enshrine relics. As a sign of the bonesetter's accredicities, it is the equivalent of the doctor's diploma.

Like the secular physician, the Pedrano bonesetter uses his hands to straighten fractures, however he may interpret the source of his dexterity and clinical judgment. In this respect he differs from his counterpart in Zinacantan where the most highly regarded bonesetters are those who "use prayers and other spiritual methods exclusively" while "a bonesetter who actually sets bones is considered far inferior" (Febrega and Silver 1973: 41-42).

In the native view, the bonesetter's medicine works because his bone is a conductor of supernatural forces. For Pedranos the manifest message of the magic bone is that religion empowers medicine. But the latent message reads in reverse: medicine empowers religion. Each instance of curing in the material world recharges faith in the existence of the spiritual world. Pedranos admire material progress. Tired of foot travel and back packs they value the efficiency of trucks and buses acquired in increasing numbers. But greater mechanical efficiency brings greater human hazards. With more trucks there are more accidents and more need for bonesetters. If setting bones is seen in progressive San Pedro la Laguna as a sacred office, this may be because the very nature of the art—making broken parts whole—so graphically symbolizes and satisfies a profound human yearning to transform disorder into order, to convert chaos into cosmos.

Bibliography

Fabrega, H. J, and D. B. Silver. 1973. Illness shamanistic Curing in Zinacantan Stanford.

Paul, I., and B. D. Paul. 1975. The Maya Midwife as Sacred Professional American Ethnologist 2: 707-726.

Rodriguez Rouanet, F. 1969. Practices medicas tradicionales de los Indigenas de Guatemala. Guatemala Indigena 4(2): 51-86.

Tax, S. 1937. The Municipios of the Midwestern Highlands of Guatemala. American Anthropologist 39: 423-444.

* *Ethnology*- Vol. xv-1976. No. 1

Chapter-6

Body, Psyche and Society: Conceptions of Illness in Ommura, Eastern Highlands, Papua New Guinea

*By Jessica R. Mayer**

Chapter-6

Knowledge of illness dimensions of sickness in Papua New Guinea cultures is still very limited although it has increased significantly over the past few years (Lewis 1975, Frankel 1980, Johannes 1980, Barth 1975 ch.15.see also Glick 1967). My present aim is to convey some aspects of the cultural meaning and significance of illness among the Ommura, a dialect group of about 800 people living on the upper slops of the Llamari River in the Dogara census division of the Eastern Highlands District. The people are shifting cultivators whose main subsistence crop is sweet potato with yams, sugarcane and maize. They also breed pigs and grow coffee as a cash crop. They are organized into dispersed patrilineal clans with strong emphasis on the maternal line. I carried out field research in 1975-6, in the villages of Samura, Yonura and Mukouri.

This paper represents one stage in a wider project dealing with Ommura representations and practices associated with illness as the products of a specific set of historical, political, economic and cultural circumstances, and with their functioning as aspects of social ideology. Analysis of medical belief and practices within their historical, social and cultural context may throw light not only on the social construction of taken-for-granted assumptions about the nature of 'health','illness' and 'medicine', but also on the way in which given systems of social relations are perpetuated and change. It has often been observed for widely differing social and cultural context how by virtue of their special emotional significance representations and practices associated with illness are charged with a particularly potent ideological force (e.g., Bordieu 1977, 218.Turner 1967:107, Sontag 1978,Young 1975).This kind of analysis may also provide fresh perspectives on aspects of social life generally treated by anthropologists within more traditional analytic domains such as 'religion', 'morality' or 'cosmology'.

While they have no single term corresponding to 'illness' Ommura certainly recognize illness in the general sense that certain 'complaints involving physical or psychological changes are categorized .....as deviations from health or from what is expected in terms of well-being .....' (Loudon 1976:37).

The states regarded as illness fall in to three general classes: *nriqa viro,vunrato afi*,and female reproductive disorders. They are all considered to be *uahi haikya* or undesirable occurrences; a very general evaluative term applicable to a wide range of events from crop failure or loss of or damage to property to certain breaches of etiquette. Beyond this these categories are distinct from one another. There is no overlap in the procedures for dealing with each of them and no covering term for them in the Ommura language.[1] Each of these types of disorder is also distinct from other types of *uahi haikya*.

In what follows I describes the nature and significance of each of these types of disorder and the distinctive behaviour of those afflicted with them. This involves taking into account notions about the person, bodily functioning, health, strength, morality, warfare, the distinctions between men and women and sources of stress or anxiety.

They are not defined in precise abstract terms any more than are 'illness' and 'disease' within the context of contemporary scientific medicine and my understanding of their nature derives from observation of the way in which people reacted to 'interpreted' and dealt with actual cases of illness and from intensive discussions with forty-four people.

Broad underlying comparison with contemporary western[2] conceptions of illness and the person—especially the pervasive body/mind dichotomy—inevitably shapes the analysis to some extent.

The general views described here were taken for granted by most adult Ommura. Within this general paradigm I found certain systematic variations according to sex, initiatory status and context. Elder men as a category were attributed with special diagnostic and therapeutic skills. However these derived from their superior magical and divinatory capacities rather than from possession of specialist knowledge about bodily functioning. The only esoteric medical knowledge is that concerning women's reproductive disorders (see below).

A full historical treatment is beyond the scope of the present paper. However it should be borne in mind that many aspects of those modes of conceptualizing and dealing with illness that prevailed during my period of fieldwork must be understood as responses to major social changes that had taken place in Ommura within the preceding fifteen years or so as the result of increasing control by the Administration, incorporation into the wider economy and exposure to new cultural influences. While one assumes that medical ideas and practices in Ommura (as elsewhere) have never been static, there is evidence that they underwent particularly major changes over this period.

Although a mission-run medical aid post had been established in the area in the late 1960s, these developments in medical belief and practices were at least in the villages in which I worked less the result of its influence than of certain changes in the political and ideological significance of illness and therapy which I shall sketch later. The people of these villages feared entering the aid post treatment hut because it was frequented by people from enemy villages who were always liable to leave dangerous substances there to harm them. Hence while they regarded western style treatment as highly efficacious, they used the aid post only for the treatment of infant's disorders and minor ailments which were treated outside the hut and occasionally as a last resort.

Body, Mind, Spirit and Society

To understand the nature and significance of illness in Ommura terms it is necessary to look first at certain aspects of the people's conceptions of relations between 'bodily','psychological','spiritual' and 'social'aspects of the person and of attitudes towards the physically unfit or incapacitated. It is necessary to appreciate the way in which visible features of the nature and state of a person's body are closely tied up with what an English-speaking person might distinguish as aspects of his or her social persona, social status, personal attributes and capacities, and the current state of his or her social relationships.

The nation of bodily *qio*, bodily 'soundness' or 'perfection,' combines 'positive health', 'physical energy' and 'attractiveness—qualities which were seen as closely related. Some people's bodies are naturedly more *qio* than those of others and illness and old age diminish one's degree of bodily *qio*.

The extent to which one approximates this ideal state has an important bearing on one's prestige and influence. It would not make sense in Ommura to praise someone for his or her, 'strength of spirit' despite the frailty of his or her body. In keeping with women's generally subsidiary role inpolitical and economic affairs, a woman's degree of physical health/attractiveness/energy is a less important aspect of her social identity than in the case of a man.

A *qio* body for either sex, is characterized by 'good skin' and 'good blood.' Good skin is full of grease so that it appears firm, bulging with muscles, smooth and sleek. The skin of the unfit and elderly is *handavenravo* 'ashlike'—dry, flakey, greyish and lacking in firmness and many curative and cosmetic procedures involve the ingestion or application of pork fat or pandanus oil 'to make the skin fat.' 'Good blood' flows freely and in the right direction so that one emanates an aura of vitality and dynamism. (As will be seen, blood flowing sluggishly and in the wrong direction causes one to become dull and lifeless).

Besides enhancing one's gardening and fighting capacities a high degree of physical health /attractiveness/energy is a source of charisma enabling one to influence people and win allies. It is also said to 'pull wealth', a notion which, given the principles underlying the giving of gifts and assistance in Ommura is not as mystical as it sounds. As one old man remarked bitterly during a food distribution from which he was excluded,'People with good skin get everything. What they plant grows large and people who distribute food think: "I'll give something to this man or woman. Later they'll help me or give me something". If someone has bad skin or eyes (he was blind in one eye), they say "nothing for that decayed man!",

Moreover, physically attractive men are highly valued by their kin groups as a source of wives. Polygyny and the relative ease with which wives can leave their husbands create a situation in which men have to compete to obtain and retain wives, and a man's physical attractiveness has an important bearing on his capacity to attract these important sources of productive and reproductive power. Ageing men or those whose health fails them often lose wives. While boys are brought up to value marriage primarily for economic reasons girls come to regard marriage as a state to be desired through a process of socialization which stresses romantic notions of the intrinsic desirability of physically attractive men as marriage partners. A common and accepted way of initiating a marriage is for a woman to 'run away' to aman whom she regards as attractive.

While a variety of factors affects one's prestige and influence in these spheres, a respectable degree of bodily *qio* is a sine *qua* non for playing an effective role in village politics and ceremonial exchange and to be positively lacking in these qualities, whether through illness, old age or chronic or endemic physical debars one (temporarily in the case of short term illness) from active participation.

To understand Ommura conceptions of illness one also needs to look at the way in which bodily states are linked to social circumstances. One's bodily state may be treated as an indication of the state of one's social relationship. It is said for example that the adequacy with which a man fulfils his exchange obligation to his affines may affect the shape of his nose. Failure to keep up to date with payments that must be rendered to them on various occasions and the resulting acrimony may cause this nose to swell out painfully causing it to become wide and flatter. There is a pervasive association between 'correct' circulation of 'blood' between affines—that is, the correct flow from wife receivers to wife givers of symbolic 'blood' equivalents (pigs, pork) in return for the wife obtained from them. In keeping with this a stoppage in the flow of a man's payments to his wife's kin may cause his blood to stagnate so that it accumulates in the nose, making it swell.

Once I had become attuned to paying the same kind of minute attention as did Ommura to variations in nose shape, I myself began to notice distinct variations in the extent to which particular people's noses appeared swollen on different occasions. Ommura culture places far more medical esthetic and symbolic significance on the nose than does contemporary English culture. It is the focal point of elaborate ritual, medical, and cosmetic procedures and while English people tend to focus on aspects of the mouth or eyes when describing facial expression or appearance in Ommura the nose is the most emphasized facial feature. There is, for example, a very wide vocabulary for different nose shapes, conditions and 'expressions'.[3]

More generally, much as English people tend to impute certain personality characteristics to people considered to have 'small piggy eyes" 'an upright bearing' or 'weak' chins, so the fact that a man's nose was naturally particularly wide, or particularly narrow and aquiline, was often cited as an indication that he was the sort of person whose relations with his affines were generally in a mess or exceptionally harmonious.

Ommura also distinguish certain named states that involve 'bodily,' 'psychological, and 'social' elements in an inseparable combination. An example is *kiaunrinro* which appears to be every similar to shame on the skin described for Hagen by Strathern. He notes that the explanations given to him of this state 'tended to stress the notion that "shame" has to do with the individual's reaction to his community relationships......' It 'has both psychological and a social reference...When persons feel "shame"in Hagen they say their skin breaks out in to sweat.....the skin' their outer self, is the immediate point of contact with the physical world outside them and can conveniently symbolize the point of contact between themselves and the social forces that surround them...(Strathern 1977:101). Like shame on the skin while kiaunrinro involves a psychological element,it cannot be understood simply as a psychological state. One only experiences this kind of shame or embarrassment in the presence of other people who are conscious of one's having performed the shameful action. It also has a bodily manifestation. The forehead of someone involved in the social situation and psychological experience of kiaunrinro is covered in beads of sweat.

The Body as a system

While there are thus complex ideas regarding relations between bodily psychological and social environmental states, conceptions about the body as a relatively independent system functioning according to principles of its own are far less elaborated.

Ommura have a large number of terms which relate to bodily processes, characteristics and states, and which they employ, for example in assessing physical attractiveness and describing personal appearance, the visible features of fighting injuries or bodily movements in fighting dancing and sexual intercourse.[4] However the structure and functioning of the body as a system has not been a subject for detailed inquiry in Ommura and ethnophysiological notions whether in the form of explicit theory or the unstated rationale underlying prophylaxis or therapy are generally far less complex than those described for many African cultures —for example Bakongo (Janzen 1978, ch. 10) or Songhay (Bissilliat 1976).

As will be seen, Ommura notions about the nature of illness and its causes stress psychosocial aspects. The most elaborated ideas I found concerning the functioning of the body as a system are those relating to the flow of blood,[5] and the antipathy between "male"and "female" parts of the body. The notion that health and vitality depend on the blood flowing freely and in a 'proper' or 'systematic' (*avu avu*) fashion pervades therapy and everyday conception of the body. While ill health is sometimes attributed in a general way to blood flowing in the wrong (*afi*) direction' there is no precise conception of what constitutes a 'correct' direction of blood flow. I did not find specific notions regarding relations between blood and other body components and functions such as those described for Songhay (Bissiliat 1976:556ff).

When blood is flowing properly one feels strong and vital because like water in a fast flowing stream, it remains fresh or new (*arakye*). This analogy is often explicit. The expression 'his blood is good, is used in much the same general sense as the English expression 'he radiates heath' or 'emanates a sense of physical well being'. Where the flow of blood slows down or its passage gets blocked causing it to flow in the wrong direction it gets stagnant or stale (*tapitaira*),so that a person becomes listless and lacking in vitality. With advancing age blood tends to flow less freely and its condition worsens. 'Bad blood' in younger people is generally associated with ill health.

Bad blood is cited in a general way as a feature of most cases of illness and symptoms common to a wide variety of illnesses (e.g.,generalized aches and pains swelling or skin rashes) are ascribed to blockages and putrefaction of the blood. Ideas concerning the relations between blood flow and illness are more specific only in the case of a category of illnesses afflicting men and seen as deriving in one way or another from antagonism between spouses or affines. Here in keeping with the feminine source of the illness it is specifically in the nose that the bad blood accumulates. (Blood is 'feminine' the nose is 'masculine'—see below). One type of illness in this category was mentioned earlier. 'Incorrect' flow of symbolic 'blood' to his affines causes the blood in a man's body to flow incorrectly and accumulate in his nose. Another type of illness involving the accumulation of bad blood in the nose is that resulting from contact with one's wife's menstrual blood. Here too blood is flowing in the wrong direction, that is from wife givers to wife receivers rather than vice versa.

The underlying rationale of several curing and prophylactic procedures is that of maintaining or restoring a 'fresh' condition of the blood. Thus the tingling sensation induced by the common practice of beating the skin with stinging nettles (*taroa*) is taken as an indication that it stimulates blood flow. Consumption of undercooked meat, the red juice of betel nut, and beer are represented as a means of adding 'new blood' to the body. There are, moreover, various blood-letting procedures for getting rid of 'stale' blood and removing blockages in the flow of blood.[6] These range from ritual nose and penis bleeding to the 'shooting' of a localized swelling with a miniature bow and arrow (*nrunda huru*). On similar grounds menstruation is represented as health giving and amenhorrhoea as harmful to the health because it involves stale blood accumulating in the body.

A general underlying opposition between antipathetic 'male' and 'female' aspects of the body is also apparent in prophylaxis and therapy and in notions of illness causation. The main distinction is between 'blood' and 'grease' (which includes saliva, semen and flesh or '*mamanta*'). In typical Papua New Guinea Highlands fashion, blood, with its connotations of childbirth and changeability is 'female' while the more substantial 'grease' is male. The lower part of the body from the waist downwards is 'female' and the upper part 'male'. Contact between 'male' and 'female' aspects is harmful. This is one reason why it is considered dangerous to the health to eat one's own pig, or as elsewhere in New Guinea (e.g., Gell 1975:259. Lewis 1975:37), to lick one's own blood (contact between one's blood and saliva). Similarly much ill health is attributed to blood (female) being trapped in the nose or penis (male parts of the body),[7] or to men ingesting food that has been in contact with the lower part of any body, including their own.

As fairly complex ideas about the physiology of conception have been reported for elsewhere in the New Guinea Highlands (e.g., Strathern 1972, 8ff; Meigs 1976:394 ff), I should note that while conception was generally explained in terms of the mother's 'blood' combining with the father's semen or 'grease,' as the result of several acts of intercourse, more specific descriptions of the physiological processes involved were not forthcoming. It is possible that more complex explanations of conception exist as part of the body of knowledge about childbirth, which is the monopoly of women who have had children, and was not available to me.[3]

I have stressed the extent to which various aspects of 'character' and 'psychological' states have visible bodily manifestations. It is also fundamental to Ommura conceptions of the person that a large part of each individuals motives, intentions; thoughts, feelings, emotions, sensations and experiences remain inside the body, invisible to others and not communicated to them.[9] This is an assumption that underlies much social interaction and communication. The distinction is important for understanding that, while there is high degree of conceptual elaboration regarding its psychological and mystical aetiology, the subjective bodily and psychological experiences of illness are generally only expressed much more diffusely through the medium of bodily stance, facial expression and song and, there is little emphasis on the precise recounting of symptoms.

Thus it was stressed that one cannot 'see' the motives, thoughts or intentions of another. They are 'inside the ear'. As elsewhere in Papua New Guinea' intellectual processes' knowledge and memory are associated with the ear.[10] The same verb '*iero*' is used to mean 'to hear' (a sound) and 'to know'or 'to understand'. It is taken for granted that people tend to keep their true (*tanruva*) thoughts, motives and intentions 'hidden', and my habit of asking questions such as 'why did he do that ?'or 'Does she likes these?' was generally regarded as rather pointless. Such questions are not treated as matters for overt speculation or analytic discourse' and the typical report was 'why ask me? I cannot see inside his ear'.[11]

Similarly, a person's feelings, emotions and physical sensation are, for the most part, invisible, to others. They may be partially expressed and communicated through bodily stance, facial expression, and song. There is a special genre of song (*ihi*) for expressing 'inner' states of this kind. The melody used may indicate to others in a general way the nature of the feelings being expressed: whether the singer is *po* (sad, depressed, grieving over a loss), *inronra hita* (angry, frustrated, irritated), in physical pain, intensely attracted to a member of the opposite sex, or hungry.

A particular named type of melody is conventionally treated as an indication of each of these general categories of feeling. Singing of this kind often constitutes an expressive medium rather than a vehicle for communication to others. The songs are frequently sung out of the earshot of other people and never to an audience. Moreover their verbal allusions tend to be private and personal rather than conventional and inter subjective as in songs for public occasions.

In large part, however, the emotions or physical sensations are 'invisible'to others. Most feeling and emotion 'remains' inside the belly, (*bvikyokya*) so that no one else can 'see it. All named feelings and emotions are associated in a non-specific way with the *bvikyokya*. In the same way a person's bodily sensations are considered to be largely 'invisible' and not a subject for precise communication to others[12].

Marauha

In certain kinds of illness the afflicted person's *marauha* is said to have been 'captured' by afflicting agent. It is therefore necessary to look at what people meant when they spoke of a person's *marauha*.

At first I understood this notion as resembling those conceptions of 'soul' or 'vital principle' that have been described for several parts of Papua New Guinea. According to Glasse, Huli 'conceive *dinini* to be the immaterial part of the human personality which survives physical death and persist indefinitely in ghostly from. The *dinini* or soul is an invisible vapour which, in the waking state, occupies the space just behind the eyes... The Huli say that the soul is the vital principle or vital essence of the human personality...' (Glasse 1965:30). For the Gnau of the West Sepik, '*wuna' at* names the part of the body where are localized vitality, thought and emotion.... for them localization is a clear attribute of consciousness... The *wuna'at* has no link to spirit or soul...' (Lewis 1975:210. See also Strathern 1979:251, Reay 1959:132, Read, 1967:212).

However, as I became more familiar with Ommura language

and culture it became apparent that to understand the term *marauha* in this way was to treat it as having a much more specific and well defined referent than was in fact the case.

It is said that at death and during possessions, serious illness and dream's the person's *marauha* leaves their *mamanta*, flesh or skin. In that it does not persist after death, *marauha* cannot be understood as 'soul': 'We do not know what happens to the *marauha* when the forehead is already dead. We just cry and cry for it until our eyes hurt.'

If *marauha* is to be described as 'vital principle' then it should be noted that this is far less specific and elaborated than the 'vital principle' or 'vital center' notions described for elsewhere in Papua New Guinea. There is, for example, no specification of bodily location for the *marauha* as with the Huli *dinini* or Gnau *wuna'at*. Nor is it represented as permeating the body.

Rather, taking into account the various contexts in which it is used, I would described *marauha* as a significantly vague concept for pointing to what are regarded as extraordinary processes the nature of which is beyond comprehension in terms of ordinary language and experience.

It is involved, for example, in the description of magical processes. Thus spells sung during sweet potato fertility ceremonies to 'call' sweet potatoes from other village are described as operating on the *marauha* of these potatoes or, where illness is attributed to contact with at taboo clump of bamboo, it is said that the *marauha* of the bamboo has harmed the *marauha* of the afflicted person rather than that 'the bamboo harmed him,' as would be the case if a bamboo without these extraordinary powers had, say, fallen on someone's head.

Similarly, the human states in relation to which the notion of *marauha* is invoked (dreaming, possession, serious illness and death) are those specifically regarded as extraordinary and beyond ordinary comprehension. The *maruauha/mamanta* contrast is not relevant to conceptualizing the person in 'normal,' everyday' circumstances. It would not make sense in Ommura to say that people 'have' *marauha*, as they might be said to 'have' souls, or (by ethnographers at least) vital centres.

It may be noted here that I did not find in Ommura a well defined conception of 'soul' or 'vital centre' such as described for other Papua New Guinea cultures. The notion of *marauha* constitutes the closest Ommura approximation to either of these kinds of concept.

A few people told me that they had heard from evangelists that after death a person's *laihor,* Ommura for 'breath,' went to *heven* (Pidgin for heaven). However, this attempt to render the Christian notion of soul in Ommura terms has had very little impact on Ommura thought.

It was necessary to describe these aspects of Ommura conceptions of the person and body in order to understand how illness is construed in terms of Ommura culture. I shall now go on to look at the nature and significance of each of the general classes of illness that are distinguished.

Nriqa Viro

Most illness (in the sense specified earlier) falls into the general category *nriqa viro*. Except in the case of children, no one other than the afflicted person has the authority to decide whether he or she is *nriqa viro*. Such a decision involves the following personal judgment about one's state. First that the bodily pain, impairment or discomfort goes beyond what one considers normal or expected for oneself. Disorders regarded as chronic or congenital or associated with the process of aging are considered part of the person's normal state and not as constituting *nriqa viro*. The label *nriqa viro* is applicable to states ranging in terms of external criteria of seriousness from minor ailments to acute incapacitating disease. Second, *nriqa viro* has distinct temporal boundaries. In contrast to congenital disorders, it has a fairly sudden onset and is not chronic or permanent. Third, the decision that a complaint constitutes *nriqa viro* involves judgment about its causes. It is always the outcome of 'invisible attack' on the afflicted person's *marauha* for one of a number of 'hidden' harmful forces which attack people under certain circumstances. Such forces may be understood, on one level as collective representations which image specific configurations of stressful experience that arise from the conditions of social life in contemporary Ommura (cf. Lienhardt 1961:170).

Nriqa viro is distinguished by the nature of its causes from *vnrato afi* or 'confused perceptions' and women's reproductive disorders, and also from pain and bodily impairment resulting from accidents or fighting ('visible attack'). While an element of bodily pain or discomfort is an essential attribute of *nriqu viro*, in keeping with what has been said about Ommura conceptions of the relations between 'bodily', 'psychological' and 'social' aspects of the person, it cannot be understood simply as a condition of the body or as a condition of the person conceived in abstraction from his or her social environment. It has (to use distinctions which are etic rather than emic) 'bodily', 'psychological', 'social', ideological and normative aspects. Besides the physical suffering or incapacity it involves, *nriqa viro*, in any specific instance, constitutes a reflection of the ill person's current social relationships and psychological state as well as of his or her attributes, capacities and general worth as person. It may also (as will be seen) be perceived as reflecting on the validity of fundamental cultural principles regarding the nature of masculinity and femininity and of relations with 'outsiders'.

Nriqa viro as a bodily state

There is far less cultural elaboration concerning purely 'bodily' aspects of *nriqa viro* than concerning the psychosocial and mystical causes to which it is attributed and its significance regarding the ill person's social situation, psychological state, attributes and capacities.

Besides its special significance for the ill person, the fact that he or she is suffering or incapacitated is clearly important to kin, who wail round the patient's bed 'because we are sorry *(po)* for him'. It also affects the sufferer's self-esteem. As was seen, absence of bodily soundness or *qio* is intrinsically degrading.

However, the specific nature of the ill persons's bodily suffering is emphatically not a subject for articulation in precise verbal terms or communication to others. It belongs in the realms of 'invisible' aspects of the person. While *nriqa viro* sufferers communicate to others through their behaviour that they are in discomfort, they will not generally speak of this discomfort even to healers.

When I questioned people about symptoms they had experienced during past episodes of *nriqa viro*, I was rarely able to obtain more precise accounts than that person had been 'short of breath', 'hot' and 'aching with bad blood': a conventional idiom for indicating *nriqa viro* and sufficiently general to be applicable to most cases. In some cases, people, noted in addition that they had suffered from back ache, or aching in the shoulders or stomach.

Thus people did not make use of the large Ommura vocabulary for bodily parts and processes to describe how they were ill. Nor did I find, as did Lewis in Gnau, 'a vocabulary which was adequate to the precise and detailed description of pain in its varieties (Lewis 1976:64). One may communicate to others through bodily stance and song that one is in pain, but the specific nature of the pain remains in large part 'inside the belly, invisible to others.'

Nor were healers or the patient's kin able to give me precise accounts of the physical signs or symptoms of an illness. My requests for such information almost invariably met with the reply: 'How can we see the pain of the illness? That is something inside the ill person himself which we cannot see.'

That the patient does not generally communicate the nature of his or her symptoms to other is consistent with the fact that the judgment of whether he or she is ill is made by afflicted person along, and also with the fact that precise discrimination of symptoms was not important in those methods of diagnosis and therapy for *nriqa viro* in use during my stay. Diagnostic categories are distinguished mainly according to psychosocial and mystical causes rather than symptoms, and with one exception ('bad blood in the nose' from tension with one's wife) particular causes do not imply particular symptoms. Healers[13] deal primarily with the causal agent or situation and their methods do not involve overt examination of the patient's body. While they always 'wash away' the illness by pouring water over the patient and 'strengthen' him or her with *kupu* bark, grease and spittle these same measures are applied routinely in all cases of *nriqa viro* whatever their causes.

Attention to specific symptoms was no greater where *nriqa viro* was considered to be *ati*—that is, too trivial to necessitate speculation over its causes. *Ati nriqa viro* is not generally felt to require treatment[14]. Clearly the fact that bodily symptoms and signs of *nriqa viro* are not verbally distinguished in any precise way must not be taken to indicate that people do not, in fact, make use of rules about the significance of particular bodily states or symptoms in judging whether or not they are ill.

* * *

There is far greater cultural emphasis on, and elaboration of, the aetiology of *nriqa viro* than its bodily symptoms or signs. Its cultural significance derives very much from the nature of the circumstances seen as leading to it.

Five general classes of causal situations or agents (*okiera*, literally 'root') are recognized: sorcery; 'pollution' caused by a man coming into contact with the menstrual blood of his wife or brother's wife, or ingesting food or drink that she has touched; breach of certain taboos; contact with a *wera*, a type of spirit associated with foreign people and places and lastly, contact with something *akiau*. *Akiau* are a class of natural phenomena which are singularly weird or anomalous in terms of Ommura world views and are attributed a special potency.

Illness as a Reflection of the Patient's Social Circumstances (Past Conduct and Attributes) and as an Affirmation of Ideological Principles

The circumstances under which each of these 'agents' is likely to 'attack' are specified in considerable detail. Each tends to attack people who have particular kinds of attributes, who are engaged in particular kinds of activities, or who are involved in latent or overt conflict with specific categories of other.

Nriqa viro, in any specific instance is thus treated very much as a reflection of the ill person's attributes, recent activities and conduct, and of the state of his or her social relationships. More generally, by virtue of the way in which it reflects on the sufferer's attributes, activities and circumstances, *nriqa viro* has normative and ideological significance. For example, the fact that someone has fallen ill through behaving in a particular way is perceived as affirming the impropriety or danger of that kind of conduct: the fact that a man is considered to have fallen ill through contact with his wife's menstrual blood may be taken as affirming the foolhardiness of ignoring one's wife's claims to household produce. Again, the fact that illness in men appears to be the outcome of attack from *wera* more often than illness in women, affirms the stereotype of men as braver than women, and hence more likely to venture into the foreign areas where *wera* lurk.

Illness as a Reflection of the Patient's Psychological State

While a mystical idiom is used for describing *nriqa viro* causation it is clear that one level this kind of disorder is seen as being psychosocially rather than mystically caused, as the outcome of psychological stress engendered by one of a number of specific sets of circumstances recognized as being particularly likely to induce fear, anxiety or emotional conflict.

When the *nriqa viro* causing 'agents' just mentioned are viewed within the context of other aspects of Ommura culture and social life, and when one examines the underlying logic of modes of therapy for *nriqa viro* attributed to particular agents, it becomes apparent that these 'agents' constitute collective representations which 'image' (Lienhardt 1961:1970) or metaphorically represent certain distinctive configurations of stressful experience arising out of the specific conditions of Ommura social life.

Thus the illness category '*nriqa viro* from attack by a *wera*' may be understood on one level as 'imaging' configurations of stressful experience arising out of exposure of strange or foreign people, places or influences[15], and *nriqa viro* from pollution by wife' as 'imaging' distinctive fears and anxieties typically arising out of a man's relations with his wife or brother's wife. Diagnosing an illness in terms of one of these categories involves attributing the patient's condition to the experience of a specific kind of stress, and a central aim of therapy is to enable the patient psychologically to 'cope with' or 'adjust to' the stressful life situation to which the illness is seen as being linked.

There are thus interesting parallels between the causes of *nriqa viro* taken as a body and some of those lists of 'stressful life events' devised by psychologists for use in predicting illness, and based on the assumption that the likelihood of becoming ill is increased by the experience of such events. (See, for example, the well known Social Readjustment Rating Scale devised by Holmes and Rahe, which consists of a list of life events believed by the authors to be stressful [Holmes and Rahe 1967]).

A recent survey of literature on 'behaviour and beliefs about illness' in the Papua New Guinea Highlands states that 'few ailments are believed to be due to "natural" causes, that is uninfluenced by sorcerers, witches or spirits.' (Brown 1978:62). This analysis of the Ommura situation suggests that these explanations of illness in terms of spirits and sorcerers may appear as far more empirically rational in relation to contemporary thinking about psychosocial causes of illness[16] than in terms of the now outmoded, predominantly 'physicalist conceptions of illness causation to which many anthropologists have tacitly subscribed[17].

Although inter-village warfare has been declared an offence by the Administration, and is far less frequent than it was a decade ago, people still feel themselves to be living in a situation in which they are surrounded by hostile enemy villages, liable to attack at any time.

For understanding the distinctive meaning and significance of illness in Ommura it is essential to appeaciate how strongly perceptions of an attitudes towards it are shaped by the warfare paradigm in terms of which it is often conceptualized. Conceptions of the causes of *nriqa viro,* its ideological and evaluative implications, its emotional significance as well as procedures for dealing with it and conventional behaviour of those afflicited with it are all coloured by a warfare metaphor. In the language for referring to *nriqa viro* and the imagery of curing ceremonies the forces that cause illness are frequently represented as dangerous 'enemies' *(nramuna)* which, in contrast to war enemies, who come from other villages, lurk round in one's own environment waiting to attack with mysterious unseen weapons. In keeping with the 'invisible' nature of the attack it is said that the victim's *marauha* has been captured by the *marauha* of the agent so that he or she has ceased to be in a 'normal' condition. A pervasive theme in therapy is that of military counterattack against the afflicting agent. In the *uaha* ceremony, for example, the men of the patient's village, dressed in full war regalia, chase away the afflicting agent by uttering war cries and snapping their bow strings at it.

Like war enemies, *nriqa viro* causing agents are essentially unpredictable in their behaviour. One can never be sure when and who they will attack.

Evaluative Attitudes to Nriqa Viro

Evaluative attitudes to *nriqa viro* are shaped by the metaphor of war attack. Just as relation with war enemies are viewed as essentially unpredictable and outside the sphere of reciprocity *(hini)* and morality, so attack from a *nriqa viro* causing agent is not something for which the victim is morally responsible or can be said to have entirely brought upon himself or herself. Procedures for dealing with *nriq a viro* are based on the idiom of retaliation against the afflicting agent rather than on restitution for wrongs committed by the sufferer.

However, while attack by a *nriqa viro* causing agent does not reflect on the sufferers moral condition it does reflect negatively on his or her social worth. In succumbing to illness one shows oneself to be lacking in power *(kyapukya)* and in the capacity for *avu* conduct (see below), qualities which are considered essential for survival in a society under threat of war, and which rank highly in terms of the way Ommura evaluate people.

It is fundamental to Ommura world views that each individual lives his or her life perpetually surrounded by a host of dangerous and threatening forces, ever liable to cause harm. Enemies from other villages, people in one's immediate environment who may secretly ensorcel or pollute one, floods and winds that may destroy one's home or food supply, and dangerous supernatural forces that lurk in the village and its environs always on the look out for people to attack.

Avu avu conduct is essentially behaving in such a way as to avert harm from these dangerous forces, conducting oneself astutely so as to steer unscathed through the maze of dangers in which one lives one's life. This requires acting always on the basis of planning and foresight rather than impulsively.

An *avu avu* person is perpetually on the alert for enemy attack and *avu avu* men are skilled at coping with and launching attacks. *Avu avu* people also store food for use in times of shortage rather than squandering it to satisfy short term needs.

Similarly, they conduct themselves in such a way as to minimize the risk of falling ill with *nriqa viro.* No matter how hungry they may be they will never risk eating food that may have been rendered harmful by a sorcerer. They are not taken in by the friendly veneer of a potential sorcerer and are capable of managing their relations with wives, neighbours and people from other villages in such a way that these people will not seek to harm their health by polluting or ensorcelling them. They are always on the alert for *akiau* or *wear* spirits that might be lurking in gardens or in the bush.

Hence falling ill with *nriqa viro* indicates that one is lacking in the capacity for conducting one's life in an *avu avu* way. One is reminded of the way in which much contemporary popular and social scientific theorizing about psychosocial causes of illness links susceptibility to illness with inadequate' social or psychological 'adjustment' (Rotman:9; and ch. 5 and ch. 6).

Being *nriqa viro* also reflects negatively on one's degree of *kyapukya,* 'power' or the ability to exert control or influence over people, natural phenomena or supernatural or magical forces. Like the capacity for *avu avu* conduct it is regarded as a quality essential for coping effectively with life in a war ridden society. Being *kyapukya* involves having the power to harm opponents in warfare, to resists succumbing to their attacks, and to carry on fighting when wounded. It also involves having the strength to work long hours and produce excellent crops, the influence to settle disputes, and the skill to exert control over magical and super-natural forces. Similarly, falling ill with *nriqa viro* is an indication that one does not have sufficient power over *nriqa viro* causing forces to resist succumbing to their influence, and hence that one is lacking in *kyapukya.*

In Ommura, then, avoiding illness is not, as for many people, a matter of fitting in with an established moral order or maintaining an ideal state of harmony between people or between humans and supernatural's[18] but of conducting one's life astutely and strategically so as to travel unscathed through the jungle of harmful and unpredictable forces that surround each individual, and of having sufficient power to harness them to one's own ends. A frequent theme in nightmares, generally interpreted as a sign that the dreamer is threatened with illness, is that massive, hostile plants are rapidly growing in on one's house, threatening to crush it. Only through mustering sufficient *kyapukya* to hack them to pieces, or sufficient cunning to wend one's way out of the maze, can one escape being choked to death.

Illness in Ommura is never, as in certain other cultures, a source of enhanced status (Turner 1967:10). Being *nriqa viro* is shameful because, as has been seen, significant absence of physical fitness or bodily sound ness is intrinsically degrading. It is also shameful because of the negative way it reflects on one's degree of *kyapukya* and capacity for *avu avu* conduct. The extent to which a person is regarded as *kyapukya* and *avu avu* has an important bearing on his prestige and authority.

Many people told me how deeply they had suffered from the lowering of their self-esteem when ill. The greater someone's claims to prestige and authority, the more they are shamed by illness. 'Big' or important men (*nronra vaisi)* suffer more deeply from lowered self esteem when they are ill than do less influential men. In keeping with their inferior political status women generally feel less disgraced than men.

By virtue of its implications regarding the ill person's *kyapukya,* not only does *nriqa viro* affect personal prestige and self-esteem, it is also perceived, in many instances, as reflecting on the validity of the principle of superior male *kyapukya* which is crucial to the perpetuation of men's authority over women in certain contexts.

If men are really so much more *kyapukya* than women then why are they not markedly less prone than the latter to fall ill? Women often taunt men with this question, and a central aim of *assochia,* one of the most elaborate procedures for dealing with illness, is to affirm the principle of superior male power against the perceived threats to it posed by men falling ill. In this ceremony, it is stressed that certain diagnostic categories imply lack of power to a far lesser extent than others, and illness in men is presented in terms of these categories while illness in women is attributed to causes which imply extreme lack of strength.[19]

Thus the significance of *nriqa viro* is such that dealing with it in specific instances often involves managing its ideological implications as well as attempting to alleviate the bodily and psychological condition of the patient.

Behviour in Nriqa viro

Someone who has decided that he or she is *nriqa viro* communicates this decision to others through withdrawal from ordinary activities and social interaction.

The extent of such withdrawal varies according to how serious the illness is felt to be, a decision which depends as much on the cause to which it is attributed as on the degree of discomfort or incapacity involved. With trivial *(ati) nriqa viro* the person maintains a relatively normal lifestyle, merely becoming less assiduous over work and personal appearance, participating less actively than usual in sociable and public events and taking extra care to avoid sorcerers, spirits, and potentially harmful foods. At the other extreme, serious *(nnronra) nriqa viro* leads to complete withdrawal from normal work and social interaction, and to conspicuous abandoning of attention to personal appearance. People in this condition cease to wash and dress. Characteristically they lie huddled in their sleeping huts, avoiding all eye contact and speaking to and spoken to by no one.

This kind of behaviour is described as *atu hiro,* a verb typically used to refer to hiding or retreating from an enemy. It is also the behaviour adopted by someone being publicly shamed *(kiaunrinro).* Several people emphasized to me that their 'shamed' behaviour while *nriqa viro* had not been merely conventional, that they had found the shame they had experienced then harder to bear than the physical suffering.

In serious *nriqa viro* there is a conspicuous absence of ordinary attention to bodily well being. People in this condition tend to subsist on food and water that would ordinarily be considered unfit for human consumption because it is indequately cooked or has been lying around on the ground. There is no attempt at symptom relief except when the patient is actually undergoing a curing ceremony. Friends and relatives are not expected to minister to the ill person's physical comfort or day to day needs beyond the provision of firewood and drinking water. They do not, for example, clear away the dirt and excrement with which he or she may be surrounded, or chase away molesting pigs, flies or dogs, and I never heard a person in this condition explicitly request assistance.

This attitude contrasts markedly with the habitual solicitousness people display for their friends' physical well-being under ordinary circumstances, massaging aching limbs, bandaging their cuts or delousing their hair. It reflects the feeling that, as one man put it, 'What is lying there is not our brother himself, but only his *mamanta* (skin, flesh). His *marauha* has been stolen.'

While friends and relatives do not thus concern themselves with the patient's immediate physical well-being, they do characteristically devote considerable time, energy and expenditure to speculating about the causes of the illness, and to arranging diagnostic and curing ceremonies. Disussion about diagnosis and therapy often takes place in the patient's presence, but I never saw a patient being consulted or attempting to participate.

Moreover, even where the illness is not regarded as a threat to life, people typically react to *nriqa viro* in a 'same blood person' (*quanranre*) — a close relative, real or fictive — with a display of emotion quite striking in its intensity to an outsider. Besides wailing *(ndatero)* round the sick bed they often engage in conventional displays of violent symbolic aggression or rage (*inronra hita)* against the afflicting agent. *Inronra hita* is a culturally learned mode of response to serious harm to oneself, one's property or a 'same blood person.' Someone who is *inronra hita* shouts war cries and outrageous verbal abuse at the agent responsible for the harm. Men shoot arrows into the air and snap their bow strings, while women brandish axes and sticks. This kind of response is explicitly identified with the response to harm to a 'same blood person' in war. The emotional intensity of this response to illness must be understood in relation to the intensity of emotion aroused by warfare or the thought of warfare in contemporary Ommura. By the same token, procedures for dealing with *nriqa viro* are explicitly aimed at treating the grief (*po*) and rage (*inronra hita)* of friends and kin as well as restoring the patient's health.

Finally, the ill person's sex, age and prestige do not in themselves have a significant bearing on the strength of the emotional response to illness and the amount of energy devoted to discussing and arranging treatment. What is important here is that the he or, she is regarded as an integral member of the 'one blood group. *Nriqa viro* in more marginal people, orphans, newly married virilocal wives and recent migrants, receives less attention.

Women's Reproductive Disorders

Certain conditions affecting women and regarded as menstrual or reproductive disorders are also treated as 'deviations from health or from what is expected in terms of well being.' These maladies are quite distinct from *nriqa viro,* and the causes to which they are attributed and the procedures for realing with them are quite different from those for *nriqa viro.*[20]

They are diagnosed and treated in the women's house by initiated women rather than publicly by male elders as in cases of *nriqa viro.* This is in keeping with the fact that knowledge about matters relating to childbirth and menstruation is the 'secret' (*uakyera)* of fully initiated women.[21] It is also consistent with the fact that in public ceremonies for diagnosing and treating *nriqa viro*, where older men have situational authority over women, women's reproductive capacities are treated as a threat to male supremacy and may not appropriately be mentioned.

I was asked not to repeat certain information given to me about the nature of specific disorders in this class and treatments for them. My account is therefore limited to some general points about aspects which are not regarded as secret.

Named categories of menstrual or reproductive disorder are distinguished according to symptoms (e.g., 'severe abdominal pain during menstruation,' 'headaches during menstruation,' bad blood from blocked menstrual flow'). Illnesses in this class are attributed to breach of the taboos and rules of sexual conduct imparted in female initiation which, incidentally, affirm rather than provide alternatives to the principle of male dominance and superiority. It is not in their secret initiation and medical practices that women's challenges to male authority are to be found. Particular disorders are often associated with breaches of specific prohibitions. 'Bad blood from blocked menstrual flow,' for example, is the outcome of failure to observe prohibitions against entering certain fields or forest areas while menstruating. Treatment, in contrast to that for *nriqa viro,* is predominantly symptom specific, and the range of symptom specific treatments is apparently far wider than for *nriqa viro,* although I was not given detailed information about them.

Menstrual and reproductive disorders do not involve dramatic role playing like *nriqa viro*. In mild cases there is no publicly visible modification of ordinary behaviour. A patient who feels too incapacitated to carry on with her normal daily activities retires to the women's hut, but there is not the same conspicuous withdrawal from communication with others or abandoning of ordinary attention to physical well-being as with *nriqa viro*. Co-wives or female relatives food, water, and firewood and make the patient comfortable. She may be rebuked by her female elders for the misdemeanour to which her condition is attributed. Yet this type of illness does not reflect negatively on her attributes, capacities or moral status, and is degrading only to the extent that it involves significant absence of physically fitness or bodily soundness (*qio*).

VUNRATO AFI: CONFUSED PERCEPTIONS

A third type of 'deviation from what is expected in terms of well being' is *vunrato afi,* or 'confused perceptions and thoughts,' literally 'confused eyes/ears.' As noted earlier, intellectual processes are associated with the ear (*nrato). Vunrato afi,* a temporarily bounded condition, quite distinct from long term 'insanity' (*werendara*) and from possession, involves disturbance of normal cognitive or thought processes. The person feels confused and anxious, incapable of thinking clearly, and may have disturbed dreams, hear voices or see visions. It is considered a distressing experience but does not involve physical pain or discomfort like *nriqa viro* or menstrual or productive disorders.

I was told that one can tell that someone is *vunrato afi* 'by the look in his eyes.' Other signs of this condition visible to others are impairment of the normal capacity to speak clearly and of muscular co-ordination. The sufferer typically behaves in what is regarded as a confused or irrational manner. The extent to which his or her normal pattern of behaviour is modified depends on the severity of the condition.

Becoming *vunrato afi* is seen as a response to finding oneself in one of several specific 'double bind' situations that Ommura people see as inherent in their social organization. Typical examples are situations in which virilocal wives are emotionally torn between loyalty to their natal kin, on the one hand, and their affinal kin, on the other, or men between solidarity with their natal villages and villages or residence with regard to intervillage warfare or sorcery. The confused *(afi)* state of the afflicted person's perceptions is represented as an inevitable reaction to the confused *(afi)* state of his or her social circumstances, and being *vunrato afi* does not reflect on one's moral state or personal worth. There is no treatment for this condition. I was told that it generally passed over as the suffer's circumstances changed or he or she managed to resolve the mental conflict.

Conclusion

As I stressed earlier, many aspects of those illness conceptions and practices described here must be understood as responses to major social changes that have taken place in Ommura life over the fifteen years or so preceding my fieldwork, as the result of increasing control by the Administration, incorporation into the wider economy and exposure to new cultural influences. While a full historical treatment represents another stage in the analysis beyond the scope of the present paper, I would like, before concluding, briefly to place in historical perspective some aspects of Ommura medical ideas and practices that I have emphasized in this paper.

A picture has emerged of a situation in which, overall, in diagnosis and therapy there is far more elaboration of, and emphasis on, psycho-social and mystical causes of illness than the identification of specific symptoms. Modes of symptom-specific treatment about which people knew or which they practised were, except for those limited to gynecological disorders, far fewer in number and less complex than those described for certain African societies at a comparable technological level (Turner 1967:299 ff).[22]

However, as I have shown elsewhere,[23] there is evidence that, in recent years, there has been a definite trend in Ommura medical ideas and practices towards increased emphasis on the aetiological level, together with a decline in the sue of symptom-specific treatment. Reminiscences indicate that modes of realing with *nriqa viro* which had passed out of fashion before y arrival, and which no one was now capable of practicing, had involved comparatively complex forms of symptom-speicific treatment. Moreover, it appears that recently creativity in the medical sphere has centered on the elaboration of theories about and methods for dealing with social and mystical causes of *nirqa viro*.

These developments must be understood as attempts to deal with new sources of stress associated with social change. They also constitute responses to a recent increase in the political and ideological significance of theories about illness causation, and diagnosis and therapy.[24] Briefly, there is a sense that the principle of superior male *kyapukya* or power, and hence the authority of initiated men over women and youths, has been seriously threatened by the Administration's measures to suppress warfare, a crucial source of male prestige and authority. Moreover, the introduction of coffee as a cash crop has provided women for the first time with a regular source of cash, hitherto a male monopoly.

Initiated men and some women explicitly treat this situation as one in which, if society is to be prevented from falling into chaos, these threats to the principle of superior male *kyapukya* must be countered by devoting far greater effort to actively and explicitly affirming it than when it was taken for granted. This has involved older men concentrating their creativity, as medical theorists and practioners, on elaborating those aspects of the medical system which have a direct bearing on this issue.

As was seen, ideas about the aetiology of *nriqa viro* are such that illness of this kind is often perceived as casting an element of doubt on the validity of the principle of superior male *kyapukya*. If men are really so much more powerful than women, then why are they not markedly less prone to fall ill? The most elaborate and spectacular innovations in the medical sphere over the past few years have been the complex of ideas and practices associated with the *assochia* ceremony mentioned earlier. A central aim of this newly established ceremony is to ensure that every case of *nirqa viro* is publicly explained or attributed to a cause in such a why that the principle of superior male *kyapukya* is situationally affirmed rather than threatened. In keeping with this, an elaborate set of new distinctions has been introduced between 'men's illnesses', the cause of which imply only minimal lack of power and 'women's illnesses', the causes of which imply far greater lack of power.

Acknowledgements

This paper is based on field research in Ommura from June 1975 to August 1976 and funded by the Social Sciences Research Council of Great Britain, whose assistance I gratefully acknowledge. I would like to thank Antuao of Samura village and Taindo Sara of Asara for explaining so much about Ommura diagnosis and therapy to me.

I am grateful to Professor A.L. Epstein and Dr. Hilary Standing for reading and criticizing the thesis chapter which provided the basis of this paper, and to Ragnar Johnson for his comments on later drafts.

References

Barth, F. (1975), *Ritual and Knowledge Among the Baktaman of New Guinea*. New Haven: Yale University Press.

Bateson, G. (1958) *Naven*, Stanford, Stanforf University Press.

Bissiliat, J. (1976). 'Village Diseases an Bush Diseases in Songhay'. In J. Loudon (ed.) 1976. *Social Anthropology and Medicine*. LOndon, Academic Press.

Bordieu, P. (1977), *outline of a Theory of Proctice*. Cambridge University Press.

Brown, P. (1978). *Highland Peoples of New Guinea*. Cambridge: Cambridge University Press.

Fabrega, H. (1979). 'Elementary Systems of Medicine'. *Culture, Medicine and Psychiatry*, Vol.3, No.2, June, 1979.

Fabrega, H. and Silver, D. (1973). *Illness and Shamanistic Curing in Zinacantan*. Stanford: Stanford University Press.

Frankel, S. (1980). "I am Dying of Man": The Pthology of Pollution'. *culture, Medicine and Psychiatry* 4 (1980) 95-117.

Gell, A.F. (1975). *Metamorphosis of the Cassowaries*. London: Athlone Press.

Gillies, E. (1976). 'Causal Criteria in African Classfications of Disease. In J. Loudon (ed.), 1976, *Social Anthropology and Medicine*, London: Academic Press.

Glass, R.M. (1965). 'The Huli of the Southern Highlands.' In P. Lawrence and M.J. Meggitt (eds), 1965, *Gods, Ghosts and Men in Melanesia*. Melbourne: Oxford University Press.

Glick, L. (1967). 'Medicine as an Ethnographic ategory: The Gimi of the New Guinea Highlands. *Ethnology* 6:31, p.56.

Harwood, A. (1970). 'Medicine as a Ethnographic Category: The Gimi of the New Glick, L. (1967). `Medicine as an Ethographic Category: The Gimi of the New Guinea Highlands. *Ethnology* 6:31, p.56.

Harwood, A. (1970). *Witchcraft, Sorcery and Social Categories Among the Safwa*. London: Oxford Unviersity Presss and the International Africa Institue.

Helman, C. (1978). 'Feed a Cold, Starve a Fever.' *Cultrure, medicine and Psychiatry* 2 (1978) 107-137.

Holmes, T. and Rahe, R.H (1967). 'The Social Readjustment Ratign Scale.' *Journal of Psychosomatic Research* II, 213-218.

Janzen, J. (1978). *The Quest for Therapy in Lower Zaire*. Berkeley, University of California Press.

Johannes, Adel (1980). 'Many Medicines in One; Curing in the Eastern Highlands of Papua New Guinea'. *Culture, Medicien and Psy-*

chiatry 4 (1980) 43-70.

Kleinman, A. (1980). *Patients and Healers in the Context of Culture.* Berkeey, University of California Press.

Lewis, G. (1975). *Knowledge of Illnes in a Sepik Society.* London. Atholone Press.

Lewis, G. (1976). 'A. View of Sickness in New Guinea.' In Louden, J.B. (ed.), *Social Anthropology and Medicline.* London, Academic Press, 49-104.

Lienhardt, G. (1961). *Divinity and Experience.* Oxford, Clarendon Press.

Loudon, J. (1976). 'Introdution' to Loudon,J. (ed.), *Social Anthropology and Medicine.* London, Academic Press.

Meigs, A. (1976). 'Male Pregnancy and the reduction of Sexual Opposition in a New Guinea HIghlands Society'. *Ethnology* 25: — 393-407.

Ngubane, H. (1977). *Body and Mind in Zulu Medicine,* London, Academic Press.

Reay, M. (1959). *The Kuma.* Melbourne University Press.

Read, K. (1967) Morality and the Concept of the Person Among the Galaku Gama'. In Middleton, J. (ed.), 1967, *Myth and Cosmos.* New York The Natural Histor Press.

Pannoff (1970). 'Maenge remedies and Conceptions of Disease.' *Ethonology,* Vol. IX, No.1, Jan., 1970. pp. 68-84.

Schachter, S. and Singer, J. (1962). 'Congnitive, social and Psychological Determinants of Emotional States.' *Psychologicl Review* 69, pp. 379-399.

Sigerist, E. (1977). 'The Special Position of the Sick.' Reprinted in Landy, D. (ed.), *Culture, Disease and Healing.* New York , Macmillan.

Strathern, A. (1977). 'Why is shame on the Skin/'. In Blacking, J. (ed.), 1977, *The Anthropologyof the Body.* London Academic Press.

Strathern, M. (1979). 'The Self in Self-Decoration.' *Oceania,* Vol. XLIX, No. 4, p. 241.

Sontag, S. (1978). *Illness as Metaphor.* New York: Farrar, Strauss and Giroux.

Totman, R. (1979). *Social Causes of Illness.* London. Souvenir Press.

Turner, V.W. (1967). *The Forest of Symbols.* Cornell University Press.

Young, A. (1976). 'Some Implications of medical Beliefs and Practices for Social Anthropology.' *American Anthropologist* 78:5-24.

NOTES

* University of Susses England.

1. I should note that the Melanesian Pidgin term 'sick' was regarded as applicable to disorders in each of these three general categories. Ommura use Melanesian Pidgin concepts mainly in communication with non-Ommura speakers.
2. Clearly, any contrast between Ommura and 'contemporary western' conceptions of illness can only be drawn in extremely broad terms. The diversity among views of the nature of illness found in contemporary western contexts is considerable. For a start, it is necessary to distinguish between views entailed by scientific medicine or 'biomedicine', by various sectors or popular culture, and by 'alternative' therapies such as homeopathy or naturopathy which are currently gaining in popularity in many western contexts (see Helman 1978, Kleinman 1980, ch. 2).
3. Other New Guinea cultures also attach a special significance to the nose. Read notes that Gahuku Gama of the Eastern Highlands will sum up (a man's) character by saying 'I know his nose. It is of such and such a type (Read 1967:213). See also Bateson (1958).
4. For example, I obtained over 35 anatomical terms.
5. It seems that elsewhere in New Guinea some of the most elaborated ideas about bodily processes in relation to illness also focus on blood flow. Lewis notes, for example, in his discussion of Gnau conceptions of 'the processes of harm in illness that 'in those views which come closest to pathology blood is the disordered element' (Lewis 1975:202). See also Panoff's (1970:473) account of Manage conceptions of illness.
6. Glick (1967) reports a similar range of therapeutic blood letting practices for Gimi of the Eastern Highlands of New Guinea.
7. Blood trapped in the nose is a source of illness for women as well as for men.
8. Fabrega (1979:171) has suggested, on the basis of a comparative analysis of several 'elementary systems of medicine', that in such systems generally 'a physically eleborated schema about bodily functions does not appear to be part of the rationale of treatment.'
9. 'While these aspects or states do not have external bodily manifestations they are not conceived as independent of the body but as 'inside' it.

10. *The same verb is used for 'to hear' (a sound) and 'to know' or 'to understand': e.g.,* Nta mmia nruua tira ienama'—*'I can hear this noise'.* 'Mmia haikya qioma ieana'-*'I understand this matter clearly'. Similarly knowledge and memories are 'stored'* (kiearo) *'in the ear': e.g.,* 'I nrato tiraea time mia'—*'If you know about this tell them-literally 'If it is in your ear tell them'.*

11. Similarly, Marilyn Strathern (1979:251) notes that in Mount Hagen, Western Highlands, it is considered that 'ordinarily a man keeps his desires, intentions and material assets hidden. . . .'

12. There are apparent parallels for other parts of New Guinea. For example, Barth (1975:245) notes that Baktaman of the Western district are not given to 'exploratory or analytical discourse about the complex constitution of the motions and motivations of other . and Lewis (1975:137) comments that The use of simple behavioural to indicate more complex human conditions, emotions or responses is charactertic of Gnau idiom'. One should bear in mind, however, the well attested nebulousness with which English speakers characteristically apply words denoting emotions. See Totman (1979:38) and Schacher and Singer (1962).

13. Public diagnosis and therapy were the monopoly of fully initiated men, although some of them were considered more skilled than others.

14. Febrega and Silver (1973:8) suggest that 'successful folk healers' are likely to have 'some general appreciation of degrees of bodily functioning, a general understanding of illness behaviour, and an intuitive knowledge of the relationship between both of these.' They criticize ethnomedical work for failing to investigate this dimension of healers' expertise. The possibility that Ommura healers operate to some extent on intuitive principles of this kind when dealing with *nriqa* viro must not be precluded.

15. Interpreted in this fashion the notion of nriqa viro from wera fits with the conclusions of many sociological studies which claim to demonstrate relationships between the occurrence of illness and the experience of rapid social change. For a summary of such studies see Totman (1979:120 ff).

16. For a survey of ideas in this field see Totman (1979).

17. Totman (1979:15 and 25).

18. As, for example, in many African contexts where illness is attributed to neglect of obligations towards ancestors or disharmony in the social group: e.g., the Zulu of whom Ngubane writes that 'good health means the harmonious working and coordination of his universe; (Ngubane 1977:27). See also Harwood (197)) and Turner (1968). Similarly, according to Fabreaga and Silver (1973-80), writing of the may of Zinacatna, 'The individual himself, his worldly contemporaries and the gods are locked in a triple web of relationships, and a frequent expression of disarticulation in this set of relationship his illness.'

19. I have described this process in detail in "Men's" and "women's" illnesses in the New Guinea Highlands,' Paper present at the conference of the British Medical Anthropological Society, November 1978, on 'Sex roles and illness.'

20. To the best of my knowledge there is no special class of male reproductive or sexual disorders.

21. It is interesting in this context that during his research in Gnau, West Sepik, Lewis noted several cases of severe beast abscesses in women whose children had died while their mothers were still lactating, and which appeared to him 'sufficiently abnormal for me to expect from them some particular explanation, which I did not obtain . . .' They did not suggest it was caused by something...' He would regard this as an example of distressing ailment accepted and natural even . . . .' (Lewis 1975: 198). One wonders, however, if these abscesses might fall into a category of `women's illnesses like those described here for Ommura, diagnosed by women in secret from men.

22. There has been a tendency among anthropologists to emphasize therapies aimed at dealing with social or mystical causes of illness at the expense of the (often less exotic) methods directed predominantly at a symptomatic level. Gillies (1976:390) has shown, with respect to African ethnography, how the fascination exerted by "who" questions' has led anthropologists to underemphasize explanations and treatments based on 'naturalistic principles.' See also Fabrega and Silver (1973:8). I should therefore note that from the start of my research I was aware of the possibility of this type of distortion and consciously sought to avoid it. Other writers on New Guinea health care systems have noted or implied a similar kind of emphasis on etiology rather than symptoms. Thus Lewis notes that Gnau of the West Sepik

`do not depend on observations of the physical signs or symptoms of illness to discriminate between them...(Lewis 1975:141). 'If you wish to know what kind of illness the patient has you may be told the name of one of the various agents causing the illness, but this tells you virtually nothing about he clinical form or pathology of the illness . . . ' (Lewis 1975:136). He observes that GNAU make farless use of Symptom Specific treatments than Lunda, Zande or Subanum (Lewis 1975:144-5) Glick (1967:39) notes similarly for the Gimi of the Eastern High-lands that what matters most about an illness is its causes.' These may thus be common features of papua New Guinea medical systems— at least during certain historical periods — related to cultural and social organizational features typical of this area. This raises a host of interesting comparative issues.

23. I have presented detailed evidence for these points in "Men's" and "women's" illness in the new Guinea Highlands', a paper presented at the conference of the British Medical Anthropological Society on 'Sex roles and illness,' November, 1978.

24. These processes are described in detail in my Ph.D. thesis in progress.

* University of Susses, England

Chapter-7

Lunda Medicine and the Treatment of Disease*

By Victor Turner

Chapter-7

In an illuminating appraisal of the literature on disease and treatment in primitive medicine, Erwin Ackerknecht (1946, 471) has pointed out that "most data on treatment, in general ethnographic monographs, consist of a list of drugs or other techniques used, of a list of the diseases in which they are applied, and of statements as to the possible objective effect that such measures have. It is obvious that such descriptions, valuable as they are, omit just the points needed for our special inquiry: *what are the the ideas underlying these therapeutic acts, and under what circumstances (with or without ritual) are they performed?"* (my italics). Since Ackerknecht wrote, there have been several praiseworthy attempts to answer his queries,[1] directly or by implication, but by and large there have been few systematic discussions of the relationship between the treatment of disease and the religious beliefs, ideas, and practices of a specific tribal society.

I am painfully aware that my own data on the treatment of disease, collected intermittently in the form of *ad hoc* observations and accounts by informants of varying intelligence and knowledge of tribal therapy, are relatively scanty and have many lacunae, but they are enough to demonstrate that Ndembu healing procedures are governed by the same principles and modes of classification as their religious rites and moral concepts. In this study I am not primarily concerned with the familiar problem of the extent to which primitive medicine is magico-religious or rational, for I am not a medical man and cannot say with authority just how "effective" a given procedure has been. My aim here is to reveal the ideas implicit in the Ndembu treatment of disease and to show that these ideas pervade wider realms of belief and action.

Disease, Misfortune, and Affliction

In the first place Ndembu conceive disease or illness (*musong'u*) as a species of misfortune (*malwa, kuhalwa, kuyindama,* or *kubula kutooka*— this last term signifying "to lack whiteness or luck or purity"). Misfortune is a class term of which other species include: bad luck at hunting, reproductive disorders, physical accidents, and the loss of property. It might be argued that words such as "misfortune," "accident," "bad luck," "mischance" are erroneous translations of *malwa* and its synonyms for there is indeed no concept of "accident" among the Ndembu, who seek to find a cause for every calamity; far from being "prelogical," they are obsessively logical, though on the basis of mystical premises, as Evans-Pritchard showed us (1937) in his classical study of Azande systems of belief. The Ndembu, like the Azande, consider that calamities and adversities of all kinds are caused by mystical forces generated or evoked and directed by conscious agents. These agents may be alive or dead, human or extrahuman. They may operate directly on their victims or indirectly through mystical intermediaries. Ancestral shades cause suffering directly; living sorcerers and witches work evil through medicines or familiars or through a combination of both. A person may also raise a "zombie" or "wraith" (*musalu),* an evil component of the personality which persists after death, by means of a curse and send it to kill someone against whom he has a grudge (*chitela).* However, shades, witches, sorcerers, and utterers of curses are not regarded as the sole causes of illness. For Ndembu talk of different kinds of *nyisong'u,* "illnesses" or "diseases," and recognize that specific symptoms are connected with each of them. At first I assumed that the Ndembu regarded these *nyisong'u* merely as conditions of the body and that they had been influenced in this respect by European notions, but when I inquired further I found that the *nyisong'u* appeared to be endowed with independent life and that part of the therapy consisted in using "bitter," "hot," or evil-smelling herbs to disgust and disconcert the *musong'u* and drive it away.

Yet Ndembu speak as though sorcery and witchcraft were

always in the background where illness is concerned. Some sicknesses are so common that the element of the untoward which makes people immediately suspect sorcery or witchcraft is lacking. Nevertheless, if these become exceptionally severe or protracted, suspicion grows. There are certain classes of calamities that are believed a *priori* t have shades as their probable cause. These are female reproductive troubles, including menstrual disorders, frequent miscarriage and stillbirth, and lack of successat hunting. Illness may or may not be caused by shades. If the patient dreams of dead relatives while he is sick, the probability is that he is begin afflicted by an ancestral shade, but the possibility of sorcery or witchcraft cannot be ruled out even here, for these evildoers are notorious deceivers and illusionists. Thus it is usual for the relatives of a person to seek out a diviner. The diviner, by means of one or another of various techniques (see Turner 1961) diagnoses a mystical cause as responsible, and a rite is performed either to propitiate a specific manifestation of a shade or to exorcise the familiars of sorcery or witchcraft.

Consulting a diviner and sponsoring a curative rite are both costly and troublesome for marginal subsistence cultivators, and there are many herbalists and lay healers in the villages who claim to be able to dispel *nyisong'u,* whether these are associated with shades and witches or not.Some Ndembu believe that all ailments are mystically caused but that most are brought on by "only little grudges" and can be dealt with by local herbalists in their early stages. It is thought that the familiars of witchcraft and sorcery are activated only by sudden violent anger or by long-cherished, smoldering "grudges" *(yitela)* resulting from some affront or the product of jealousy or envy. A minor grudge or quarrel might induce a sorcerer to send a minor ailment against his rival, but in this case there is little public interest in who did it. It is mainly a matter for the patient and his close kin and affines who desire the restoration of his health.

Some illnesses are believed to be caused by the breach of a ritual prohibition which is disclosed by the nature of its symptoms. For example, leprosy *(mbumba)* is thought to be the result of transgressing one of the taboos of *Mukanda,* the boys' circumcision ceremony. A form of fever, associated with foaming at the mouth and believed to attack only young children, is said to be caused by eating the meat of the hyrax (*chibatata)* or wild pig *(chombu)*. Other diseases, such as elephantiasis of the scrotum, may result, according to Ndembu ideas, from coming in contact with protective medicine against adultery, though it is conceded that the disease may not always have this cause, for a newborn child may have it.

Other diseases again, such as tuberculosis (*musong'u wantulu,* "the disease of the chest") and dysentery (*kapokota)* are held to have been imported by the Europeans, though treatments based on traditional Ndembu pharmacological principles have been developed to cope with them, as we shall see. These may or may not be connected by Ndembu with indigenous notions of witchcraft or spirit possession. In the case of severe tuberculosis the rite of Tukuka, introduced from the Cnokwe and Luvale territories, is often performed. Its aim is to propitiate the souls of living aliens,but principally those of Europeans, which are believed to fly about at night, to possess Ndembu, causing them to tremble violently and to feed on their lungs.[2] Nevertheless, before Ndembu have recourse to *Tukuka* specialists, they treat tuberculosis as if it were *musong'u* with herbal and other kinds of "medicines."

Ackerknecht has shows (1946, 472) that of the diseases regarded as "natural" by primitives, three groups seem to stand out: "the very slight diseases (colds); the very common diseases (old age, tuberculosis, venereal diseases, malaria, filariasis, yaws, food poisoning, sunstroke, skin diseases); and the diseases imported by the Whites." Children's diseases are often added to the very common diseases. The word "natural" is not apposite here, for Ndembu do not distinguish, as we do, between natural and supernatural orders. For them there is only a single cosmic order, though some parts of its are "quite clear" and others are "dark" and obscure, some things are visible and others cannot be seen. The process of therapy, as we shall see, is partly a process of making hidden and secret things visible and thereby accessible, if they are harmful, to redressive and remedial action. Ackerknecht's formulation would fit the Ndembu facts if we substituted for "natural diseases" the phrase "diseases in their own right," that is to say, not as brought on by spirits or witches. perhaps the only instance of disease regarded as inexplicable in its origin, if not natural, is the influenza epidemic of 1918 which followed the First World War and swept destructively through Ndembu territory, as it did through the rest of the world.

Color Symbolism, Medicines, and Treatment

The classification of reality in terms of the tripartite color division between white, red, and black, which I have discussed elsewhere, is also of crucial importance in the rapeutic procedures. For among the many senses of whiteness are: strength (*wukolu),* life (*wumi),* health (*kuhanda),* making visible (*kusolola),* sweeping clean (*kukomba),* and washing (impurities from) oneself (*Kuwela).* It also stands for "prosperity" and "freedom from misfortune." Thus the state of health is a "white," "clean," and Pure" state. The state of ill health is, on the contrary, a "black" state, and indeed one of the attributes of blackness is "having diseases" (*yikweti yikatu—* from the verb *kukata,* "to be ill"; *yikatu* is synonymous with *nusong'u*). "Black" is also to "lack luck" (*kubula kutooka)* or "purity," to have "sufferings" *(yihung'u)* and "misfortune" (*malwa).* It also represents "darkness" *(mwidima)* and "what is secret" (*chakujindaP* or "what is hidden" *(chakusweka).* One of the aims of therapy therefore, is to restore his former "witness" to the patient who is in a "black" state. Symbolic action directed to that end include sweeping the patient's body with a medicine broom to get rid of the "impure things" on it or in it and washing him with decoctions of pounded herbs. Some medicines are literally "white" substances, made from plants with white bark, wood, roots or fruits, or from birds or animals with white feathers or fur. Others have analogous qualities to "whiteness" or "purity," like the tree *mukombukombu (Tricalysia angolensis [Leptactina]),* whose leaves are used in the making of a medicine broom (*chisampu).* The name of this tree is homonymous with *kukomba* (to sweep), and from the name alone, and not from any physical property of the tree—its leaves are small and unsuitable for sweeping—*mukombukombu* has acquired its ritual role as an instrument of purification.

However, "to make white" (*kutookisha)* is more than these: it is to make clear and explicit, to leave nothing hidden or confused. The herbal and other "medicines" applied to the patient as potions, lotions, or poultices are substances each of which has its own specific "virtue"—each reveals either some aspect of the disease or points forward to some aspect of the desired state of health or "whiteness." The pharmacopoeia for each disease is nothing less than a description of the disease in symbolic terms and a statement of the attributes of health and wholeness. behind the symbols and their interpretation lies the pattern of values peculiar to Ndembu, the fundamental frame of their thinking and feeling. Thus, the act of treatment is itself a "white" action, directed against the "black" action of the disease.

Redness also has its part to play in therapy, its usual equivocal part. For in some respects, it represents, as we have seen, "power" *(ng'ovu),* "life" *(wumi),* the strength and joy that comes from eating the flesh of animals, and the blood tie linking together matrilineal kin and mother and child. It also stands for murder, necrophagous wichcraft, and the impure blood of menstruation. Thus some diseases, in addition to being "black", also have a "red' lethal character. Bilharziasis (*kaseli kamashi)* is such a disease for one of its symptoms is blood *(mashi)* in the urine. The use of certain red medicines in its treatment is therefore appropriate, for these "reveal" the essential character of the disease.

Although this fundamental classification governs the symbolic articles and symbolic actions of Ndembu treatments, nevertheless there are other features to be considered here. Most important is the Ndembu concept of "medicines." C.M.N. White has outlined the main features of Luvale beliefs in medicines (1961, 35—38) and for the most part his conclusions apply to the Ndembu, who are neighbors of the Luvale. Like the Luvale, Ndembu distinguish between two classes of dedicate, *yitumbu* (Luvale *vitumbo)* and *mpelu* (Luvale *lupelo).* White describes the former as "of vegetable or inorganic nature" and the latter as "organi material." I would like to distinguish these clases further by the mode of association thought to exist between the symbol and its object and associated concepts. In the case of *yitumbu,* the associative link is dominantlyone of sympathy; thy symbol shares an aspect of the object's existence or state. For example, the root of the *kapumbwa* plant *(Ancylobothrys amoena)* secretes white gum which resembles pus *(mashina). Yitumbu* made from this root is used in the treatment of gonorrhea *(kaseli kamashina),* one symptom of which for Ndembu is the presence of pus in the urine. In the case of *mpelu,* the associative link is one of contagion—to borrow a useful term from Sir James Frazer which indicates that the symbol has in fact been part of the object it signifies or has been in close physical contact with it. Thus, as part of the materia medical employed to cure tuberculosis, we find portions of the diaphragm of an antbear *(itandantulu dachibudi).* This animal has a strong chest and *mpelu* taken from it will, so it is believed, strengthen the chest of the patient. Similarly, the hair of an albino *(mwabi)* is considered "strengthening," for a albino is a "white" or auspicious being.

Yitumbu has much the same range of senses as the East Central which Goddall, writing of the Bemba, defined (1921), 80) as "medicine, simple, charm, drug, poison (almost entirely prepared fromthe bark, leaves, wood or roots of trees)." Here I shall be concerned only with its use as medicine, drug, and simple, not as poison or charm.

I propose to describe a series of diseases and their treatments, just as my informants told me of them. In the course of these accounts, we shall encounter different kinds and classes of medicines and ways in which they are applied. It is in these contexts of situation that we shall get to understand their properties and uses best.

Inventory of Diseases

The following list of diseases makes no claim to completeness or even adequacy, but it represents some of the more common types which spring readily to the mind of a Kandembu. I give the vernacular term for the disease, informants' comments on its name and symptcms (*yuma yakutiyayi muntu mumujimba hakukata),* and finally the term by which it is known in English. In this matter of translation I have followed the advice of Dr. Cahal who points out that the *chimbuki* treats symptoms and signs, not specific diseases. The vernacular terms correspond to symtoms, Thus *Kaseli kamashi* is hematuria, not necessarily bilharziasis, although bilharziasis may well be the most common cause of hematuria among the Ndembu.

Mbumba yaluzong'a or mbumba yachula

"This disease causes people to lose toes and fingers. They have white spots." [Almost certainly leprosy.]

mbumba yichinana "

"Red leprosy." [Possibly yaws.]

Kaseli kamashi

"Blood is seen in the urine." [I lematuria.]

Kaseli kamashina

"There is pus in the urine." [Pyuria.]

Musong'u wantulu

"The disease of the chest; the patient spits blood." [Chest disease (hemoptysis).]

Musongu wamesesi

"The disease of sore eyes. A cream-colored liquid, called *mpota* comes out of th eeyes. A white film covers the eyes. But only a few go blind with it." [Possibly conjunctivo-keratitis and corneal opacities.]

Musong'u wamatu

"Disease of the ears. Pus comes out of the ear, following earache. The patient may become deaf (wajika matu)." [Otiis media.]

Musong'u wevumu

"Disease of the stomach. There are several kinds: (I) pains in the stomach, (2) inability to defecate; (3) a 'running' stomach; (4) *'Kapokota,'* a disease which perforates the intestine. This disease comes from the Northern Rhodesian Copperbelt." [(I)

Stomach ache; (2) constipation; (3) diarrhea; (4) dysentery.]

Musong'u wakalepa

"The patient cannot move. This disease is incurable, and has been known by Ndembu from time immemorial." [Paralysis.]

Musong'u wakuzaluka

"The patient talks much, sleeps or goes away without giving warning, curses wildly. Once there are a woman called Nyasoneka of Nswanakamawu Village in Chief Mukang'ala's area. Her illness started with a headache. Then she had great fever. Her relatives thought she had some ordinary illness. After some months she became weak and tired. This was followed by a time when she stole food. Then she grew garrulous and began to tell lies. She did not seem to take any notice of the opinions of others. She took to sleeping in different villages, a night in each. Finally she went away into the bush where she got lost and died—no one foudn her body. People generally reckoned her to be mad *(kuzaluka).* About four years elapsed from the beginning of her illness to her death." [Insanity.]

Musong'u wanyima

"Disease of the back. The patient feels a pain in the back which gradually grows worse. In bad cases the person's back becomes bent *(wukuheng'nyima)."* [Backache.]

Musong'u wachinkomya

"This is to fall down in a fit *(kukonya).*" [Epilepsy.]

Musong'u wawansi

"The disease of childhood. First the child cries a lot. This is followed by shivering and fever. After one day it begins to move its limbs convulsively. If the disease started in the morning, it will do this once that day, but on the following day will do it twice or thrice. These limb movements will continue for two or three weeks and then stop. If it goes on for longer the people will think it is epilepsy. This disease is caused by eating the flesh of the hyrax or of the wild pig, for these animals make a bubbling sound and move their limbs independently of their bodies."[?]

Musong'u wakanwa

"Disease of the mouth. It starts with a pain in the gums,

with small boils (*mabobela).* The gums become swollen and discharge blood and pus. Teeth drop out." [Pyorrhea.]

Musong'u wachingongu

"Disease of smallpox. *Tungongu* are small tattoo marks, the raised scars of tattooing, i.e., cheloids. The patient is isolated from the village and treated in the bush (European influence?)." [Probably smallpox, with occasionally severe chickenpox being included.]

Musong'u wamutu

"Disease of the head. A person first feels very cold and his head feels very heavy. Then he has pain in his whole body. Sometimes it ends in death. Since much pain is felt in the temples, incisions are made in them and medicines are rubbed in." [Headache with fever.]

Musong'u watupepa

"A person feels sharp pains in his feet, just as when one suddenly withdraws one's feet from the neighborhood of a hot fire in very cold weather. The pain proceeds up the leg to the hips where it stops. He cannot walk.The cure is to keep the feet warm." [Severe cramps.]

Musong'u wawunonu (also called *musong'u wakaswendi)*

"Pus flows from the genitals, and from the ears, nose and throat."

[Possibly Lymphogranuloma venereum.]

Musong'u wampang'a

"It attacks the testicles and causes them to swell." [Swelling of the scrotum; it probably includes hydrocele, hernia, varicocele, as well as elephantiasis.]

Musong'u wanshing'u

"A person feels as though the inside of his neck is broken." [Stiff neck.]

Musong'u wakunong'oka

"A person often falls into a doze." [Possibly sleeping sickness, but may also include encephalitis, some forms of epilepsy, and brain tumors.]

Treatment of Specific Diseases

I now present some accounts of treatments given to me by a number of informants, including Muchona, my best informant on ritual and medicine, Kasonda my cook, Ihembi, a famed doctor and herbalist, Sandombu, the principal "actor" in the "social dramas" of my book *Schism and Continuity,* Chakadyi, a village headman, Windson Kashnakaji, a village schoolmaster, and Jackson, a young educated man.

MBUMBA YALUZONG'A, LEPROSY

"Leprosy attacks a woman if she walks in the former site of a circumcision lodge, where the men were making *nfunda* medicine (the major protective medicine of the lodge which contains cindered foreskins, the urine of apprentice—circumcisers, the ashes of the burned lodge and of various sacred fires, and a number of other highly dangerous symbolic substances). *Mbumba* attacks people in the air where the boys were circumcised (a site known as *ifwilu,* the place of dying). But if your blood can fight *mbumba* you will not be attacked."

The curative procedure is as follows. "First you collect medicines *(kuhuka yitumbu).* The first thing is to go to a former circumcision site *(ifwilu)* to the *mudyi* tree *(Diplorryncus condylocarpon)* under which *Kambanji* (war leader), the senior novice, was circumcised and take aa single piece of its root.

"Next you go to the streamside evergreen forest *(itu)* where the *mbumba yachula* tree (*Landolphia rubescens)* grows. (This means 'leprosy of the frog' and refers to the pale mottling an spots on a frog's skin which resembles the marks of leprosy.) A branch of this tree is cut, and some bark scrapings (*nyemba)* are removed by a ax *(kazemba)* or knife (*mpoku).* These are put either in a potsherd (*chizanda),* a round, flat winnowing basket (*lwalu),* or any kind of discarded basket.

"Next a root (*muzaji or muji)* of *kavulawumi (Maprounea africana)* is collected. After this they go to the former site of the fire near which the novice *Kambanji* slept at a lodge and take a root from the ground beneath it, of any species. They also take a root of any species from the earth beneath the fire of the novice called *kajika* ('the little-one-who-closes'), who was the last to be circumcised. They then go into the bush to find the tree with white-spotted bark (called *mutondu wamabeng'a,* 'the tree of spots') and collect bark-scrapings.

"They return, scrape the skin from the roots and burn the bark and root-scrapings they have collected. The ashes are then mixed with castor oil (*imonu)* to form an ointment.

"Now the patient is brought and the doctors (*ayimbuki or ayimbanda)* make circular cuts around the sores and patches or spots *mabeng'a ambumba)* of leprosy. They rub the ointment into these incisions, then rub what is left into the patient's whole body."

No explanations were given of the significance of these actions and medicines, but it is clear that the main principle underlying the treatment is to collect a number of substances that exhibit sympathetic associations with leprosy, or with boys circumcision (of which one of the main mystical sanctions is leprosy), and to incinerate these, thereby destroying the disease (by sympathetic magic). This would be in accordance with the principle underlying the burning of the seclusion lodge (*ng'ula)* itself. it is sid that "all disease re burned if they are thrown into the burning *ng'ula,"* presumably in symbolic guise.

It is interesting that *mudyi,* normally employed in ritual to signify such "good" things as "mother's milk," "womanhood," "Matriliny" and "tribal custom" should here be connected with leprosy. *Mudyi* is a "white' symbol according to Ndembu principles of classification, and leprosy is a "white" disease, so that it would appear that whiteness (*wutooka)* is ambivalent in meaning. It is said that if a novice dies during *Mukanda,* no case may be brought against the lodge officials for compensation, since "God (*Nzambi)* took him." God is represented by white symbols, and it is likely that leprosy, a ritual sanction in other contexts also—if a Paramount Chief's *lukanu* bracelet of royalty is polluted the incumbent will become a leper—is regarded as a divine punishment, a punishment by the *Deus absconditus*.

KASELI KAMASHI, HEMATURIA
(Probably caused by bilharzia)

"Doctors begin to give medicines to the patient when they see that his urine contains blood or pus. If they see blood they know that it is *kaseli Kamashi;* if pus, that it is *kaseli kamashina* (gonorrhea).

"Red gum is collected from the *mupuchi* tree (*Brachystegia spiciformis).* Then some roots of the *katunya* tree (*Uvariastrom hexaloboides)* which grows on the banks of rivers, are dug up. Its roots are red. They are cut up into small pieces, mixed with *mupuchi* gum and put in water in a clay jug (mulondu*).* The jug is then warmed on a fire and when it is warm the patient drinks this medicine. He goes on taking it at intervals from two days to a week.

"If the patient does not get better the doctor collects the roots of the *ywutotu (Gardenia imperialis)* and *kansanying'a* shrubs, which grow near rivers or on large termite-hills (*tuwumbu).* These are cut up, mixed with water in a jug, warmed, then drunk by the patient. *Wutotu* has white roots and produces white gum. *Kansañying'a* has white roots and stinks strongly *(kanunka hama).*" Other roots are used in this treatment but the informant who told me of it had forgotten them.

The beginnings of a explanation appear in this account, for the informant, unsolicited thought it necessary to mention the color of the roots and gums employed as medicine. The red medicines seem to refer to the blood passed in the urine. *Wutotu* is used in the treatment of *kaseli kamashina,* thought by Ndembu to be closely connected with *kaseli kamashi.* The basic principle here seems to be homeopathic; give the patient a medcine that has similar properties to the symptoms of the disease and he will recover. It should be noted that medicine is in this instance taken internally—the *musong'u* affects the internal organs—whereas in the case of leprosy, medicines, representing spotted and discolored skin, were applied to the body surfaces.

Kaseli Kamashina, Pyuria

The doctor collects and cuts up *wutotu* and *kapumbwa* roots and puts them into an earthenware vessel *(nsaba)* or jug *(mulondu)*. Water is added, the pot is warmed, and the patient drinks. This is repeated every day for several weeks. If the patient does not recover, the medicines of *kaseli kamashi* are tried. Sometimes a potion of *mudy (Diplorrhyncus condylocarpon)* and *Kajing'a ludi*[3] roots is given.

It was explained that in the context of *wumbuki*, "treatment with medicines," whitish exudations from trees and shrubs are called *mashina*, "pus," while red secretions are called *mashi*, "blood." The *kapumbwa* plant produces white gum, which drops on the ground and is said to resemble pus. *Mudyi*, of course, secretes a milky latex which in more auspicious ritual contexts represents mother's milk.

Musong'u Wantulu, Chest disease (Hemoptysis)

(a) *First potion.* "The doctor goes first to an old burrow where red army ants *(nsalafu)* live. He digs and finds roots in it, cuts them up, puts them in a clay jug with water, and gives this potion to the patient to drink."

An abandoned burrow, now inhabited by the migratory red ants, is known as *itala dawansalafu*, "the hut of the red ants." Roots that have come in contact with these ants share their characteristics, prominent among which is their sharp, needlelike bite. "The pain in the chest is like the bites of red ants."

(b) *Second potion.* "The doctor locates and cuts up roots of the *mukula* tree *(Pterocarpus angolensis)* and mixes them in a clay jug with the diaphragm of an antbear, *muhanu (Ficus sp.)* roots, and the scale of a pangolin. Water is added, the mixture is warmed, and the patient *(myyeji)* drinks."

"The *mukula* tree drops red gum; it is the tree of blood (indeed, it has many ritual uses with this significance; see Turner, 1962b). It represents the spitting of blood.The diaphragm of an antbear *(itandantulu dachibudi)* is used because the antbear has a strong chest and they want the patient to have a strong chest too. The scale *(ikalu)* of a pangolin *(nkaka)* is put in: because the pangolin moves slowly and curls up if it sees anyone coming. A hunter can carry it easily curled up. In the some way, the disease can be caught and taken away to die. *Muhanu* roots are used because *muhanu* grows up a hole in another tree—it will break the obstruction in a patient's chest. It does not matter which of these two potions is given first."

Three of the ingredients listed above are classed as *mpelu* (pl.*jipelu)* i.e., as operating by contagious magic. These are the roots from the he red ants' nest, and the portions of antbear and pangolin. It would seem logical to a European observer, once he knew that hemoptysis was likened to the biting of red ants, to suppose that the Ndembu used anteater medicines to destroy the disease just as anteaters consume ants, but no informant gave me this explanation. Moral: One should guess meanings as little as possible and collect native explanations, as Professor Monica Wilson has always urged (1957, 6).

MUSONG'U WAMATU, DISCHARGE FROM THE EARS (OTTIS MEDIA)

"Yellowish fruits of the *chikoli* tree (*Strychnos spinosa)* are cut in two, the pulp is stirred up and lukewarm water is poured into the fruit. It is then left to soak in thoroughly. After a time some drops of the juice are allowed to fall into the patient's affected ear.

"Alternatively, bark is scraped from the *Mushokotu* tree (*Faurea saligna),* mixed with water in a large clay pot, the mixture is warmed, and drops are inserted in the patient's ear."

No explanations of the use of these vegetable medicines in terms of sympathetic or contagious magic were forthcoming. I have known Ndembu, treated in this way, who asserted strongly that they experienced an improvement in their condition. It is possible that these medicines are employed because they are objectively effective.

Musong'u Wevumu, Disease of the Stomach

There are two kinds of this disease. One is for women and one is for children. The kind for women is called *chisumi* or *mukung'a.* It affects the stomach in a line that crosses it completely just above the navel in front. A woman may have this pain whether she is expecting a child or not. It is continuous until medicines are given. The one for children is called *musong'u wevumu* with no other name.

(a) *Chisumi or m'kung'a.* "Two old potsherds *(yizanda)* or cooking pots *(Manung'u)* are found in the village and taken by the doctor to a stream. One potsherd is put on either bank of the stream at a place where an old tree has fallen across the water. Bark from the root of any species of tree is scraped off and some scrapings are placed in both potsherds. Then warm water is poured in one, and cold water in the other. After that both potsherds are put on the same side of the stream. The roots used as medicine must go right across the stream. Water must have flowed over and pushed against them.

"When all has been made ready, the doctor and his helpers bring a razor *(ntewula)* and make two cuts in the woman's abdomen, one on each side of the navel. Then they fetch cupping horns *(tusumu)*[4] and the doctor *(chimbanda)* sucks *(ku-sumika)* one horn on the adbdomen, and one on the woman's back immediately opposite. He waits for a short while, then grasps both horns at once, pulls them off abruptly and empties the blood into the stream.

"Next, the doctor makes an incision at the outer side of each of the two cuts on the patient's abdomen and others on the outer side of those on her back. The horns are applied and removed as before. Afterwards the doctor takes medicine from the potsherbd and rubs it into the cuts. He then tells the patient to return to her village. Meanwhile, he remains at the site of the operation and makes a barrage *(kafuza)* across the steam just where he threw in the blood. Then he throws in the potsherds and the dregs of the medicine at the same place. But he does not throw the cupping horns away. When he is ready to go, he pulls the barrage away and releases the water. Everything he has thrown in is completely carried away.

"After he has returned to the village with his cupping horns, the doctor goes into the bush and collects the root of the *mwala* tree *(Afzelia quanzensis)*, which is very bitter in taste. One largeroot is taken, cut up and warmed in an earthenware vessel *(nsaba)*. It is then given to the patient to drink and she takes it for about a week.

"If there is no improvement he goes to a *mutata* tree *(Securidaca longipedunculata)*, digs up and removes one long root which he cuts in pieces. These he puts in a pot with water, warms the medicine and cuts in pieces. These he puts in a pot with water, warms the medicine and gives it to the patient to drink. This she does for several days until she gets quite better. But if she is still sick, roots of *molu wawubwang'u*[5] are cut up and mixed with the chopped roots of the *kakwema* tree (*Uvaria angolensis or Enneastemon schweinforthii)*. These are then heated in a earthenware vessel and given to the patient until she gets better, perhaps for as long as two weeks."

"The name *chisumi* is from *ku-suma*, 'to bite.' Its other name, Mukung'a, is from *ku-kung'ama*, 'to lie across, traverse.' Thus the root used for medicine lies across the stream just as the disease lies across the stomach. *Ku-kungika* stands for the pilling up of flotsam *(ntotujahameji)* against the traversing root. This flotsam or rubbish resembles the disease. Medicine is rubbed into the cuts to rid the women's stomach of the rubbish. When the doctor pulls down the barrage, the disease goes away like the rubbish.

"The bitterness *(kulula)* of the *mwala* root can kill the disease. *Mutata* has a very nasty smell. The woman should drink its medicine to make her stomach smell very much. The disease will smell it and die because of its stink. *Molu wawubwang'u* also has strong smell to kill the disease. So has *kakwema*. Medicines that are used because they stink *(ku-nunka)* are called '*yitumbu yanunka or yitumbu yevumba.*'

"A disease (*musong'*u) is something which remains alive in the body. If it goes on and on the patient is *wahalwa* or *mukwakuyindama*, an inauspicious person[6]."

This treatment stands on the borderline between the taking of more or less rational therapeutic measures and the performance of magical rite. The first part of the treatment consists almost entirely of acts in accordance with the principles of sympathetic magic. A pain "crosses" the stomach, which is like a stream in that through it fluids and solids pass, and from it (since it is thought to be continuous with the womb) flow children; hence a doctor goes to a stream with his patient and performs symbolic actions indicative of the removal of obstructions that impede the flow of the water and cause flotsam (=the disease) to pile up. The symbolism of two banks or sides is repeated in another form with the cupping horns-one in front and one at the back of the patient-and in the cutting of incisions on either side of the navel. Some informants connected the treatment with dysmenorrhea, for it was also the cure for this. The disease was believed to hold up the normal flow of the menses and hence to cause temporary sterility, for Ndembu recognize that normal periodicity is a perquisite of pregnancy. The pain, they feel, is connected with the damming up of the ordinary flow.

The quasi-rational aspect merges in the second part of the treatment in which potions are given to the patient to drink. Given the premise that the disease is a living entity inhabiting the stomach, it is quite rational to suppose that bitter or evil-smelling, substances, disliked on the whole by human beings, animals, and birds, will drive it away or kill it. I am in full agreement with Ackerknecht's strictures on Malinowski for calling "scientific" the rational elements in primitive medicine, for, as he says (1946, 489), "Practical behaviour is not yet science. A butcher is no scientist. Science, full of disinterested curiosity, aims primarily at truth, not at practical success of psychic relaxation.... Science is unthinkable without the experiment.... presupposes a quality of scepticism..... is a late invention of humanity." This is very different from acting medically, as Rivers pointed out (1924, 52) with perfect logic and rationality, but on the basis of false, supernaturalistic premises. Yet it must be admitted that medicine in our culture relies to a certain extent on suggestion. The general practitioner in British rural areas administered "nasty" medicines, partly on account of their curative properties and partly to satisfy the patient that they were "strong" enough to "kill" the ailment.

For all I know, *mwala* root juice may be empirically effective in curing stomach-ache, but if this is so, it is effective for the wrong reasons. It is possible that many "medicines" have been tried out by Ndembu doctors and some have been found to procure relief, but the next step has not been to set up a series of carefully controlled experiments to isolate the substance causing the beneficial effect. Rather it is to examine the sensorily perceptible attributes of the plant to see which of them might be regarded as an expression or embodiment of auspicious mystical powers, or which of them exhibited some virtue opposed to the putative properties of the disease. It is a question of allocating the item to a pre-existent category and not of making new discoveries by experimental method.

(b) *Musong'u wevumu watwansi.* "The doctor collects and cuts up long roots of *kapwipu (Swartzie madagascariensis)* and *musong'a-song'a* (or *lusong' wasong'wa, Ximenia americana*). The root skin (*nyemba*) of *kapwipu* is scraped off and put in two different potsherds. Hot water is put in one pot of *kapwipu* medicine, cold water in the other; the *musong' asong's* medicine is dealt with likewise. The doctor and his child-patient then sit under the *kapwipu* tree from which medicine was obtained and the doctor makes incisions on the patient's stomach beside the navel and on his back, just as for *Chisumi*, and applies *tusumu* cupping horns. When a girdle of horn-scars has been made round the patient's waist, *kapwipu* medicine is rubbed into them. When all is over, the doctor *(chimbuki)* buries *(wavumbika* or *wajika)* the potsherd containers, together with the blood sucked from the patient and kept in a small calabash, in the hole in the ground left by the long taproot taken for medicine.

"Next day the same process is repeated under the *musong'asong's* tree with medicine obtained from that tree.

"Afterwards roots of the *chiputa mazala* tree (*Erythrina tomentosa*) are cut up into pieces (*yikunku*), put into a clay pot, and heated until lukewarm *(kavuyenki)*. The patient is then given this decoction to drink.

"If the disease continues, *kanshinshi* root medicine is given lukewarm to the patient as a draught. Finally, *kakung'ami* root medicine is given as a lukewarm potion."

The reasons for using these roots are as follows. "*Kapwipu* medicine is used because it is a hard tree. Hardness (*ku-kola*) represents health and strength. *Musong' asong' a* is used for the same reason. *Chiputa mazala* medicine is given because it has a strong smell, *kanshinshi* because it has both a strong smell and a bitter taste.

"*Kakung'ami* is used not only because of its stink, but also because of its bubbling sound (*chilululu*—sounds of flatulence) which drives the disease to one side, so that it no longer lies across the stomach. The disease fears (*watiya woma*) the medicine. If the stomach cannot fight it the disease spreads right over it, but the medicine chases it into one place where it will die.

"When the doctor goes to the *kapwipu* tree, he makes an address *(ku-lang'ula)* before collecting this, the principal *(mukulumpi)* medicine of the treatment. He mentions the doctor who taught him how to administer, it the name of the patient, and the circumstances leading up to the treatment."

(c) When men have stomach ache, also called *musong'u wevumu*. "The doctor collects, cuts, up and puts in a pot with lukewarm water the roots of *katong'a* (*Strychnos cocculoides*), which are very bitter, and gives the potion to the patient to drink. *Mulolu* roots (*Annonanana*) may be given as a decoction, because they have a strong smell. If the disease continues, *chikwata* roots *(Zizyphus mucronata)* may be given as above, because they are a little bitter."

Ackerknecht has observed (1946, 482) that bloodletting "is effective in some diseases although we do not know why, and have discarded it (in the West), therefore, almost entirely. In most cases its magico-religious 'purificative' character or its objective to drive out disease demons is obvious." The use of cupping techniques among the Ndembu would provide an example of "magic-religious" beliefs. In the case of "stomach disease," one of the main aims is to introduce substances possessing mystical power into the body of the patient. Although this was not stated by Ndembu informants, it is probable that there is here some notion of "replacement." Blood is taken out (and in the case of (b) poured into the hole from which the medicine root was removed) and replaced by medicine which it is hoped will force away the disease or give toughness and health to the patient. We meet once more in these treatments the notion that a disease is animate and vulnerable to obnoxious tastes and smells.

Musong'u Wamesesi, Conjunctivo-keratyitis, corneal opacities and other eye Diseases

Bark is scraped from the trunk of a *muhuma tree (strychnos spinosa* or stropanthus *welwitschii)* and mixed with warm water in a clay pot. The patient's eyes are then bathed in the lotion. If this is not enough, the tiny leaves of *lweng'eng'i (Dracaena reflexa)* are crushed between the fingers (a process knows as *kuchikita*), put in a leat-funnel (*lutotu*), and allowed to drop in the patient's eyes.

Finally, steam treatment may be tried. Leaves of the *wadikalanziza tree,* sometimes known as *kayiza* (*Strychnos stuhlmannii*), are collected, put in a pot with water, and heated to the boiling point. The patient covers his head with a blanket and puts his face in rising stream (*luya*).

In the case of each of these three medicines, informants told me that the efficacy (*ng'ovu*) of the herb is derived from its "bitterness." "Bitterness" is *wukawu* or the verbal noun *kulula*. Ndembu say that "*wukmau*" can "stick to" (*ku-lamata*) the disease, "like a leach" *(neyiizambu),* until it dies.

One informant gave me a little information about *kayiza*, which might help to identify it correctly. He said, "*Kayiza* is very bitter in taste. It can grow into a big tree. Its fruits when ripe are as black as ink. They blacken your tongue when you eat them. That is why it is called also *wadikalanziza*, from *wadikala*, 'you deny,' for you can't deny having eaten it since it makes your tongue black."

MUSONG'U WAKUZALUKA, INSANITY

"The doctor first collects old bones of a mad dog. Then he goes to a *musoli* tree *(Vangueriopiies lanciflora)* and collects a root and some leaves. Next he takes a root and leaves of *ikamba dachihamba* (or *musambanjita) (Cryptosepalum maraviense)* and a root of *musong'asong'a* (*Ximenia americana*), followed by leafy branches and roots of *mukombukombu* (*Tricalysia angolensis*), *mututambululu* (*Xylopiaadoraissima*), and *muhotuhotu (Canthium venosum)*. Next a root and leaves of *mukandachina* which grows on termite-hills are collected.

"The doctor then goes to a place where a wild pig (*chombu*) was lying or trampling and there collects grasses and twigs. The doctor and his assistants go to the termite-hill from which they obtained *mukandachina* (*Rhus longipes*, or possibly *Eriocoelum sp.*) medicine. There they cut up all the roots they have collected, mix them together well, and fill two pots (*mazawu*) with the mixture. Old calabashes *(yipwepu)* can be used. Then they add any part of a dead leopard, a piece of wild pig's meat, and a mad dog's bone to each pot. These portions are classed as *jipelu*. *Mpelu* from the coney or hyrax *(Chibila, chibatata),* the *mamba (ntoka),* the lion (*mutupa*), and of a fish called *muvundu* are also added to the contents of each pot.

"Now water is brought and poured in each *izawu*. There is no pounding of the tree medicines *(nyitondu)* in a mortar, as is often done. A medicine broom *(chisampu)* is made of the leafy branches of *mukombukombu, muhotuhotu, mututambululu,* and *musoli.* Both pots contain only cold medicine, the pots must not be warmed. One pot is carried to the top of the termite-hill, the other is left as the foot of it. The patient, the crazy person, is made to kneel while the doctor gives him the medicine to drink, first from the pot at the top of the termitary, then from the one at the bottom. Then he sprinkles the patient's eyes and face with his medicine broom. He repeats this treatment twice a day until the patient is able to say that he has recovered. No drums are played at this treatment."

The procedure is explained thus. "The musoli tree is the *ishikenu*, 'the place of greeting,'where an invocation is made. It is the senior of the medicines. It has many edible fruits, yellow and purple, called *nsoli* much eaten by duiker *(nkayi)* and other antelope from September to November. Its name is from *ku-solola.*', ' to reveal' Here it means 'to make everything clear,' for a mad person does not see things clearly.

'*Musambanjita* used to be a war medicine to make people invulnerable to bullets or spears. Here it does the eyes good, for person suffering from this disease feels dizzy in the eyes. This medicine clears the eyes.

'*Musong'asong'a* feels bitter *(kutiya wukawu)* to the eyes. This tree produces red edible fruits—*ku-song'a* signifies 'to produce fruits.'

Mukandachina is collected because its has the habit of growing on top of termite-hills. A mad person is like a person who passes above (things). *(Muntu wazaluka wudi neyi muntu wahita kwiwulu.)* He wanders about in the air *(nynepela,)* on the tops of hills and even of tress. He can do nothing in a peaceful way. It is seldom that he talks while sitting, but he talks in the air (while standing?). That is also why a pot of medicine is placed on top of a termitary. There is a *mukishi*[7], (a manifestation of) an ancestral spirit (in the form of a hunter of long ago), who also behaves like a mad person and ascends to the tops or crests of places.

"*Mpelu* taken from a leopard (*chisumpa*) is used because a leopard is like a madman and kills for no reason, only for sport *(nakuhemahohu)*. *Mpelu* of a wild pig is used because it moves about just like a mad person *(randomly)*. So does a coney.

"The *muvundu* fish may swim upside down, it changes its direction, it is a mad fish. Its name is connected with *ku-vundumuka,* 'to pack up and go away without giving any reason.'

"This disease of insanity comes in the air."

The special case of rabies. "If a person has been bitten by a mad dog, he will, in the first instance, be given a medicine to make him vomit.

"The doctor goes to a *kavulawumi* tree (*Maprounea africana*), digs down and exposes the root, and cuts off a piece about six inches long.

"He then scrapes off the skin or bark of the root with the help of an old piece of calabash and puts these scrapings (*nyemba*) in the sunshine to dry. When dry they are pounded into powder (*luseng'a*) in a mortar. The doctor next brings some thin cassava porridge (*kapudyi*), to which he adds the powder, mixing it in well.

"He gives this mixture to the patient to drink. After drinking, the patient vomits very much, and has frequent motions of the bowels.

"Another treatment is to cut up the root of *mudiansefu* (possibly *Craterosiphon quarrei*), which secretes a white gum, add water to the portions in a pot and boil for about a quarter of an hour. While the water is still boiling, *kapudyi* gruel is brought and the medicine is added to it hot. The patient must then drink it while it is still very hot. The medicine stays within a short while, then the patient vomits and excretes at short intervals until his stomach is cleared out.

"These emetics and aperients, *kavulawumi* and *mudiansefu*, are equally strong. If they fail, the full medicines for *musong'u wakuzaluka* are used."

My informants gave this explanation. "A person bitten by a mad dog froths at mouth (*ku-tupula*), just like the dog. Such frothy saliva is called *izeng'i* (singular), while ordinary saliva is called *mazeng'i* (plural). 'To foam at the mouth like a madman' is *kutupulaizeng'i-zeng'i.* The poison given to a man by a mad dog in just like arrow-poison *(wulembi)* taken from the *Strophanthus* plant (also *wulembi).*"

The *treatment of madness as a rite of affliction*[8]. "The drum (or rite) of mad ancestral spirits *(ng'oma yawakishi akuzaluka)* is 'played' (performed) if all these medicines fail. It is then supposed that the spirits of people who died insane have 'caught' (possessed) the patient."

My best informant, Muchona[9], described the rite as follows:

"The relative responsible for the patient [literally the 'owner of the patient' (*mwenimuyeji*)] starts the proceedings by bringing the doctor (*chimbuki*—as in herbal therapy) a cock or a goat, which may be of any color. The doctor agrees and fetches *mpelu* made from an *'mpompa'* a wooden fetter used to fasten the limbs of madmen, slaves, and criminals.

"Next he goes to an old site of the *Mung'ong'i* cult rites[10] and collects five or six roots from any species of tree that grows there. What is important is not the species but the place—the *izembi* shelter of the sacred mysteries. Then he goes to the site of a former circumcision lodge and collects about six roots from the *ifwilu* or *'place of dying'* where the boys are actually circumcised.

"Next, he and his assistants (an assistant or apprentice doctor is called *kadize,'* one who learning') go to a stream and collect in the gallery forest (*itu*) roots and leaves of the *kaleng ang'ombi* thornbush[11]. Two clay pots are used, each containing the same medicine. One *izawu* pot is taken to the top of a termite-hill *(kawumbu),* the other is left on the ground. Then the goat's throat is cut and its blood poured in each pot. The pots contain cut and pounded roots collected by the doctor.

"Next the patient drinks from both pots. The whole following night is spent in splashing medicine *(ku-kupula)* on the patient's body, washing it which medicine, and giving him a medicine draught at intervals.

"Drums are played near the medicine pot on the ground.

The site is in the bush not far from the village. They begin by singing *Mung'ong'i* songs, then *Mukanda* songs, and follow these with songs from the *Kayong'u* rite [Turner 1961, 23-26]—performed to propitiate an ancestral spirit which causes chest trouble and confers the power to divine by tossing symbolic objects in a basket—and from the *Kaluwi* or *Mukala* rite [see below] performed to placate a particularly troublesome manifestation of a hunter ancestor. These spirits are regarded as 'mad' (*akuzalka*), for they make those possessed[12] by them jerk about convulsively (*ku-zakuka*). Both patient and doctor jerk and shiver. The doctor must treat himself with medicine along with the patient, otherwise the mad spirit may possess him also. When he shivers, the spirit is temporarily in him too.

"After drumming, the doctor continues to administer these medicines to the patient, for days or maybe weeks, until he is better."

It is interesting to note in what respects the treatment of insanity as a "disease" (*musong'u*) resembles the rite of affliction, where madness is regarded as a sign and symptom of affliction by an ancestral spirit. Both procedures stress the opposition of "above" and "below" (*hewulu* as opposed to *hamaseki*, literally "in the air" and "on the ground"), both take place on and near termite-hills, both involve the splashing of the patient—although Muchona did not mention the collection of the usual components of a medicine broom, *mukombukombu, muhotuhotu* and *mututambululu* fronds, this was probably done before the affliction rite.

There are also profound differences between them, for the rite deals with the spirit of a deceased kinsman as well as with a disease. Since ancestral spirits are said "to be pleased by the playing of drums," drumming and singing must accompany the administration of medicines. Indeed, among the objects in a diviner's basket, a piece of wood crudely carved to represent a drum stands for "rites to propitiate ancestral spirits" (Turner 1961, 65).

The slaughter of an animal or fowl is another recurrent

feature of rites of affliction that is not found in the direct treatment of disease. It is not always easy to see such slaughters as "sacrifices," for often the animal or chicken represents the ancestral spirit himself. If there is sacrifice, it is a sacrifice (in symbolic guise) of the ancestor, not to the ancestor, on behalf of the ritual participants and as a sign of reconciliation and communion between the spirit and his kin. Nevertheless, however it may be regarded, the slaughter of an animal is a characteristic feature of manistic rites among the Ndembu.

There may be a connection with the slaughter of a goat at this rite and at *Kayong'u*. At *Kayong'u*, too, a cock is slaughtered by the patient himself, who bites the bird's head off. About this act Muchona said (Turner 1961, 32), "*Kayong'u* makes a person a little mad. He feels as if he were drunk or epileptic." It looks as though the spirit responsible for insanity were a species of the *Kayong'u* manifestation. The classical association between soothsaying and madness is made in a tribal milieu, for *Kayng'u* is usually regarded as the mode of affliction assumed by a dead diviner's spirit.

This comparison of treatment and rite enables us to see that a "rite of affliction" is a combination of therapy, aimed at treating the pathological condition (cataract, madness, reproductive disorder) and religious service (veneration and propitiation of ancestral spirits). There has been a considerable fusion of these procedures, so that some medicines have become symbols for modes of spirit manifestation, while something of the "law" bound character of magic has influenced the relationship held to exist between ancestral spirits and their living kin. Thus it seems to be assumed that if one collects the medicines appropriate to a rite and applies them correctly, the ancestral spirit is more or less compelled to stop afflicting the patient. This situation differs at any rate from invocations made to village shrine trees, outside the rite of affliction context, in which appeals are made to ancestors to "change their livers" (i.e. "minds") and cease causing trouble to their relatives. Here "free will" apparently prevails over "necessity."

MUAONG'U WANYIMA, BACKACHE

(*a*) "The doctor takes part of a broken hoe blade. Then he goes to a tree that has been struck by lightning and takes a portion of the splintered wood. After that he goes to an old village site to the place where a mortar once stood for pounding cassava roots and grain. There he digs and removes the first root he finds—of any species of tree.

"He now brings the patient and makes him lie under a *mudyi* tree (*Diplorrhyncus condylocarpon*) that is naturally bent. With his knife, he scrapes off bark from underneath the band in the tree. Then he collects some bark scrapings (*nyemba*) from the upper side. His next task is to place a pounding pole (*mwishi*) at right angles to the tree. He then adds to the medicine in his basket (*lwalu*, a flat round winnowing basket) some scrapings from the top of a tortoise's shell.

"The patient is then allowed to leave the *mudyi* site for a moment while the doctor brings a potsherd (*chizanda*) in which he puts red *ing'aji* oil (palm oil?). He scrapes some iron dust from broken hoe on to the oil. Then he burns the piece of lightning-struck tree and adds its ash to the mixture. In go the tortoise shell scrapings and finally the *nyemba* of the *mudyi* tree. The medicine is thoroughly mixed with the oil.

"The doctor then makes two or three lines of small incisions across the small of the patient's back, where the pain is, with his razor (*ntewula*). When the blood begins to ooze, the doctor rubs the medicine into those cuts. The medicine goes into the blood right to the part where the pain is felt.

"When that is done, the doctor takes the pounding pole (*mwishi*) and presses (*ku-kanda*) it on the patient's back where the incisions are. The doctor presses the pestle lengthwise on the back with both hands. He then puts the razor and medicines in a pot and removes them from the scene.

"Now the doctor tells the patient to hold the pounding pole up vertically and to go under the crook in the *mudyi* tree once more. The patient must then straighten himself up, with the help of the pounding pole, and push the *mudyi* up with his back (a process known as *kudyikanda*).

"Now he must address the tree (*ku-subwila mutondu*) as follows:

'I have already left this disease with you (*nakushiyili dehi musong'u*). I must go home feeling no more pain, because I have left it already with you'. Then the patient returns home bearing the pounding pole,"

(b) *Another treatment*. "The doctor goes in the early morning to where a mortar stands. He gets women to shift its position, digs down and removes a piece of any root he finds there. Then he scrapes some dirt from the base of the mortar itself. He mixes the scrapings from the root and the earth scrapings with castor oil (*imonu*) or palm oil (*ing'aji*) in a potsherd.

"Next he makes the patient lie across the hole where he removed the root at the former site of the mortar. Then he makes three lines of cuts with his razor on the patient's back where he felt pain and rubs medicine into the incisions. After that, he orders the patient to pull himself upright by means of the pounding pole that usually goes with the mortar. He must leave the pounding pole upright[13] against a tree near his hut and never let it lie on its side."

In the first of these treatments "the doctor took a broken hoe blade because hoe blades snap suddenly (*koto-o*) when people are digging. In the same way a person with backache (*lumbago*) feels as though he has suddenly been broken.

"A meal mortar is used because of the pounding (*ku-twa*). This represents 'hitting.' Having backache is like being hit very hard.

"A tortoise shell is used because a tortoise has a hard shell and a hard body so be never feels backache. Its medicine strengthens the back.

"The *mudyi* tree has white gum, so it is a white or lucky tree. The patient leaves bad things with mudyi, and its whiteness gives him health *(wukolu).*"

In the second treatment, the earth from the mortar "is a kind of *mpelu* for strenghening (*nakukolesha*)."

"A lightning-smitten tree is used because lightning gives a sudden shock (expressed by the ideophone *bele-e).* 'To strike' is kw-anda. `Thunder' *is chivumina, `o thunder' ku-dulumwina.* Lightning is an animal. A mole rat (*mpumba*) makes a sound similar to that of thunder. The lightning grows jealous and tries to hit the mole rat and kill it. That is why lightning follows the holes and 'hills' of mole rats all the way along."

The treatment for backache appears to be almost entirely magical. In less severe cases, it is possible to imagine that there may be some psychological benefit.

MUSONG'U WACHINKONYA, EPILEPSY

"The doctor goes first to a *museng'u* tree (*Ochna pulchra*) and collects leaves which are rolled up into a curl backward from the tip (*mafu adikonya adivung'a mafunda*) to form bundles (*mafunda*).

"Next he brings an old calabash cut across (*chipwepu*) and puts into to both pounded and unpounded *museng'u* leaves. He then adds several kinds of *mpelu*: a portion of coney or hyrax (*chibatata*), a piece of the beak of a *samunkambu* bird, and scale of a pangolin.

"The doctor then takes a reed (*iteti*) and blows into it to make the water (which contains all these ingredients) bubble (*wapepa mwiteti nakubukumwina meji*). At intervals he washes the patient's face with the bubbling, foaming water.

"If this treatment fails after several days, the doctor collects the same kinds of *jipelu*, then goes to a *mulendi* tree (*Sterculia quinqueloba*) and cuts from it a part of a root. Then he goes to a place where a lion, leopard, or wild pig has scratched and collects grass scratched by their claws or hooves. He brings along another *chipwepu* calabash, cuts the *mulendi* roots into pieces and adds them to cold water in the *chipwepw*. Then he puts all the *jipelu* (including those of the previous treatment) in the medicine, adding thereto the scratched grass and takes the *chiwepu* to the village ash pile (*izalelu*). He puts it on top of the ash pile and gives the patient medicine to drink from his cupped hand. After this he washes the face, head and chest of the patient and repeats the treatment for several days.

The procedure is explained as follows.'*Museng'u* is used because the epileptic patient shoots out his arms then folds them again like curled *museng'u* leaves.

"*Chibatata* (*mpelu*) is used because it is an animal which makes a sound like an epileptic.

"*Samunkambu* is a bird which flies up and down spasmodically like an epileptic,making a whirring sound.

"The pangolin (*nkaka*) curls itself into a ball like an epileptic's spasm.

"The doctor blows through the reed so that the foam rises (*kulonda kafulolu*[14] *kanyamuki)* like the foam on an epileptic's lips.

"*Mulendi* is a very slippery or glossy (=*senena*) tree difficult to climb. The patient's disease will slip down and fall just like the climber of *mulendi*.

"The scratched grass is used because a lion, leopard, or wild pig scratches just like an epileptic in his fit.

"The ash pile is used because everything is thrown there so the disease should be thrown there too."

This is another treatment which appears to rely entirely upon the principles of contagious and sympathetic magic. It is possible that the more severe the disease the greater the recourse to magical techniques (*q.v.*, leprosy, insanity, lumbago).

Musong'u wakanwa, Disease of the Mouth

(a variety of conditions,including pyorrhea and toothache)

(*a*) *For blisters in the mouth* (*mabobela mukanwa*). One educated informant a mission out-school teacher, described this condition marked by blisters and sores in the mouth as "scurvy",which is indeed characterized by swollen gums. It is probable that he picked up the term at the mission hospital at Kalene Hill. Dr.Cahal writes that while some conditions under this heading may be scurvy, others may well be apthous ulcers, herpetic ulcers and so forth. For as mentioned above the Ndembu doctor treats symptoms not diseases.

The procedure is described thus."First the doctor goes to a *mwalu* tree (also called *kalukuta,* possibly *Olax obtusifolius*), collects roots, cuts them up, puts them in a pot with water and boils them for several minutes.When he judges it hot enough he puts the pot between the patient's open legs, makes him put his head over the pot, covers him entirely with a blanket and tells him to open his mouth directly in the path of the rising steam. To cover oneself with a cloth (so that the wind will not blow the steam away) is termed *kudibutililamu or kudijikililamu*. When the patient's body begins to sweat the doctor removes the blanket or skin, takes medicine from the pot and tells the patient to rinse his mouth out with it (*ku-mumika*—to wash out the mouth with water is *ku-kucha*). This treatment continues for three or four days.

"If the results are not good the doctor goes to a *mwang alala tree* (*paropsia brazzeana*),takes roots, cuts them up and warms them gently on a fire in a pot with water, then gives the medicine to the patient as a mouthwash.

"Another mouthwash is made by splitting large pieces (*nakusea yibalu*) of the *musosu* plant (*Boscia corymbosa*) which grows on termite-hills. These laths are then soaked in warm water and the water is given to the patient to rinse his mouth with. He may do this for a week.

"Finally, roots of *kambanjibanji* are cut into piece and warmed in water. The resultant mouthwash is retained in the patient's mouth for several minutes. He repeats this at intervals for several days."

My informants explained the treatment this way."*Mwalu* is

used because it is bitter and can kill the disease.

"*Mwang'alala* is used because it sets the teeth on edge; also it is hot (*ku-yeya*).

"*Musosu* is used because it lacks saltiness, is insipid."

One doctor said when discussing *musosu*, that doctors test out different medicine until they find one to deaden the pain—a remark which implies some degree of rational experimentation.

"*Kambanjibanji* is used because it is hot (*ku-yeya*)."[15]

(*b*) *Toothache with mouth soreness* (*kakeleketi*, possibly from *kukeleketa*,"to gnaw").This is a condition in which "bad teeth are left to fall out on their own", i.e. are not extracted. It is said that the following "medicines" will remove the pain and the teeth will drop out.

"The doctor cuts up the root of an *ipupa' puts* the pieces in a pot with warm water and gives them to the patient as a mouth-wash. He must rinse his mouth in the mixture frequently for several days. *Ipupa* is used because it is rather hot (*dayeya chanti*)."

(*c*) *Pyorrhea,chivukuta*. If the above treatment proves, ineffectual and the doctor finds blood on the front of the gums he may suspect that the patient is suffering from *chivukuta*,"the disease that eats the gums" (*musong'u wadyang'a wushinshinyi*).

"The doctor (chimbuki) fetches *ilengi* reeds and burns them into ash—often used for salt. Then he goes to the nest of a species of tiny ants called *masoha* and takes from it a ball (of organic material) known as *isoha*. Then he burns the *isoha* into ash and mixes it with *ileng'i* ash. He brings part of a calabash and makes little holes (*walokola nyiteta*) in it. Then a large leaf such as a *mubula* leaf (*Uapacasp*) is put into the calabash as a loose lining. The ashes are placed on top of the leaf. Next another old calabash is set beneath the first one. Water is gently poured over the ash and then strained (*ku-keleka*) through the holes of the upper calabash into the lower one. The same process is used for straining salt from grass ashes to add to food. The leaf prevents the ash itself from coming through. When the doctor estimates that enough strained liquid is in the lower calabash he pours it off into his medicine pot. Then he goes to a *kapepi* tree (*Hymenocardia acida*), takes a root and scrapes the outside bark (*nyemba*) into an empty *chipwepu* calabash container.

"The doctor boils the water from the strained ashes until it has all evaporated leaving only salty powder (*mung'wa*). He mixes this with the *kapepi* scraping, then crushes the mixture very fine with a knife handle. He now adds just enough water to make the mixture into a paste.

"Taking this paste he rubs it very gently into the painful part of the patient's gums. Sometimes blood comes from the rubbing and the patient begins to spit blood and paste. After a while the patient rubs the paste on himself resting when the pain becomes too great. He goes on rubbing until blood ceases to flow from the painful spot. This is a very good treatment."

The treatment is explained further"*Ileng'i* ash is used because it is very pungently salty (*ku-tukuma*). *Isoha* is used because it resembles blisters (*mabobela*) or boils (*mahuti*). *Kapepi* is used because of its bitterness (*wukawu*)."

Pyorrhea is said by the mission doctors at Kalene Hospital to be very common among the Ndembu. Some attributed its prevalence to their dependence on cassava as a staple crop—almost pure carbohydrate.

MUSONG'U WAMPANG'A, SWELLING OF THE SCROTUM

This disease is thought to be most commonly caused by *mukayu* "medicines"used by husbands to protect their wives from adultery and by the owners of hives and gardens against thieves. White (1961,36) discusses similar protective medicines among the Luvale and concludes that they "contain a selective power within them which enables them to function .....medicine to keep adulterers from a wife will not injure the husband but only adulterers." It is this selective power so it is believed which causes the scrotum—and in some cases the *membrum virile*—of the adulterer to swell up. Ndembu are quick to point out that the disease is not invariably caused by *mukayu*—for even a newborn infant may have it."

"The first thing doctor (*chimbuki*) does is to go to an *ivung'u-vung'u* tree (*Kigelia pinnata*—the sausage tree with long pods) and make an address to it (*ku-shahu mpandula*). He carries his ax and hoe and says: "You,O tree I received you from another doctor.[16] The medicine we will collect from you here must have the power of killing the diseases."(*Eyi mutondu nawutambwili kudi chimbanda mukwawu yitumbu yinukuhukaku yikali nang'ovu yakujaha nyisong'u.*)

"Then the doctor digs up a root, takes some leaves, and collects fruit from the tree. He puts one piece of root in a pot then cuts the long pod into two parts of which one is chopped up and put in the pot. Warm water is added and the patient drinks the potion repeatedly for several days.

"The doctor next brings two potsherds in each of which he places some *ivung'uvung'u* medicine. Then he scrapes the root and puts some scrapings in each potsherd. The leaves are pounded into pulped leaf medicine, known as *nsompu*,which is put in a third potsherd in cold water. Hot water is poured in one of the original potsherds and cold water into the other. Now the patient is taken to the village ash pile *(izalelu)*. The doctor then drinks nsompu leaf medicine gives some to the patient and then makes his assistant who will tap the patient's blood (*ku-sumuna muyeji*), have a draught.That potsherd is then removed.

"The operator makes cuts on the lower half of the patient's abdomen and applies a cupping horn *(kasumu);* makes another cut just to the right of the navel and applies a horn; applies another to the right of the stomach and another just above the right hip. The operator rubs hot medicine from one potsherd into the cuts and presses it in (*ku-kanda*). After the horns have been removed a hole is made in the ash pile and the patient's blood is poured into it from the cupping horns and lightly covered with ashes. During the operation the patient is made to drink medicine from the pot. Afterwards the potsherds are taken away and kept for further use. The *epoch* goes with the patient to this hut. He must go on drinking medicine after the treatment. Next day the operator and patient come back to the ash pile with the pot and three potsherds and the treatment is repeated. This continues for two or three days and after it is over the patient must go on drinking the medicine for a long time.

"The doctor afterward goes and collects a pumpkin vine (*molu weyang'wa*), cuts a piece off it and takes its roots. He conceals these in his hut. Then he goes to a bundle of *nsama*, used to smoke out bees. The *nsama* consists of a cone-or poke-shaped bundle of small leafy twigs (*nsonsu*) containing dry twigs and grass and tied around with bark string. A bark rope (*isosu*) is tied to its narrow top end. When a man goes to get honey he lifts the *nsama* by this rope as he climbs the tree to the beehive or nest. He sets fire to the *nsama* and ties it to a bough above the hive so that it dangles just below the hive and smokes out the bees. Very often the rope breaks or burns through and is left hanging from the branch by the honey gatherer. It is this abandoned portion that is collected by the doctor. He then goes to a *muhwila* tree (*Strychnos spinosa*)—which produces large round fruits—and removes a fruit, a root, and some leaves.

"At his village he pounds the leaves he has collected into *nsompu* and puts into a calabash cup (*lupanda*). Other *nsompu* is put into a pot also the roots of the pumpkin vine and the *muhwila* tree. This is for the patient to drink.

"Then cupping horns and medicine are applied as before and medicine is drunk by the patient."

Further comments were these. "*Ivung'uvung'u* is used because the fruits in its pod resemble testicles (*nyisokwa* or *makutu*). *Iyang'wa* the pumpkin is used because it is like a swollen testicle. The fruit of *muhwila* is used for the same reason. *Isosu dansama* the piece of rope is a kind of *mpelu*. It is used because the nsama bundle hangs from it. With elephantiasis the testicles hang down because of their weight.

MUSONG'U WAMUTU, HEADACHE

Two kinds of *musong'u wamutu* are recognized: (a) *Musong'u wamutu* proper which begins when "a person feels that the skin of his temples is moving about (throbbing). His head feels heavy and pain comes in his temples first then spreads to his whole head." (b) *Musong'u wanyembu wamutu* or *kakenka* which starts with a pain just above the eyes in mid-brow and spreads till it covers the whole eye then spreads to the ears. It gives '*ku-kena*' a word which describes the very bright light made when lightning falls on a hut—such a light comes very suddenly' it is a sharp stab of pain."

(*a*) "The doctor (*chimbuki*) goes to a *kapwipu* tree (*Swartzia madagascariensis*) and cuts from it some large chips of bark (*yitumbu yakusea*). He then puts these in a pot and adds either hot or cold water. After a time the patient washes his whole head with it. He may do this at any time of the day or evening and continues with the washing for several days.

"If the *kapwipu* medicine fails the doctor goes to a *chikoli* tree (*Strychnos spinosa*), carrying a flaming bundle of grass with which he burns some of its leaves. He collects burned leaves and puts them in a mortar where they are pounded into nsompu.This is put into a pot and warm water is added. The doctor tells his patient to wash his head in the medicine. If the patient has suffered from the disease before he can collect these medicine himself, otherwise he must seek out a doctor. This treatment continues throughout the day. The washing is known as ku-boba where the water is taken in the hollowed hand and splashed vigorously on the head. *Ku-boba* strictly refers to this splashing of the head. This treatment may last for several days.

"If *chikoli* fails the doctor collects a root of *kambanjibanji* [see also p.197, scrapes it and puts the scrapings in an old potsherd. He then goes to a *lwengi or lweng'i* plant (*Dracaena reflexa*) and takes some leaves. These are mixed with the *kambanjibanji* bark scrapings, after having first been crushed in the doctor's fingers. He then takes his razor and makes incisions from the right temple along the hairline to the left temple. He rubs the medicine into the cut marks. This medicine is wanted so that it can fight the disease in order to kill it.

"If the disease still continues, two further cuts are made in each temple and horns are sucked onto them. No medicine is used with these *tusumu*".

Explanation for this procedure is given thus:

"*Kapwipu* is used because of its bitterness (*wukawu*) and its heat (*ku-yeya*), like that of chillies or pepper. When it is mixed with water it can enter the whole head and fight the disease.

"*Chikoli* is used for its bitterness (*wukawu*), but also because it is a strong medicine (*ku-kola*—to be strong or well').

"*Kambanjibanji* is used because of its heat (*ku-yeya*) and slight astringency.

"*Lweng'i* smells strongly and has heat. It causes pain when rubbed in. When you burn leaves this means that you burn a *chisaku*.[17] When you burn leaves you burn insects (*wbubu*—a euphemism for witche's familiars here) and *ndumba* (witches familiars), in fact everything with bad magical power; you make the chisaku go away (*wafumisha chisaku*).

"Headache is usually caused by a *chisaku*; if a patient has one it will be burned with the leaves. *Chisaku* is bad luck *(malwa)* which causes death or suffering, causes someone to be beaten to death, or makes a man break an arm or leg. It is the same as a grudge (*chitela*) which a man cherishes secretly against another. One kind of *chisaku* is from familiars of witchcraft, another is from ghosts *(chisaku chikwawu chawafu)*.

"Lweng'i grows near the edge of village; it is used in many treatments. It is also used by sorcerers *(aloji)*[18]

(*b*) *Musong'u wanyembu*. "The doctor goes to a *mudyi* tree (*Diplorrhyncus condylocarpon*) and splits off a portion *(chibalu)*. Then he goes to a tree smitten by lightning and takes another portion. Then one from a *kapepi* tree *(Hynenocardia acida)* and another from a *kapwipu* tree *(Swartzia madagascariensis)* and from a *chikwata* tree *(Zizyphus mucronata)* and another from a *chikoli* tree *(Strychnos spinosa)*. All these yibalu are brought to the patient's hut. An old pot is then fetched. All the medicines are put into it. Then a piece of *mpemba* (white clay) and a piece of *ngula* or *mukundu* (red clay), already softened are brought and the doctor draws a line of white clay (*mufunda wampemba*) around the rim of the pot and a line of red clay (*mufunda wangula*) underneath it. The pot is then suspended by bark string over the patient's doorway. Sometimes a pangolin's scale is added to the medicine. Water is added to the pot which is now called *izawu*, a container of medicine.

"At dawn one of the patient's relatives comes with two ax blades. The doctor comes too and washes the patients head, pressing on medicine where he feels pain. As he does this the relative clinks (*kukenkumwina*) the ax blades together near the front of the patient's head. When he has been thoroughly washed with medicine his relative drops the ax heads at his feet. This treatment is repeated at sunset, and at dawn and sunset for several days, until the headache is cured."

The reasoning behind the treatment is this. "*Mudyi* is used because it was used at *Nkang'a* the girls puberty rites. Also because it is bitter. *Mudyi* is a strong tree (*mutindu wakola*)

"A lightning-struck tree is used because lightning is like the stabbing pain of a headache.

"*Kapepi* is used because of its bitterness (*wukawu*).

"*Kapwipu* is used because of its bitterness and heat.

"*Chikwata* (which has strong thorns) is used because it can pierce the disease.

"*Chikoli* is used because it is strong.

"The line of *mpemba* is just for purifying *(ku-tookesha)*; the line of *mukundu* means blood (mashi) or bad luck *(ku-halwa)*. The pangolin is used because it can kill the disease. It is used in many treatments. For the pangolin lies on an *isoha*, a kind of round ant's nest, waiting for the ants to come out to eat them. The clinking ax blades represent the pain of the headache. The relative drops them suddenly at his feet so that the disease may instantly leave the patient.

"When the sun comes, it brings the proper light. The sun (*itang'wa*)comes for all things, it is the elder of the country *(itang'wa wudinakwinza nayuma yejima,diyi mukulumpi wampata).* We say that (the application of) medicines must begin early just when the sun itself begins to appear. We have all found, we Africans, that if we do this our diseases become weak *(nyisong'u yetu yifomoki).* We believe too that diseases must die with the sun in the evening; that is why they also treat the patient in the evening.

"A long time ago the sun was said to be '*Nzambi*'[19] (the name now given to the Deity). *Nzambi* looks after the rain, the animals, and people. Once there was a man who came from Luunda[20] called *Mweni*. 'The Owner' or *mweniwamatung'a*, The Owner of the Realms' an important chief. He spokes personally to *Nzambi*. If he wanted more food for his people he would ask *Nzambi* for it. He reached the Lukoji river in the Congo. Now people come together to venerate *Mweni* in the *Musolu* rite—performed by chiefs when the rains are late in coming.

"Headache is a condition that seems more clearly associated with belief in witchcraft and sorcery than many other diseases. Possibly this is because the head is regarded as peculiarly the seat of one's individual life. A pain in the head may be the sign of a mystical attack on one's life by a sorcerer or witch, but the treatment of headache is directed against a vague and unspecified crowd of malevolent agencies rather than a particular witch or ghost. In this respect it falls together with the treatment of insanity into a borderline category between therapy and ritual. When Ndembu speak about "the bitterness," "the heat," "the sourness," "the strength", "the saltiness,"or "the pungency" of medicine it is clear that they think of them as having some empirically remedial effect on the patient's state even though we would consider that the principles underlying their use are those of sympathetic, contagious, and homeopathic magic. When they make medicine from a lightning-struck tree to cure headache simply because they sense an analogy between lightning and sudden headache, they would be the first to admit that the medicine was used not because of its empirically verified curative effects, but because "the disease resembles lightning" and therefore is imbued with the same sort of mystical power. Once embodied in a symbol that power can be controlled by the doctor for the patient's benefit. A step further in the direction of ritual is exemplified by the burning of the *chikoli* leaves. This is done explicitly to destroy the harm brought on by mystical agencies. The action is directed against the malignant agency rather than against the disease. Yet the *kapwipu* medicine which is employed because of its "heat and bitterness" and the *chikoli* medicine which is burned "to destroy witches familiars" are both applied in exactly the same manner—as a headwash.[21]

The distinction between "medicine"as "drug" and as "ritual symbol" is a very fine one and it is not always possible to make it clearly. All things are felt to be charged with powers of various kinds and it is the job both of the herbalist and of the ritual specialist to manipulate these for the benefit of society. The ritual specialist may be said to deal primarily with powers that have already come under the control of conscious and purposive beings visible or invisible, alive or dead, who use them, in general, to afflict the living with illness and misfortune. "Diseases," although they are sometimes said to "think" are certainly regarded as "alive" but are more like animals than persons, and motiveless in their malignancy. They might almost be said to come lowest in a hierarchy of afflicting agencies and to be controlled and directed by those above them. The Ndembu theory of affliction decrees that when conscious voluntary beings decide to afflict human beings with illness they rarely do so alone or in their own right but usually with the help of another conscious being, or through an intermediary being or power. Thus a witch has her familiar homunculi, the *tuyebela* or *andumba*; a sorcerer has his *ilomba* the human faced serpent or his figurines activated by human blood; the invoker of a curse raises by it a zombie (*musalu*)to do his fell work; while an ancestral spirit, as in *Chihamba*, may afflict in association with a demigod or may assume the guise of a specific "mode of affliction"(among the Luvale known as *lihamba*[22]). The *musong'u* the "disease" is believed to be strengthened by these intermediaries which act on behalf of conscious beings who desire either the death or punishment of the patient.

MUSONG'U WANSHING'U, DISEASE OF THE NECK, STIFF NECK

Ndembu say that the sufferer from this disease "feels as though the inside of his neck is broken he has a pain in the back of his neck and his neck is stiff and immovable."

(*a*) "The doctor first goes to a *mubang'a* tree(*Alfrormosia angolensis*) and breaks off a branch retaining all its twigs. He then ties a string to its broken end and to the tip to make a small bow (*kawuta*). Next he goes to collect some grass or reeds called *ntengwiji* (*Phrag-mites*); he takes two individual pieces broken off at the joints. He puts blobs of wax (*ndunda*) of the small *chilundi* bee on the tips of the grass stems. With branch for bow and grass stem as arrow' he approaches close to the spot where the pain is and releases 'the arrow'. Then he repeats the procedure at another part of the patient's neck. Next he puts the patient's arm between the bow and string and hangs the bow over his shoulder (*ku-pakatisha kawuta*).

"The doctor also takes some portions of the outer bark of the *mubaang'a* tree, chews them, and spits the juice on the painful place and also on the place where there is no pain. Then the patient lifts the bow over his head and presses (*ku-kanda)* it into his neck all the way around. Afterwards the doctor puts the bow and arrow in the over hanging thatch of the patient's hut above the veranda.

(*b*) "Should the above treatment be unsuccessful the doctor goes into the bush to look for a place where a python (*mboma*) died, leaving its bones. If he is lucky he takes three of the vertebrae and puts them on a string to form a necklace. The procedure is first to warm these bones over a fire then to press them into the sore place, and finally to tie them on a string around the patient's neck. This treatment continues for several days."

These treatments are further explained. "A branch of the *mmusbang'a* tree stands stiffly; to bend it with a string means to make it yield to pressure. The disease pushes the patients neck straight like the branch of the hard *mubang'a*—the tree against which novices urinate in seclusion after circumcision to make their wounds heal and give them a hard erection. *Nteng'wiji* grass is used because when it hits someone it is just like the pain he feels in the neck. The beeswax is soft *(yayovu)* so the disease will become soft (supple) too. A python is used in the second treatment because it is strong and supple *(mamovu);* thus the neck will become flexible instead of stiff."

MUSONG'U WACHINGONGU, SMALLPOX (WITH SEVERE CHIKEN POX)

Smallpox is not considered to be the result of witchcraft or sorcery or of ancestral affliction. It is said "to come to you in the air from Europeans." It is thought by Ndembu to be very deadly and formerly its victims were secluded in the bush far from their villages. If a mother fell sick with smallpox her child could accompany her and vice versa. One of my informants Sandombu considered it to be the second worst disease, leprosy being the more feared. Several Ndembu know the "true" *(yalala)* medicines but there are no great specialists as there are for insanity and leprosy. Treatment is usually given in the bush itself.

The doctor collects bark-scrapings from the following trees: *Mufung'u (Anisophyllea sp.),* the wild plum which has reddish bark and bears either reddish or purple plumlike edible fruits; *mukula(ptercarpus anglensis)*,which secretes red gum; *Luvung'u* (*Anisophyllea boehmii*), which has round orange-colored fruits. These bark-scrapings *(nyemba)* are mixed with *musengeleli* grass and a European disinfectant such as Jeyes Fluid bought at the local store is added. The mixture is rubbed on the pustules.

When the smallpox victim shivers with fever, the pounded leaves of the *wululushrub (Khaya nyassica?)* are rubbed on his body. This treatment is continued for two successive days. *Wululu* is a legume with yellow flowers and small, round paired leaves in a spray of light green color. The pounded leaves are also used in the preparation of fish poison. I have not been able to identify this plant: it is possibly the *mululu* of the Bemba, Yombe, Ila, Lamba, Kaonde, and many other tribes identified by the Northern Rhodesia Forest Department as *Khaya nyassica*. Fanshawe suggests it might be a species of *Cassia*.

Concluding Note on Treatment of Diseases

The above makes up the full tally of my systematic accounts of the treatment of various diseases. What follows consists of the organization of comments and remarks made to me at various times during my fieldwork by a variety of informants. Before we consider them, however, it is worth mentioning that Ndembu recognize the originators of new curative procedures under the titles "*Sayitmbu*," Father of the Medicine or "*Sakuuka*," Father of Treatment. For example, it was said that Katontu of Kalema Village in Chief Kanongesha Ndembi's area was a Sayitumbu. A former Kanongesha Chief Izemba is declared to have introduced many curative techniques—and also the *Kaneng'a* rite against illness caused by witchcraft or sorcery. Although there is an element of standardization in the procedures I have listed particularly with regard to quasi-ritual acts such as straightening a bent *mudyi* tree to cure backche, yet there is considerable variation in herbalists recommendations of medicines to be used for particular diseases. For example, some herbalists recommended that the pounded leaves and roots of the *musenzi (Combretum zeyheri)* plant should be steeped in cold water for two days and then given to men suffering from dysentery *(kapokota)* rather than the chikwata roots mentioned in the description above of the treatment of men's *musong'u wevumu*.

Among the accounts I collected are data on some of the mechanical devices and "surgical procedures" of the Ndembu. Much of this material was collected in Mbamvu Village in Chief Mwininyilamba's area. The villagers had come fairly recently—three years before—from the Lovwa River in Angola and were still relatively uninfluenced by the behavior and values of a changing society. Their views may fairly be said to be those of traditional Ndembu.

SURVEY OF MECHANICAL DEVICES USED IN MEDICINE

(Mainly from recent Angolan immigrants)

Massage

To cure constipation, the stomach is rubbed with castor oil and then massaged gently.

Circular Bandages

If muscles are displaced or joints dislocated, circular bandages, consisting of sheets of bark fibre bound round by bark strings are tied tightly around the affected area. The bandage is called *chisesa*, a term that also denotes a split palm mat. A *chisesa* is also used in one treatment of headache. First, small incisions are made between each eye and ear and then medicine made from the bark of the *kalayi*, plant is rubbed into them. Finally, a *chisesa* is tied round the head to cover the cuts.

Bleeding

To prevent bleeding, cold water is quickly applied to a wound. If the nose bleeds, it is plugged with leaves.

***Abscesses* (mahuti)**

Abscesses may be cut with a knife or pierced with a sharp stick and washed out with warm water.

Snake Bite

First, a ligature is tied at the nearest joint—below the knee or elbow as the case may be—then the flesh is cut out around the snake bite and medicine is applied to the wound. The medicine consists of:

(*a*) powder known as *ndakala;* made from the dried and pounded heads of all the poisonous snakes known to the Ndembu. (b)powdered root bark of the *mukeketi* (*Veptoderris nabilis*) tree—also known as *musombu;* (*c*) powdered root bark of *mupembi*

(*Ekebergia arborea*); powdered root bark of *Mundoyi* (*Chrysophyllum* [*Magalismontanum*] *bangweolense*); and (*e*) powdered root bark of *mutokatoka* (*Ilex mitis*).

At the same times as the medicine is applied to the wound the patient must chew the leaves of *musombu, mupembi, mundoyi, mutokatoka,* and *mwang'alala* (*Paropsia brazzeana*) and swallow the juice mixed with his saliva.

Next purse (*masaku*) made from the skin of three species of mongoose *(kabunshi, mungeli* and *kangamba)* are tighly bound around the ligature. Before they are tied on, they are rubbed on the patient's calf and forearm. If the blood is not flowing freely from the wound as it ought to do, the doctor takes some *ndakala* medicine from a tortoise shell container *(mbachi),* chews it in his mouth, sucks the wound, then applies the medicine.

Treatment of Severe Cuts

Bark scrapings of *mupuchi (Brachystegia spiciformis)*, *muvuka* (*Marquesia macrova*), *mwanda* (*Julbernardia paniculata*), *mundoyi* (*Chrysophyllum sp.*), *mwang'alala* (*paropsia brazzeana*) and *mudyi (Diplorrhyncus condylocarpon)* are boiled in a pot, and the hot mixture is applied in a sheet of bark fiber to the affected part and tied over it. Then a grass hut *(nkunka)* is built for the patient outside the village where he may lie quietly until he recuperates.

Emetics

If a person has swallowed something poisonous, he is given root scrapings of *mundoyi* which are mixed with thin warmed gruel (*kapudyi*) and eaten; root peelings of *kavulawumi (Maprounea africana)* are also dropped in beer which is then drunk.

If a person has drunk a large amount of beer but cannot vomit he chews leaves of any available species and swallows the sap.

Enemas

Enemas are made of small calabashes *(tuswaha)* with reeds inserted through the necks. They are filled with warm water and given to the patient to administer himself. They are used in cases of dysentery (*kapokota*) and if the patient has become very thin, of hook worm.

Splints

Splints are used for broken limbs. They are made of mats of split palm (*yisesa*), split sugar cane, or tough reed, tied round with bark string. The patient is segregated from the village in a grass hut, as in the treatment for severe cuts. Medicine leaves are applied to the skin under the mats. The famous *Sayitumbu, Katontu,* is said to have cured broken limbs by breaking the legs of a chicken and treating patient and chicken together. When the chicken stars to walk again so (in theory!) will the patient.

Amputation is unknown.

Stitches

Stitches are never made in wounds. If a cut is deep, the doctor closes one eye "so that the medicine may sink in deeply."

Burns

"If someone has a burn the doctor brings him *chitakachi* leaves (*Phyllanthus discoideus*),which are pounded, then soaked in water. He rubs this medicine on the burn. This treatment continues for two days.

"If the burn made a severe wound, the doctor burns a wild pig's bones to ash. Then he takes the patient to a *mukula* tree rubs *mukula*gum on the wound, and finishes by rubbing bone ash (*mula*) on it. This treatment is repeated for several days.

"If the wound does not heal, the doctor goes to a *kampandi* tree *(Maytenus cymosus),* collects some pieces of bark, pounds them and puts them, in the sun to dry. When dry, they are sieved so as to form a powder. The patient is brought and his wound is well washed with water. When it is clean this powder is applied while the burn is still wet. The water and powder should meet together and form a scab. This treatment goes on for as many weeks as the burn requires to be healed.

"*Chitakachi* is *wazema* or 'tacky'; it comes off in a long string, all in one piece. Its leaves are treacly like that just like the leaves of the relish plant *wusi*; they are difficult to separate, like honey.They are used so that the wound will not spread but will remain in one piece.

"*Mukula* is used so that the burn will form a hard dry scab like *mukula* gum. The wild pig's bone meal mixed with *mukula* gum is used to make the burn hard like a dry paste.

"*Kampanddi* is used to make the wound form a scab for the bark of *kampandi* is hard."

Steam Bath

We have already noted the use of the steam bath in the treatment of eye disease. It is also used occasionally during the "*kayong'u* rite, which may be performed for a patient who shows signs of asthma or bronchitis, thought to be the result of ancestral affliction (Turner 1961,5,23-26).

Scarification

Scarification is a standard Ndembu therapeutic practice, as we have seen.

Cupping

This is employed in several rites of affliction (e.g., *Ihamba, Kaneng'a)* with the avowed aim of removing harmful objects, mystically propelled into it from the patient's body. Cupping is also used in several kinds of therapy.

Further notes on Treatment and Medicines

Sores (Yilonda, *sing.* chiloṇda)

(*a*)The pounded leaves of *wunkomukomu* (possibly *Aphrohiza nitida*) are mixed with copper ore obtained from returned labor migrants from the Copperbelt in Zambia and are rubbed on the sores. *Wunkomukomu* is a small shrub with large lanceolate leaves.

(*b*)Either pounded *muvuka* (*Marquesia macrova*) roots mixed with salt or pounded *kapwipu* (*Swartzia madagascariensis*) leaves mixed with salt are rubbed into the sores.

Infantile Disorders

(*a*) If an infant is very feeble, his father collects leaves of *chikan'g anjamba,* another name for the *chikoli* tree mentioned above in several treatments; the name *chikang'anjamba* means "(the tree) the elephant fails to (break)"; it is used because it is very tough and enduring. The name *chikoli* is from *ku-kola,* "to be strong, hard or healthy." The leaves are pounded and left to steep in cold water.

(*b*) If a child is slow in learning to walk, his father collects *kambanjibanji leaves* (used also as a toothache cure), pounds them, allows them to steep in cold water for three days then gives them to the child to drink.

Hookworm

The pounded leaves of *kavulawumi (Maprounea africana)* are administered in cold water to induce vomiting.

Lactation Troubles

"If a woman's breast milk (*mayeli*) becomes 'red' or 'yellow,' it is called *nshidi,* 'guilt' or 'sin'. If her baby drinks it, may die. If the creeper or vine *molu wawubwang'u* is twined around the breast that is not giving white milk, it will become white.'

In the *Wubwang'u* rites performed for a mother of twins, *molu wawubwang'u* is one of the principal medicines and is regarded as the dominant symbol of the *itu,* or streamside forest.

Masculine Sterility

"If the color of a man's semen is 'red' or 'yellow' he will become a sterile person *(nshinta).* But if he eats medicine made from the *mucheki* plant mixed with thin gruel *(kapudyi)* his semen will become white. After he has finished eating *mucheki,* he must dig a little hole in the ground and urinate into it."

Mucheki is the dominant symbol of the *kutumbuka* or major phase of the great *Chilhamba* rite (Turner 1962a),where its root is regarded as epitomizing the purest "whiteness" and all the values and ideas annexed thereto. In these two medicines, *molu wawubwang'u* and *mucheki,*we get a glimpse of the relationship between religious rite and lay treatment. Here it would seem the treatment derives from the rite the "magical"practice from the "religious"observance.

Analysis and Conclusions

It has been said (Ackerman 1942) that in the primitive treatment of disease,"an invisible force is dealt with visibly by means that are meant and understood to be symbolic." This formulation would account for much that goes on at Ndembu curative procedures. It seems to bé the case, however, that some scope is permitted for experiment, but in the main it is held that to make visible by symbolic means is to make a disease accessible to therapeutic action, also of a symbolic character. A glance at the "Alphabetical List of Trees and Plants Used in Treatments" illustrates this point sufficiently. Sympathetic, contagious and homeopathic magic appear to account for the employment of the majority of the "medicines." All the senses—sight, hearing, taste smell, and touch—are enlisted in the service of association and analogy. *Mucheki* is used because its wood is white and its medicine will hence make "red" semen "white" and fruitful. The "sound" of *kung'ami* as it bubbles in a child's stomach will drive the disease to one side." The bitter taste of *kapepi or nwalu* will kill disease of the mouth. The nasty smell of *mutata* will "kill stomach disease in women." The "stiffness" of *mubang'a* is communicated to a homeopathic medicine made from it which will cure stiff neck.

There is no attempt to distinguish between medicines the effect of which are thought to depend on one kind of sensorily distinguishable property and medicines dependent on other kinds, and to reserve one kind for a single curative procedure. All kinds are interlinked in a single procedure. The procedure itself may often contain actions and episodes that we in the West might consider to be "religious." I refer to the invocations made by doctor to the principal medicine trees, to the formal washings aspersions and anointings. The prescribed, stereotyped behavior of the curative specialists seems often to fall more within the sphere of ritual than of therapeutic action. This consideration brings me back to Ackerknecht's query with which this study began: 'What are the ideas underlying these therapeutic acts and under what circumstances (with or without ritual) are they performed?"

We have partly answered these questions in commenting on specific treatments. The central idea behind both Ndembu therapy and Ndembu ritual is that the visible world is permeated by and perhaps is but a manifestation of a "powers" (*jing'oju*) assembled ultimately under the treble rubric of white-red-black and capable of being evoked by those with specialized knowledge either for good or ill. Such powers conceived sometimes as personal, sometimes as animate but without purposiveness or rationality, may be evoked by various means. In the first place, there must be a specialist, a *chimbuki* or *chimbanda* who "knows"(*weluka*) what medicines are efficacious against a given disease, how they should be administered, and why they are used. Knowledge among the Ndembu is far more literally "power" than it is with us. To know more is to *be* more fully, and to possess greater power with respect to the field of action to which that knowledge pertains. It is also to increase in social status and authority in that field of action and knowledge. Knowledge in short has existential implications. It may be acquired by participation in a full-scale *rite de passage* ,where the novices or candidates are taught the properties of herbal and other medicines, it may be taught by a senior relative—and this is particularly common where therapeutic knowledge is concerned—or it may be bought from another, unrelated specialist. In whatever way such knowledge may have been obtained it confers some kind of mys-

Alphabetical List of Trees and Shrubs Used inTreatments

Prefix	*Root*	*Botanical Name*	*Disease or Injury*	*Reason for Use*
Nw	*ala*	*Afzeliaquanzenis*	Stomach disease	"Bitterness will kill disease" (contains a high proportion of
		tannins with marked astringent effect—Dr. Cahal)		
Nw	*alu or*	*?Olax obtusifolius*	Blisters in mouth	
Ka-	*lukuta*		(Scurvy?)	"Bitter, can kill disease"
Mw-	*anda*	*Julbernardia paniculata*		
Mw-	*angalala*	*Paropsia brazzeana*	Blitsters in mouth (Scurvy?)	"It is hot and sets teeth on edge"
Mw-	*ang'alala*	*Paropsia brazzeana*	Snake bite	
Mw-	*ang'alala*	*Paropsia brazzeana*	Severe cuts	
Mu-	*bang'a*	*Afromosia angolensis*	Stiff neck	"Stiff tree to bend"
M-	*bumba yachula*	*Lamdolphia rufescens*	Leprosy	"Has mottled bark like leper's skin"
Mu-	*cheki*	*Creamaspora triflora*	Male sterility	"Al `white' medicine, makes semen
		white"		
Wa-	*dikalanziza or*	*(memecylon flavovirens)*	Eye disease	"Bitter"
Ka-	*yiza*	*Strychnos stuhlmannii*		
Mu-	*diansefu*	*? Craterosiphon quarrei*	Rabies	"Aperient"
Mu-	*dyi*	*Diplorrhyncus condylo*	Backache	Auspicious tree (hhere it *Carpon*
		refers also to bent		
				specimen—like patient's back)
Mu-	*dyi*	*Diplorrhyncus condylo-*	Gonorrhea	White latex resembles pus of

		gonorrheea *carpon*		
Mu	*dyi*	*Diplorrhyncus condylo carpon*	Headache	Auspicious, biter
Mu	*dyi*	*Diplorrhyncus condylo carpon*	Leprosy	White like leprous sports, sym bolic role in
		Mukanda rites, sanctioned by		leprosy
Mu-	*dyi*	*Diplorrhyncus condylo carpon*	Severe cuts	
Lw-	*eng'engi'*		Eye disease	"Bitter"
Lw-	*eng'i*	*Draecena reflexa var. mitens*	Headache	"Strong smell and hot"
My-	*fung'u*	*? Arisophyllea boehmii*	Small pox	"Reddish fruits"
Mu-	*hanu*	*Ficus sp.*	Tuberculosis	Grows in hol ein other trees; will
		break		obstruction in chest"
Mu-	*hotuhotu*	*Canthium venosum*	Insanity	Traditiona component of medicien broom
My-	*huma*	*Strychnos spinosa* (Stro		
Mu-	*hwila*	*phanthus welwitschii)*	Eye disease	"Bitter"
Ka	*jing'a ludi*	*? Apocycnaceae creepet. Landolphia*	Gonorrhea	"Creeper with whte flowers" (=pus)
I-	*kamba da Chihamba*	*Cryptosepalum mara viense*	Insanity	"Clears the eyes"
Mu-	*kandachina*	*(Eriocoelum sp.) Rhus longipes*	Insanity	"Grows on top of termitte hills; a madman goes to top of things"

Chi-	*kang'anjamba (see chi koli)*	*Strychnos spinosa*		
Mu-	*keketi*	*(veptoderris nabilis)*	Snake bite	
		Syzygium quineense		
Chi-	*koli*	*Strychnos spinosa*	Earache	"Yellow fruits"
Chi-	*kolit*	*strychnos spinosa*	headache	"Bitter and strong"
Chi	*koli*	*Strychnos spinosa*	Slow infant development	"Strong tree"
Mu-	*kombukombu*	*Tricalysia angolensis (Leptactina)*	Insanity	Component of medicne broom
Mu-	*kula*	*Pterocarpus angolensis*	Burns	"Red gum dries like scab"
Mu-	*kula*	*Pterocarpus angolensis*	Smallpox	"Red gum like pustules"
Mu-	*kula*	*Pterocarpus angolensis*	Smallpox	"Red gum like putsules"
Mu-	*Kula*	*terocarpus angolensis*	Tuberculosis	"Red gum—spittign blood"
Ka-	*kung'ami*		Children's stomach	"Stinks, bubbles, drives disease aside" trouble
Chi-	*kwata*	*Zizyphus mucronata* disease	men's stomach	"Bitter"
Chi-	*kwata*	*Zizyphys mucronata*	Headache	"Strong throns pierce disease"
Ka-	*kwema*	*(Enneastemon schwein forthii)* Uvaria angolensis	Stomach disease	"Its nasty smell kills disease"
Mu-	*lendi*	*Sterculia quinqueloba* from patient"	Epilepsy	"Very slippery; so disease will slip
Ka-	*leng'anag'ombi*	Thornbush of gallery forest	Instanity	"Used in Mukanda boys' circumci sion rites'

I-	*leng's*	*(? Uapaca sansibarica) cyperus sp.*	Pyorhea	"Reeds from which salt is made Saltiness can cure"
Mu-	*lolu*	*Anonanana*	Men's stomach disease	"Strong smell"
Ka-	*lukuta*	*See mwalu*		
Wu-	*lulu*	*(Khaya nyassica) Cassia* sp.	Smallpox	
Ka-	*mbanjibanji*		Headache	"Strong and astringent"
Ka-	*mbanjoibanji*		*Blisters in mouth (Scurvy?)*	"Hot"
Ka-	*mbanjibanji*			
Ka-	*mbanjibanji*		*Slow infant development*	
Ka-	*mpandi*	*Maytenus cymosus*	Burns	"Its bark is hard and scablike"
Mu-	*ndoyi*	*Chrysophyllum*	Severe cuts	
Mu-	*ndoyi*	*(Mgahis montanum)*	Snake bite	
Mu-	*ndoyi*	*bangweolense*	Poison in stomach	Emetic
Wu-	*ukomukomu*	*(? Aphrohiza nitida)*	Sores	
			small shrub, largc lanceolate leaves	
Ka-	*nsanying'a*	(?)	Bilharziasis	"Has white roots and stron smell"
Ka-	*nshinshi*	(?)	Stomach disease of children	"Strong smell and bitter taste
M (w)	*olu wawubwang'u*	creeper.	Grows in gallery forest Can make milk flow	Lactation diorders "A 'white white"
(Mu-	*Lu wawubwang'u)*		Stomach disease	"Strong smell kills disease"
Mu-	*pembi*	*Ekebergia arborea*	Snake bite	
Ka-	*pepi*	*Hymenocardia acida*	Headache	"Bitter"
Ka-	*pepi*	*Hymenocardia acida*	Pyorrhea	"Bitter"

Mu-	*puchi*	*Brahystegia spiciformis*	Bilharziasis	"Red gum, like blood of bilharziasis"
Mu-	*puchi*	*Brahystegia spiciformis*	Severe cuts	
Ka-	*pumbwa*	*Ancylobothrys amoena*	Gonorrhea	"Its white gum drops on the ground, resembles pus of gonorrhea"
Chi-	*Puta mazala*	*Erythina tomentosa*	Stomach disease of children	"Strong smell"
Ka-	*Pwipu*	*Swartzia madagazcarienses*	Headache	"Bitter and hot"
Ka-	*pwipu*	*Swartiza madagascariensis*	Sores	
Ka-	*puipu*	*Swartzia madagascariensis*	Stomach disease of children	"Hardness of tree = health and strength"
Mu-	*Seng'u*	*Ochna pulchra*	Epilepsy	"its leves are curled like someone in an epileptic fit"
Mu-	*senzi*	*Conbretum zeyheri*	Dysentery	
Mu-	*Shokotu*	*Faurea saligna*	Earache	
Mu-	*soli*	*Vangueriopsis Lanciflora*	*Insanity*	"Tɔ clear madman's mind"
Mu-	*sombu*	*Syzygium guineense*		
Mu-	*song'ason'a*	*Ximenia americana*	Stomach disease of children	"Has hard wood,makes strong and healthy"
Mu-	*song'ason'a*	*(Olax obtuifolius)*	Insanity	"Bitter for the eyes. Clears them"
Mu-	*sosu*	*Boscia corymbosa*	Blisters in mouth (Scurvy?)	"lacks salt, mild"
Chi-	*takachi*	*(phyllanthus discoideus)*	Burns	"Stickines of leaves coagulates burn
Mu-	*tata*	*Securidaca longipedunculata*	Stomach disease	"Its nasty smell will kill disease"
Mu-	*tokatoka*	*Ilex mitis*	Snake bite	
Ka-	*tong'a*	*Strychnos cocculoides*	Stomach disease of men	"Very bitter"

Wu-	*totu*	*Gardenia imperialis/*	Bilharziasis	"White roots and gum resemble pus"
Wu=	*totu*	*Taberanaemontana angolensis*	Gonorrhea	"White roots and gum resemble pus of gonorrhea"
Ka-	*tunya*	*(Uvariastrom hexalobiodes) Harungana madagascariensis*	Bilharziasis	"Red roots like blood of Bilharziasis"
Mu-	*tutambululu*	*Zylopia adoratissima*	Insanity	Component of medicine broom
Mu-	*vuka*	*Marquesia macrova*	Severe cuts	
Mu-	*vuka*	*Marwuesia macrova*	Sores	
Ka-	*vulawumi*	*Maprounea africana*	Hookworm	"Brings on vomiting"
Ka-	*vulawumi*	*Maprounea africana*	Leprosy	
Ka-	*vulawumi*	*maprounea africana*	Poison in stomach	Emetic
Ka-	*voluwumi*	*Maprounea africana*	Rabies	Emetic
Lu-	*vung'u*	*Anisophyllea boehmii*	Smallpox	"Round ornge fruits" (like pustulles?)
I-	*vung'uvung'u*	*Kigelia pinnata*	Elephantiais of scrotum	"fruits resemble testicles"
I-	*yang'wa*	*? Agauria salicifolia*	Elehantiaisi of scrotum	"Resembles swollen testicles"
Ka-	*Yiza*	*(Memecylon flovovirens) strychnos stuhlmannii*		

tical power on its possessor, gives him or her an affinity with the materia medica used, and enables the herbalist to activate the latent virtues in the herbs he uses.

However, it is not enough merely to possess power and knowledge. The herbalist must take positive steps to awaken—and here the term *ku-tonisha*, "to awaken" is actually employed—the powers hidden and slumbering in herbs. Sometimes he and his assistants do this by singing traditional songs associated in some way with the disease as they go into the bush to collect medicine. Sometimes the herbalists may "address" the principal medicine tree before he cuts portions from it for his special *lwalu* basket . I have given an example of such an address on "O tree' , I received you from another doctor. The medicine we will collect from you here must have the power of killing disease". After making the address (*mpanddula*), the doctor often takes a leaf from the tree, places it on the back of his clenched left fist and claps his flattened right hand down on it. The sharp report thus made—sometimes compared with a gun shot—is also intended to "wake up" the medicine or—in rites proper—the ancestral spirits who act as tutelaries to the doctor adepts.

This right-left contrast has importance in a number of ritual con texts where it may represent: male/female husband/wife, arrow (held in the right hand)/bow (held in the left)—and indeed the "arrow"may symbolize the male genital and power of begetting while the "bow"represents female fertility.

Again, right may be associated with whiteness, while left may be associated with redness. Often they are conceptualized as a complementary pair in which the left hand is called *nkwashi*, "the helper," the one which enables the right hand to accomplish its act, just as a wife helps her husband in his activities.

In medicine it is thought the the power of a *chimbuki* passes through his right arm into his ax when he cuts medicine from a tree. This power evokes the power possessed by the tree. The smell of the slashed bark or cut root, the gum or latex oozing from the excision, these too are regarded as expressions of roused power. Each tree is felt to have its specific "virtue"which is now informed by mystical power.

Such rousing preliminaries—which may also include the use of musical instruments such as stridulators, drums, hunting bells, and clashing bars of iron—are themselves only a part of a configuration of symbolic actions and symbolic articles, and it is the form of the total procedure which most signally evokes contains, and controls the mystical powers employed by the healer or herbalist. It is impossible to overstate the importance of the mode of arrangement of the parts of a curative procedure. Out of the randomness and incoherence of the environment, the *chimbuki* selects certain items and arrays them in a coherent structure in accordance with his sensitivity to Ndembu evaluations and symbolism and in accordance with his intention of curing a specific culturally defined disease. When I say that "the *chimbuki* selects" I mean no more than that he follows precedent, whether that of the doctor who taught him the medicine or of the tradition within which that doctor was working. Incidentally it is no surprise to find that many doctors became so because they began as patients who learned the medicines and curative procedure for a particular disease in the course of being treated for it. There are more than practical considerations at work here, for Ndembu have a tendency to regard like or shared experience as creating a mystical bond between all persons (including, so Ndembu believe, the dead), things, and activities comprising the experience or closely associated with it. From the point of view Western science' such a bond or association may be merely adventitious or superficial; from the point of view of the Ndembu persons and things which "were together" in space and time at a moment of critical significance for an individual or a group may acquire a deep and permanent relationship of "mystical participation" to use Levy-Bruhl's useful term.

To understand Ndembu therapy, therefore, it is necessary to turn away from an atomistic consideration of particular symbolic and pragmatic items of medicine and treatment to an examination of the principles underlying the total procedure. From this standpoint it is unimportant that a particular medicine owes its employment to a particular mode of sensory or mental association. For, behind the configuration of symbolic medicines and acts stand a few principles which articulate the separate items into a whole. This can be seen if a particular treatment is analyzed for, example, that of *musong'u wanyembu* ("splitting" headache).

In this treatment there are five components: (1) the disease; (2) color symbolism; (3) the medicines; (4) the mode of treatment ; and (5) the times of treatment. These components are interarticulated by a few ruling ideas. The disease is considered in this instance to be partly the result of witchcraft or sorcery. It has in terms of Ndembu thought, a "black" character. This gives us the key to the color symbolism, for here white and red are regarded at one level as working in combination to rid the patient of the black, deathly taint of the witch's grudge (*chitela*) or malevolent action (*chisaku*). The white decoration of the pot represent the "purification of the patient," while the red line stands for "blood"or killing. Here it may represent the "strength" desired for the patient and would link up with the "strong" medicines used (*mudyi, chikwata, chikoli*), for Ndembu say that blood is "life," though it also stands for the taking of life. It may stand here also for the taking of the "life" of the *musong'u*, the disease regarded as an animate being. Red is an ambivalent symbol in Ndembu ritual and here would represent both a wish for the patient's recovery of life and a wish for the "killing" of the disease and the "bad luck" (*ku-halwa*). The medicines all have a "strong" (*kola*) aggressive character, associated with redness and the level of color symbolism. They have a "bitter" taste, they are "'hot", they have thorns "to pierce (or stab) the disease." The disease itself has this very quality, for it is described as resembling "the very bright light made when lightning falls on a hut— such a light comes suddenly, it is sharp stab of pain" . It must, so Ndembu seem to think, be fought by its own weapons. Hence the use of a lightning-struck tree as medicine "because lightning is like the pain of headache". Hence the mode of treatment by clinking ax blades together near the patient's head—not by any means a treatment that would strike us as soothing! Behind this simulation in the treatment of the supposed properties of the disease may also lie the notion (common in another aspects of Ndembu symbolic practices) that to reveal or portray is to expose, and that exposure of the "true" character of a disease or "grudge" is half the therapeutic battle, for the known is not nearly so dangerous as the hidden and unknown. Action can be taken against something visible and classified in terms of traditional thought and belief and positive action, as has often been said, reduces anxiety and promotes confidence. Nor can we rule out of the picture the possibility that noise and shock themselves may have a therapeutic value. As Lessa and Vogt (1958,343) have said: "The typical primitive supernatural treatment involves elements of shock or stress analogous to modern shock treatment—treatment which stimulates an internal reaction capable of returning the organism to health."

The times of performance—at sunset and sunrise—link up with the color symbolism, with the medicines, and with the disease. For the sun is considered a "white" object and a symbol of *Nzambi*, the High God, source of all power. Here the rising of the sun seems to be associated with an increase in the effect of the medicines, while the declining sun is connected with the declining strength of the disease.

A number of symbols actions actually performed or implicit in the symbolism, represent the death or decline or elimination of the disease. There is the setting of the sun just mentioned—"disease must die with the sun in the evening." Then there is the sudden dropping of the ax blades at the patient's feet,"so that the disease may instantly leave him." There is the *chikwata* thorn tree which can "pierce" the disease. Finally, there is the use of the pangolin's scale as *mpelu*, contagious magical medicine for the reason that the pangolin eats up stinging ants, which are identified with the disease.

The symbolic contrast of "above" with "below" influences the procedure. We have noted the supposed effects of the rising and setting sun on the strength of medicine and disease. The white line above the red line on the pot may mean many things, but one of them is the wished-for ascendancy of "purification," a term that embraces the curative procedure, over "bad luck," a multivocal term that includes the disease add the witch's grudge that probably caused it. In the case of headache, it is, of course the head (the "above") that is itself being attacked by witchcraft which, with its necrophagous attributes, is associated in many contexts with the "below." This is why the medicine pot is hung over the patient's doorway, head high, why the ax blades are clinked in front of his head, and why sun symbolism plays such a major part. Healthful powers are thus enlisted against the "disease of the head," wherein the patient's life (*wumi*) is felt to reside.

There are a number of echoes from Ndembu rites proper in the symbolic pattern of this treatment which indicate how deeply their pharmacopoeia is influenced by ritual beliefs and practices. For example, *chikoli, chikwata,* and indeed the *mudyi* tree itself, under which novices are circumcised, are important symbols in *Mukanda,* the boy's circumcision rites. *Chikoli* there represent *inter alia* an erect phallus, a tought, healthy body, and masculinity. *Chikwata* is though to confer healing power on the boys' penes after the operation. Again, in *Mukanda,* the circumcisers' protective medicine has to be lifted above the ground or it will lose its efficacy, and when a certain song (the *ng'ung'u*) is sung by circumcisers, the novices must climb up trees or onto the shoulders of adult men, otherwise they will suffer, it is said, from incontinence of urine for the rest of their lives. Thus, what is above is auspicious and what is below or on the ground is contextually inauspicious, as in the treatment of headache. It is probable that there is here a connection between a potent and erect male member and what is above, and a slack, impotent member and what is below. Pain is certainly associated with lying on the ground, for this is the posture of circumcision. Several informants have given me this interpretation. It might not be fanciful to conjecture that Ndembu associate, the head of a healthy man with the glans of the potent member, and headache (produced by witchcraft) with impotence (also produced by witchcraft).

Other symbolic links with virility are perhaps provided by the use by *kepepi* and *Kapwipu* medicines, for both these trees play an important role in the symbolism of hunting rites. I have discussed this role elsewhere and here merely mention that in addition to their specific properties these trees are held to share the following characteristics:

(1) string cannot be made from their bark—thus they do not "tie up huntsmanship," i.e., the hunter's power and skill in killing animals; (2) they have a tough, termite-and weather-resistant wood-the hunter should posses toughness and power of endurance; and (3) their wood is white and is thus an embodiment of the power of whiteness, supreme auspiciousness.

Kapepi and *Kapwipu* are trees from which the most common type of shrine created for the spirits of hunter ancestors is made; a forked branch stripped of leaves and adorned with trophies of the chase. Offerings of blood are smeared on the branches and poured at the base, and portions of internal organs of the slain animal, consecrated to the use of hunters alone, are transfixed on the sharpened points. The sharpness of the point represents the acuity of huntsmanship (*ku-wambuka kwaW ubinda*).

Viewed in this wider framework, it seems likely that these medicines are not employed solely on account of their bitter taste or "heat," since they are believed to confer robustness and endurance on the person enfeebled by a splitting headache. If the connection between the treatment and hunting ritual is a valid one, there would be yet another reference to the relationship between white and red, for blood, the most direct expression of the principle of redness, is brought to the white shrine and the two are combined in the act of veneration.

The treatment of headache thus reveals itself as a formal procedure controlled by religious ideas that are expressed in symbolic actions and symbolic articles: whiteness/redness; above/below; strength/weakness; health/disease (a mode of blackness); sunrise/sunset; links between the power of God, the sun, whiteness, strength, endurance, virility; between lightning, metallic noise, stabbing headache, thorns, circumcision, the killing of animals. As in all diseases, the aim is to restore the patient from a "black" to a "white" condition (one aspect of which is purification). In the particular case of headache this process of restoration is directed towards the head (with overtones of operations on the upper parts of other extremities). The notion of lightning plays an important part here because lightning is said to strike the topknot of grass at the apex of a hut (resembling the head of a person) as well as on account of its analogy with sudden, splitting, pain in the head. Lighting, in its suddenness and ferocity, is a symbol for sorcery and witchcraft, and indeed Ndembu believe that certain sorcerers use medicine (*wang'a wanzaji, "lightning magic*") to bring lightning down (even from a clear sky) to kill their personal enemies. Violent headache, spreading out into constant pain, is for Ndembu a sign that an unknown witch or sorcerer is assailing therm in their most vital center. Against this assault must be mobilized medicines borrowed from rites that most signally promote health, strength and virility, and other "white" qualities: such rites as girls' puberty (with its *mudyi* tree symbol), boys's circumcision, and those of the hunting cults.

In these and other ways, ultimate and axiomatic values of Ndembu religion and ethics enter into such an everyday matter as curing a headache. The meaning existence has for a Ndembu tribesman is present in many of his minor ends as well as in the great ends of a full-scale life-crisis rite. To restore order, health, or peace the powers that make for these must be brought into play by the correct use and combination of symbols, viewed as repositories of power as well as semantic systems. For Ndembu, again unlike ourselves, to "know" something, to understand the meaning of a symbol or the use of a "medicine", for example, is to increase in "power."

After reading the above account people may ask: "Why do such treatments continue to be practiced, since it is clear that they have little empirical derivation and are based on mystical ideas?" One reason for their persistence lies, no doubt, in the very fact that they are part of a religious system which itself constitutes an explanation of the universe and guarantees the norms and values on which orderly social arrangements rest. To query the premises on which Ndembu medicine rests would be to query the axioms underlying the Ndembu *Welibild*. Another more practical reason would be that many diseases are self-curing; in the course of time, regardless of the treatment they are given, many people recover from illness, but the recovery is attributed to the treatment. Then again, psychological considerations must play a part in the case of mild psychosomatic conditions and in the milder cases of somatic illness. Such considerations would include the authoritative air of the doctor-herbalist, the purposive structure of the procedure, the "shock treatment' aspect mentioned above, and the sense that something traditional is being done about a known and named condition. Here we have an instance of the well-known placebo effect, where medicine is given to humor rather than to cure the patient, but where improvement in health nevertheless results.

Yet when all is said, the public health situation of the Ndembu, as of most Africans, is highly unsatisfactory. Charles. C. Hughes, in an admirable conspectus of the topic in nonliterate groups (1961), surveys a wide spread of literature bearing on health to reach the conclusion, with George H. T. Kimball (1960, 159), that "in the African social drama sickness has a strong claim to being arch-villain." Poor hygiene, malnutrition, dietetic imbalance (partly produced by food taboos of a ritual character), the presence of liver disease, worm infestations or other intestinal diseases which interfere with absorption or storage, famine—all these and other environmentally and culturally determined conditions maintain health at a chronically low level. The fact that a rich and elaborate system of ritual and magical beliefs and practices provides a set of explanations for sickness and death and gives people a false sense of confidence that they have the means of coping with disease does nothing towards raising the level of health or increasing the life expectancy. Only better hygiene, a bigger and well-balanced diet, the widespread use of prophylactic medicine and the extension of hospital facilities will slay the "arch-villain" disease and free the African from its ancient mastery.

Bibliography

Acherknecht, E. H. 1942. "Problems of Primitive Medicine," *Bulletin of the History of Medicine*, XI, 503-521.

—. 1946. "Natural Diseases and Rational Treatment in Primitive Medicine," *Bulletin of the History of Medicine*, XIX, No. 5.

Baumann, H. 1935. *Lunda; Bei Bauen und Jagern in Inner Angola*. Berlin; Wurfel-Verlag.

Evans-Pritchard, E. 1937. *Witchcraft, Oracles and Magic among the Azande*. London: Oxford University Press.

Goodall, E. B. H. 1921. *Some wemba Words*. London: Oxford University Press.

Hughes, C. C. 1961. "Hygiene and Public Health in Nonliterate Societies." Paper presented at the Conference on Medicine and Anthropology at Arden House, Harriman, New York, in November, 1961.

Kimball, H. TO. 1960. *Tropical Africa*. 2 vols. New York: twentieth Century Fund.

Lessa, W. A., and Vogt, E. Z., eds, 1958. *Reader in Comparative Religion*. Evanston: Row, Peterson and Co.

McCulloch, M. 1951. *The Southern Lunda and Related Peoples*. Ed. by Daryll Forde. London: International African Institute.

Reynolds, Barrie, 1963, *Magic, Divination and Witchcraft among the Barotse of Northern Rhodesia* (Robins Series, Rhodes Livingstone Museum) London: Chatto and Windus.

Rivers, W. H. R. 1924. *Medicine, Magic and Religion*. London: Oxford University Press.

Turner, V. W. 1953. *Lunda Rites and Ceremonies* (Occasional Papers of the Rhodes Livingstone Museum, N.S.). No. 10. Livingstone: Zambia.

Turner, V.W. 1957. *Schism and Continuity in an African Society: A Study of Ndembu Village Life*. Manchester University Press.

—. 1961. *Ndembu Divination: Its Symbolism and techniques* (Rhodes-Livingstone Paper 31). Manchester University Press.

—. 1962a. *Chihamba, the White Spirit* (Rhodes-Livingstone Paper 33). Manchester University Press.

—. 1962b. "Three Symbols of Passage in Ndembu Circumcision Ritual," in M. Gluckman, ed., *Essays on the Ritual of Social Relations*. Man-chester University Press.

White, C. M. N. 1961. *Element in Luvale Beliefs and Rituals* (Rhodes-Livingston Paper 32). Manchester University Press.

Wilson, M. 1957. *Rituals of Kinship among the Nyakyusa*. London;

Oxford University Press, for the International African Institute.

References

1. In the field of African studies there have been analyses of tribal therapies by Monica Wilson, S.F. Nadel, and Michael Gelfand.

2. H. Baumann mentions (1935, 205-206) that the Chokew themselves connect *Tukuka* with Europeans, and that two clay models of bellows (reresenting lungs?) "are important for the cult."

3. This is creeper with small white, five-pointed starlike flowers, possibly *Storphanthus welwitschii*. Fanshawe suggests that *Kajings'a ludi* might also be applied to a *Landolphia* or *Apocynaceae* creeper (personal communication).

4. These are usually goats' horns with tips removed. After they have been sucked on over an incision in the patient's body, the open top end is plugged with beeswax by the operator and left for a time before removal. *Tusumu* are used in several rites to suck from a patient's body substances that have been injected into it by magical or mystical means. For example, the upper middle incisor of a dead hunter is believed to "bite" (*ke-suma*) a living relative of that hunter for neglect of his memory or as a punishment for quarreling between intolerable pain. It is extracted by the joint action of ritual and cuppong. again, sorcerers are supposed to shoot teeth, pieces of human bone and soil from graves into the bodies of those they wish to kill. They use a miniature gun carved from a human tibia and known as the "night gun" (*wuta wawufuku*). A full desceiption of night guns and the ways in ways in which they are used may be found in Barrie Reynolds, 1963.

5. A creeper found near strema. It is hung around the shoulders of the patinet-candidate in the *Wubwang'u* rite performed for mothers of twins—it is supposed also to whiten the milk of a mother who has been yielding "red" or "yellow" milk—the result of some infection of the mammary glands, no doubt.

6. Ndembu mean many things by these terms. Such person is in a "black," or impure and unhealthy state; he is either afflicted by an ancesstral spirit in punishment of his own or of his kin-group's transgressions or is under attack by witchcraft or sorcery. In other words, the *musong'u* had been mystically intensified and is

now associated with other malignant agencies.

7. *Mukala* or *Kaluwi*, see above, p. 293.

8. See my *Schiam and Continuity* (1957, 292-303), for a discussion of this class of rites.

9. A character sketch of Muchona appears above in "Muchona the Hornet, Interpreter of Religion," pp. 131-151, and his interpreations from a considererbale part of *Ndembu Divination* (1961).

10. A funerary association which performs elaborate initiation rites on the death of its members. Among the Northern Lunda, or Luunda, it appears to have been connected with circumcision; but among the Ndembu, and other Southern Lunda and culturally similar tribes as the Luvale, Chokwe, and Luchazi, the circumcision rites, called *Mukanda*, are performed independently of *Mung'ong'i*.

11. Used as a symbol during the rite accompanying circumcision and explained in terms of the foundation myth of *Mukanda*. For a fuller accounts, see above, pp. 219-220.

12. Ndembu say "*waheta mukishi*," "you have a spirit," when they wish to indicate possession by a spirit. Often, too, they speak of a spirit which "catches" (*wakwata*) a patinet.

13. To lean upright is *Ku-kunjika*.

14. This term is also applied to the fermentation of beer.

15. This root is also used as a female aphrodisic for the same reason—"to heat desire."

16. He learned the properties and use of the tree as a therapy for elephantiasis from another doctor.

17. According to White (1961, 38) the Luvale cognate term *chisako* "denotes anything afflicting a person, be it illness, bad luck or failure such as lack of success in hunting, or a troublesome spirit."

18. For its use in divination, see Turner (1961, 73).

19. See H. Baumann's views (1935, 104-105) on the solar concept of death and resurrecion among the Chokwe.

20. The traditional homeland of the Ndembu in the Katanga.

21. As many investigation have pointed out, it is the theoretical basis which demarcates primitive from Western medicine most

clearly. It is possible that *chikoli* ash contains an ingredient that objectively reduces headache, but the ash is not used for this reason; curative medicins are epiphenomena of mystical beliefs, not the results of scientific experiment.

22. White (1961, 47) says *Mahamba* may originally have been earth-spirits which later became syncretized with ancestral spirits and now appear as the culturally standardized mode of manifestation—in terms of illness and ill luck—of the latter.

* *The Forest of Symbols: Aspects of Ndembu Rituals* by Victor Turner, 1967

Chapter-8

Processes for the Articulation of Meaning and Ritual Healing among the Northern Yaka (Zaïre)*

By René Devisch

Chapter-8

More and more studies in cultural anthropology are being directed towards the problems of symbolism: what it is, what we are to understand by special symbolic phenomena and how we are to go about studying it.

Both R. FIRTH (1973) and N. D. MUNN(1973) have given their own personal critical reviews of the different directions the study of symbolism has taken. V. TURNER's so-called cryptological approach to ritual symbolism and C. LEVI-STRAUSS' structural analysis approach have recently been criticized by D. SPERBER (1974; 1975) for their lack of relevance in studying the meaning of ritual symbolism.

Taking into account the results of the research already mentioned, I will attempt to give a personal approach which I will call semiological. This approach concerns the processes by which the significance of ritual symbols is brought about and comes to light, i.e., its "articulation".

I will be making an analysis of certain aspects of the ritual therapeutic institution known as *khita* among the Yaka population of Northern Kwaango in the Bandundu Region of the Republic of Zaire. This institution concerns the origin, the transmission and the ritual treatment of gynaecological disorders (sterility, menstrual anomalies, miscarriage and a high mortality rate among children born of the same mother)[1] and constitutional anomalies which affect the mother as much as they do twins, dwarves, albinos and deformed children.

In this present anthropological study, I will try to show how far my approach compares with and differs from conventional semiological approaches. Semiology in the Saussurean tradition is the science that studies the life of signs within society, and considers those signs as systems of communication, i. e. a language, and also as elements which give significance to meaning.

I will show how far my approach results from a partial transposition in the filed of rites—of concepts in linguistic analysis and semiotics[2] in particular.

The results of recent semiotic analyses have led me away from the concept of the single symbol as the basic unit of analysis in favour of the whole process of articulation involved in a complete unit of meaning such as a sentence. The study of rites and more specifically the analysis of the metaphoric and metonymic articulations of meaning have made it possible to redefine the specific characteristics of the process of the ritual articulation of symbolic meaning and to rethink the question of the effect of symbolism in healing rites.

The extent of the relevance of this semiological approach can be judged through a brief examination of D. SPERBER's critical work on "Rethinking Symbolism".

1. Elements in the social organization of the Northern Yaka

This study only concerns a small number[3] of the rural and traditional Yala population in Northern Kwaango[4].

The Yaka inhabit a region of sparsely wooded steppe and tree covered savannah situated on sandy plateaux. The river-valleys are covered by dense forest. Aside from their political and common ritual activities, their time is taken up with hunting are game. And yet hunting is still very clearly a male occupation which is very highly valued by the community; a good catch can be a sign of prosperity, whereas the opposite might indicate that all is not well within the community. The work of the women is confined to the house and to the field.

In order to study the ritual *khita* institution, it is important to describe the basic principles of the kinship system. In fact, it is in a kinship or alliance context that the *khita* anomalies appear. Ritual intervention also implicates the reorganization of those kin or alliance relations.

The kin relationships among the Northern Yaka link up each member of the patrilineage on the father's side as well as each member of the matrilineage on the mother's side by consanguineal ties. The privileged descent is patrilineal traced from one male ancestor to his descendants through the male line. This descent includes in particular the passing on of the name of the lineage, of some collective privileges or rights and of some professional or ritual skills acquired through inheritance. A patrilineage is divided into non-residential maximal lineage segments, into minor lineage segments, which are residential groups headed by an elder; finally, a minimal lineage segment consists of a man, his sons and their wives which represents the smallest cooperative.

On his mother's side, and individual finds himself caught up in a matrilineal network or "kindred" (*yikhanda* or *yingudi*) which goes back at least three generations. The individual has a special relationship with the elders who represent the three ascendant in-law groups: the elder brother (primary or classificatory brother) of this individual's mother, the elder brother of her mother and the elder brother of the matrilateral grandmother of the individual's mother or the man who represents him through patrilineal descent. Those eldest brothers have an "uncle-function" for the individual or are his "male mother" or *ngudyakhasi* (term of address). Those matrilineal avuncular relations are seen as a tree: the individual is related to his first or primary uncle or *leemba dyamathaandu* (term of reference, literally "upper uncle"), to his great uncle or *leemba dyamakati* (lit. "intermediate uncle"), who represents the eldest brother of his mother's mother and to his great-great uncle or *leemba dyamasina* (lit. "uncle at the root") who represents the eldest brother of his matrilateral great-grandmother.

People are individualized in their patrilineal descent groups by their matrilineal relations; in this way, semi-siblings and classificatory brothers are distinguished by their respective mothers. It will be shown later how the "avuncular role" or *buleemba* has an important existential significance. Indeed, an individual is related to his mother's brother, to his mother's mothers brother and to the brother of his matrilateral great-grandmother, who all represent for him the origin of life itself and the line down which all "hereditary" influence has been passed into him.

It is the primary uncle who fills the avuncular role by intervening in crises (death, marriage, birth) and misfortune (illness, ill luck, etc.) in the life of his sister's children. Afterwards, he informs the other uncles and shares the reward offered for services rendered. The great uncle assumes the avuncular role if the primary uncle neglects his duties or abuses his power by taking the life of one of the people under his protection. In cases of matrilineal "heredity" such as a gynaecological disorder, only the great-great uncle is able to intervene by means of ritual in the matrilineal transmission of those disorders.

Marriage is patrilocal. At the age of 35, a man generally acquires or inherits a second wife. Extended polygyny is a privilege enjoyed only by the political head of the group.

The last invaders to settle in the Kwaango region were the Luunda who set up a political hierarchy similar to the one in the Luunda State of Mwaantayaaf of Koola (in the Shaba Region)[5]. Seniority is mainly based on age and on the degree of proximity of the individual to his patrilineal ancestors. Only senior citizens are allowed to make decisions involving the group, to establish norms and to see people respect those norms, imposing sanctions if necessary and to control the exchange of rare commodities as well as the produce from hunting the agriculture. Duties requiring special skills are performed solely by the elders.

2. Towards a pertinent approach to ritual symbolism

As a result of my experiences "in the field", I took a special interest in the study of rites, more specifically their significance, i. e. the relationship beween the elements of a single rite and of those elements to the elements of other rites, and to other activities and to other institutions or organizations and to collective representations.

My experience has taught me the importance of rites to the Northern Yaka in the carrying on of tradition and of the established norms. It has also become apparent that rites and especially ritual institutions have the particular function of articulating or expressing meanings relating to facts or events which challenge the established order and which concern individuals on the fringe of the community,or who are in the process of losing their previous status within that community. Amongst the ritual institutions—about twenty in all—*khita* is the one which involves the greatest number of people and which represents structurally the other ritual institutions.

Khita firstly involves finding out the origin and the matrilineal transmission of gynecological and constitutional disorders which are seen as the result of transgressions by matrilineal ascendants of the victim of such a disorder. Secondly Rhita also concerns the root of the disorder which physically and socially affects a particular individual. Thirdly ,it concerns the process of ritual intervention which has the effect of reintegrating the individual affected by a khita disorder by reorganizing the group and thereby curing the individual of that affliction.

Challenged by the unknown nature of the ritual activities I had witnessed and being very careful to approach the subject with an open mind, I began to look at the problem from the following partially different angles: from the point of view of the vocabulary used during the rites, of the exegesis given by the ritual officers, by the skilled informants and by the participants in the rite; of the "semantic categorization" ("decoupage semantique") particularly in the way vocabulary used in the rite and the exegesis lexicalize, i.e. provide divisions and ategories of meaning. I looked to,the interaction of the participants, of their gestures, of the objects involved and the whole human and phenomenal environment of the rite, as well as their method of preparation and of establishing the causes of the disorder or of the disease[6].

After having witnessed several of these rites and having adopted several different viewpoints on the subject, there were still a few problems left hanging in the air: how to understand the internal organization of a complex rite and its development, and how it is linked with the etiological interpretation of the disorder in question, the nature of its relations to other levels of social life, and how to understand the effect of symbolism in the healing process.

This specific approach to the articulation of meaning was developed over a long period of participant observation of those rites. I will first mention other approaches which seem to lack validity as they do not seem to understand the process of articulation of meaning, namely the functional approach, the substantial a approach—which studies religious experience seen in terms of expressive or religious versus instrumental or magical attitudes—, the psychological approach of the "sens vecu", or of meaningful states of consciousness. On the other hand, I find TURNER's approach (1972:48-58) very enlightening. Its validity however is questionable in the light of certain speculative statements, which are non-anthropological in nature,which appear in his explanation of the process of articulation of meaning and of how all the participants similarly interpret the symbols.

Using a semiological approach, I finally found a relevant way to study the ritual articulation of meaning. It is not the semiology of social sings as systems of communication, but the semiology of sings which give significance to meaning I have used in my study of the khita rites.

3. Semiological approach

The semiological approach, as I already said, is based on a partial transposition of concepts in structural linguistics.

Here are the fields of linguistics I have employed in my study. Linguistics has been developed as the general science of language, of now meaning only comes about at the moment of its articulation. Since we can use different words for the same thing and use the same word for different things, a word is not intrinsically tied to one meaning, nor is it able to describe one thing. In linguistics, meaning only comes about through the articulation of signs put in a specific relationship one to the other. Identifying the meaning of a sentence consists in identifying intuitively the relationship between each of its elements. This articulation of meaning consists in establishing "signifier" ("signifiant") -"signified" ("signifie") -relationships. The "signifier" gives substance to the "signified" in the sense that a "signified" effect comes about or is produced. "Signifiers" only give substance to "signifieds" by their opposition to and their link with adjacent "signifiers". The "signified" is the other face of the "signifier" whose expression and meaning are interdependable, i.e. expression and meaning of the latter being totally dependant on the former. The relationship between the "signifier" and "signified" can be described not so much as a distinction between a form and a meaning slotted into it, but rather as a connection which is continually produced in the sign by the articulation of meaning during the course of the sentence. Phonological analysis concerns the study of the different stages in the process of this articulation of meaning. Phonology has developed models for the analysis of the double articulation of language, notably as much in the articulation of minimal units of meaning (morphemes), as in the relevant or differential elements (phonemes) which go to make them up. this linguistic model gains in complexity through the principle of the double axis or the two-dimensional structure of language. The relationship which bring together these linguistic elements are based either on substitutions and selections on a paradigmatic plane, or on connections on a syntagmatic plane. Moreover the basic process of articulation is studied today more on the level of a whole sentence or a "text" through semiotic or "semanalytic" approaches[7] done by KRISTEVA (1969) and other linguists[8].

I would like to elaborate further my approach which I have called semiological by mentioning briefly some semiological studies in the field of social science such as those carried out by C. LEVI-STRAUSS and R. BARTHES. This brief account will show how my approach is based on a similar approach to recent linguistic and semiotic analysis of the meaning of words, sentences and "texts" from the viewpoint of their articulation or production of meaning. The problem is to find out whether the articulation of meaning in a rite can be seen as similar to the articulation of meaning in a "text" and under which conditions the transposition of the linguistic model is a valid one. Finally, I will show in what ways my definitions of metaphoric and metonymic forms of the articulation of meaning are different from those established by JAKOBSON (1963:43-67) by associating the paradigmatic and syntagmatic on the one hand with the metaphoric and metonymic on the other.

3.1. The semiological approaches of Levi-Strautss and Barthes

The semiological approaches of LEVI-STRAUTSS and BARTHES to the analysis of systems of signs within society, i. e. a language, follows the Saussurean tradition. Looking at his work as a whole, it appears that LEVI-STRAUTSS did not succeed in his semiological approach to the study of systems of communication (1958:399, 404). In one way, his semiological study of the systems of social as systems of communication, i.e. a language, did not achieve its aim. It was only in the elementary structure of kinship that he almost succeeded in discovering double articulation, a fundamental characteristic of human language. He did not succeed in identifying a second articulation either in totemic classificatory systems, rites, myths or in exchange systems, that is to say to isolate the relevant differential traits which go to make up their units of meaning. Because he did not succeed in identifying the second articulation, this invalidates any consideration of this system of signs as a system of communication, i.e. a language[9]. LEVI-STRAUSS links the notions of flow ("circulation"), exchange and communication of words, commodities, services rendered, and women (e.g. 1958:95, 326 f.) because they have analogous functions. However, he was unable to find a successful method of analysis that could be used similarly in the study of these associations, neither did he discover a similar structure behind those associated phenomena. On the other hand, if you consider the semiological approach as a science of significance, then LEVI-STRAUTSS failed here too in some way because he did not succeed in discovering the process by which the internal organization of systems which have meaning is brought about, i.e. he did not succeed in finding out how the significance of signs and symbols comes to light. He defines the symbolic unit as a potential sign, capable of making a link between one "signifier" and another. To the structuralist, sense is formal meaning arising solely from the structure of its expression or from the structure of its "signifiers".

In his "elements de Semiologie" (1964), R. BARTHES discussed the conditions in which a linguistic model might be used for the study of non-linguistic systems of meaning. In his study of the system of fashion promoted through descriptions, BARTHERS (1967) pays most attention to the structure of articulation of the "signifier" -component in significant units of the system of clothes-design. This kind of analysis can be termed "semiotic[10].

Does this application of a linguistic model imply what SAPIR and WHORF said about the influence of lexical and grammatical structure of language on men in their relationships and in their relationship with their environment? However, my approach, although also termed semiological, implies only the transposition of a few linguistic concepts. Moreover, this approach will deal in particular with the study of the semantic categorization in the field of khita and with the internal organization of the activities involved in, and the relations between the participants of a khita rite. So, in my analysis of ritual symbolism, I uphold the concept that the human, interhuman and phenomenal environment is fashioned after the way people speak about it and interact and work in it. This concept takes up a position in the question of the basic difference between the approach to ritual symbolism adopted by MONICA WILSON and that adopted by VICTOR TURNER. This concept does claim to complement, from a different angle the specifically cognitive approach to symbolism taken up by D. SPERBER (1974).

In fact, the ritual texts, the exegesis and the commentaries that the ritual officers, the skilled informants and the participants give in connection with the rite do not fully cover the rite as a whole. what is said in fact is a development of the rite rather than a clarification of meaning. Besides, what is said does not always give a full account of what is done, as is the case of the contextual meaning which emerges from the positions and the relations of the participants in the rite. For example[11], in the sequence preceding the confinement of the woman affected by a gynecological or constitutional disorder, the *khita* rites bring together again the representatives of the alliance: the wife, her uncle and sometimes, her father, her husband and occasionally his father. It is also through the meaning inherent in the context of the sequences, the gestures and the objects appertaining to the rite, that representative of the alliance succeed in creating a meaning of renewed fertility for the patient which is the "ration d'etre" of the alliance.

We know, for example, that what is said does not fully cover the latent function of ritual activities which help to integrate individuals moved out to the fringe of society or to get round or conceal a deeper conflicts, as in the ihamba rite among the Ndembu (cf. TURNER 1968:128-197). Moreover, all that is said in commentaries and exegesis hides more or less latent, unclarified meaning which is articulated only through the process of transmutation of "signifiers". These "signifiers" are taken from semantic contexts different from the ones in which they are called to be actualized, in an unexpected way, so that the "signified" appears only as a result of the whole process. As will be shown later, this process of transmutation of "signifiers" is comparable to the process of metaphorical articulation of meaning. In the part of the khita rite just mentioned, the renewed fertility or fertilization appears as a "signified" established by the articulation of meaning. This "signified" is not brought about by connections the "signifiers" had with "signifieds" in other semantic contexts.

The distinction between metonymic and metaphoric forms of articulation of meaning-in the field of ritual analysis-seems to cast new light on the problem of this disparity of meaning or of the differences between exegesis, contextual sense and meaning articulated by transmutation of "signifiers". As I will show after giving them a definition, metonym and metaphor seen as analytical concepts make it possible to solve several of the problem with which this approach is faced.

3.2. Metaphor and metonym

Here, I will show the way in which concepts of metonymic and metaphoric forms of articulation of meaning have been elaborated.

It was R. JAKOBSON whom, in his study of the problem of aphasia (1963:43-67), became the first to attempt to transpose the model of the double axis of linguistic articulation into one showing how significance comes about in non-linguistic contexts and by doing so, thus enlarged the field of linguistics to include semiology. Here are the main characteristics of this linguistic articulation shown on a double axis.

(a) The *syntagmatic* plane corresponds to a continuous development of speech. It is through a connection of successive units that elements of meaning become articulate: those elements are linked with preceding and following elements of the same level, "in praesentia", by dint of differential and referential ties. JAKOBSON considers that the metonymic process of articulation is brought about and appears on the level of predicative or syntagmatic articulation. This methonymic process can be considered as a characteristic of the so-called magic by contagion for example.

(*b*) *The Paradigmatic* associative or systematic plane treats language as a system. This articulation is set up through selection within categories of elements which evoke each other and which are interchangeable by dint of their mutual similarity. Those correlates from virtual mnemonic series or categories existing through memory association of which only a few see the light of day during the process of articulation. In other words, the paradigmatic relations link actually occurring elements with elements "in absentia" which might have been actualized in their place. JAKOBSON sees the building up of *metaphoric* articulation in relation to the paradigmatic articulation axis. He also claims that this kind of articulation is a characteristic of the process of homeopathic magical activities based on imitation or similarity between the symbolic act and its intended result.

Those two planes are very closely related: the elements of the vertical paradigmatic axis have significance when they are put in syntagmatic, linear juxtaposition. This means that a sentence is only meaningful through the syntagmatic articulation of the elements which go to make up its meaning (as e. g. "he makes a journey", "he travels", "by car", by bus".).

However, the trans-linguistic application of this model initiated by JAKOBSON, still leaves us with an important methodological problem, namely how to identify the minimal units of meaning or the minimal significant units in the ritual articulation of meaning. At this stage in our study, it seems only possibly to identify some units of meaning and these only within the specific context in which they are used. So, analytically, an element whose meaning is affected by splitting the "signifier"— component, can be seen as a significant unit of meaning. It is however almost impossible to identify these minimal units of meaning-units from the first articulation—but it would be even less possible, should the chance ever occur, to find out the pertinent or differential traits—from the second articulation-making up those minimal units.

Because the linguistic model of double articulation is not applicable to the field of rites, several methodological consequences arise. Firstly, the impossibility of identifying the ritual unit off meaning by its composition means that this unit cannot be taken as a basic unit of analysis such as a linguistic sign identifiable by its "signifier-signified" relationship. Therefore, the term "ritual *element* of meaning" here is to be used in preference to "ritual *unit* of meaning". Secondly, unable to start studying basic units—such as signs in a language—, attention must be given instead to the process of linear evolution or the building up of meaning itself. This approach will later by put forward in opposition to some of JAKOBSON's statements, in which we can find evidence of some metaphorical forms of articulation of meaning at the level of syntagmatic articulation.

I would again like to point out that my definitions of metonymic and metaphoric forms of articulation are analytical ones which will be elaborated here only in connection with the study for rites. The process of *metaphoric* articulation seen in progress is of a paradigmatic order. In this process of articulation some "signifiers" are substituted for others, but the new semantic context resulting from this substitution, differs from the individuals semantic fields from which the elements are taken. For example, in one of Moustaki's songs, the metaphoric expression "drink bitterness" takes on a new specific meaning which results from the bringing together of two terms taken from two separate semantic fields which are different from each other and from the new meaning created. The meaning which comes to light through this articulation is not directly determined by the semantic fields from which the "signifiers" have been taken, i.e. by the semantic fields. The effect of meaning can only be perceived on the syntagmatic or linear level of articulation : it is in the same process that this effect of meaning comes about or reveals itself. The metaphoric articulation of meaning is a semantic innovation which includes the transposition or transmutation of "signifiers" from their conventional semantic field to a new or unconventional one. The relationship of those "signifiers" to their original or conventional "signifieds" —has· no little influence on those "signifiers" in their new role in an unusual semantic context set up by the metaphoric articulation although those original relationships have no further bearing on the new effect of meaning. e. g. although "drink" might be conventionally lined with "a bitter drink" and influence the metaphoric expression "drink bitterness", the metaphoric effect of meaning does not result in any way from this original link, but from a semantic transmutation of the original links. The more real this semantic transmutation is, the more it loses its semantic connections to the conventional semantic field, and the clearer a new or metaphoric appears through the process of articulation, i.e. a meaning which is structurally new. In other words, the links between "signifiers" and "signifieds" in other semantic contexts do not set up this new meaning, neither are they linked by copresence or by superimposition and neither do they hide behind the new meaning. In an entirely metaphoric articulation of meaning, the new meaning replaces another which did not exist before, in any from whatsoever[12]. Moreover, it is the "signifier"—component which predominates in a metaphor.

The *metonymic* articulation of meaning can be seen to function paradig matically and is created as a result of the substitution or superimposition of "signifiers". Semantic ties, i.e. relations which are seen as significant links like those existing between a cause and its effect, a part and its whole, a container and its contents, a phenomenon and its spatial or temporal surroundings, etc., are based on replacements or substitutions of "signifiers' The effect of meaning results from our combined or syntagmatic perception of the "signifiers", together with the ones they replace, the one's hidden behind or virtually connected with them. The connections those "signifiers" had with "signifieds", in other or in original semantic contexts, underlay these new links. Because of the fact that those connections had already been established when this new articulation appeared those former connections not only outline the character of the new articulation, but they also partially make up or help to make up the new meaning. These original connections are the metonymic "referents" or paradigms associated with the elements of meaning that go to make up a metonym. The metonymic articulation of meaning does not involve real semantic transmutation; it is the "signified"—component which predominates in a metonym, and which points out the way in order to identify the former connections or "referents". In the following example of a matonymic expression, it can be clearly seen how the elements still retain some of their original meaning: "time flashes past" means that the years pass by at the speed of light. Commentaries and exegesis are almost predominantly metonymic approaches of the phenomena under examination, and only rarely metaphoric. In this way, some "signifiers" in a rite are identifiable through the connections with "signifieds" they could have had in other semantic contexts. In addition, one predominant "signified" points out the way to identify certain "signifiers" by paying attention to some of their partial characteristics. Therefore popular exegesis and commentaries, popular etiological interpretations of a disorder or a disease, and superficial initiation or transmission of ritual knowledge colour the meaning already articulated with sentiments and beliefs calling this meaning into an almost palpable and autonomous existence filling the subject of this articulation with life. That is to say that the meaning undergoes a reification or sacralization, and resembles what is known as fetichism. Anything potentially symbolic or metaphoric in "signifiers" is limited to having one specific connection with "signifieds" in former semantic contexts as a result of this process of reification or sacralization. As such, a rite loses its symbolic or metaphoric role and is virtually taken over by supernatural or extrahuman forces which can be brought to life, through the process of metonymic articulation of an effect of meaning. For example, an act of aggression against a kinsman, although symbolically represented, in real life takes on a menacing appearance of extrahuman proportions.

To summarize, the approach, I have termed semiological, concerns the study of the processes involved in the ritual articulation of meaning either in metaphoric or metonymic form; those processes are interpreted according to each of the different levels where we find meaning undergoing a process of articulation. Those levels concern:

1. the whole process by which the sense of a ritual intervention emerges from an etiological examination of a disorder removing the causes of this disorder and filling up the gaps revealed by the etiological inquiry;
2. the meaning built up through the vocabulary used during the rites and also through the exegesis in accordance with the different categories of informants present[13];
3. the context formed by each of the sequences of the rite, or by the specific relationship which exist between those sequences, the context formed by the relationships between each of the participants in the rite, by their social positions, by their gestures, by the various intervening objects, as well

as the whole human and phenomenal environment existing within the rite.

This semiological approach differs from formal structuralist semiology, it being essentially a study of the way social signs seen as system of communication are built up.

4. Some aspects of the significance of therapeutic rites in the *khita* institution

The semiological analysis of the articulation of meaning at each of its different levels in the ritual *khita* institution brings to light a set of meanings of which it will be only possible here to point out some of the aspects.

The therapeutic *khita* rites are called upon to intervene in question of a social or physical nature, in the gynaecological or constitutional disorders themselves, in fact. The social aspect of the problem concerns the patient's role of procreation in the context of alliance. The disorder confuses the pattern of positions and relations in which the patient and her relatives are involved. The constitutional anomalies also have a social character, in that the deformed individual—before the ritual intervention—is moved out to the fringe of the community and so has to take up an almost subhuman position. And yet this present study only concerns gynaecological disorder, whose etiological examination and ritual intervention, formally, differ little from those of a constitutional disorder.

In order to study better the effect of ritual intervention and the process by which meaning comes to light, it is first necessary to point out the link between ritual intervention and social definitions of a disorder.

4.1. Social definitions of a gynaecological disorder

The definitions which sum up the social aspects represented by a gynecological disorder are established by studying the reactions of the people involved when threatened with the disorder, and then by the reactions of the representatives of the matrimonial alliance, and by the content of the divinatory oracle.

By noticing who intervene when a gynaecological disorder appears and the way in which he intervenes, it becomes clear that the meaning attributed to the disorder is based on the meaning attributed to fertility in the context of the alliance.

Through alliance, the original kin group of the wife gives up the latter to the husband and to his kin group for the purpose of procreation. When the young wife fails to become pregnant after the period arranged or when other anomalies of a similar nature appear, first of all the husband and his father examine the question of the bridewealth, that is to say the setting up of the alliance which is now in a state of compromise. The husband or his father or occasionally the husband's mother give bouquets of herbs to the young wife: to represent the bringing of bad luck upon the disorder, she is invited to take potions made from these plants which are to be administered anally. Then, in turn, the father of the wife and the uncle, more carefully still, intervene ritually to bring bad luck upon the hereditary disorders[14] which might be affecting the wife.

The wife suffering from this problem of infertility is placed somewhat on the fringe of her alliance group or her wider residential group. The strange habit of often returning to her family of origin to stay and the nick-names they give her are testimonies of her having been moved away from her group.

When the disorder gives no sign of clearing up or starts becoming serious, she is handed over to the diviner for examination. The divinatory oracles give some explanation of the problem by establishing the social origins of the disorder. The nature of the ritual intervention will depend on what is told in the oracle.

A comparative analysis of twenty-five oracles dealing with gyanecological or constitutional disorders has shown how the etiological interpretation given by the divinatory oracles sees the problem from three different angles.

(a) The first approach deals with the supposition that "life" (*m-mooyi*) is transmitted through the mother and is a result of the matrimonial alliances. It is the mothers' eldest brother who is chiefly responsible for the life of the children of his sister's marriage: he is the "male mother" or "uncle" of those children. As has been said already, this responsibility for the transmission of life through the maternal line sometimes involves at least three generations linking the matrilineal descendance of the great-great uncle to the children of this man's sisters, or linking the matrilineal déscendance of the great-great uncle to a woman and to the children of this woman's daughters and of her sister's daughters. Certain rights and privileges have the aim of protecting the transmitted life from dying out, and can take the form of "prohibitions" (*n-taiku* or *tauku*) transmitted also through the maternal line[15]. The uncle is equally responsible for the transmission and the safeguarding of these prohibitions.

(b) The second approach deals with those cases, in the matrilineal ascendance, where those rights have been ignored, that is to say in cases where the rule to prohibition has been broken or has been transgressed. According to divinatory etiology, any abuse of rights calls for a sanction which has been brought about by a victim of such an abuse. In defense of the abuse hurled at him, the wronged person retaliates by chanting a "conventional curse" (*n-sasu*), calling for the appropriate sanction to be brought into force. The step from abuse to sanction is a purely metaphorical one, which tansmutes a neutral fact into one which is highly valued from an ethical or a penal point of view[16]. And yet when the actual disorder is submitted to the divinatory oracle for attention, this oracle regards a recent transgression in the same light and looks on it as analogous with a previous transgression from the past whose reparation has been demanded by the wronged person. In fact, the oracle looks at the actual disorder as being the reason why it affected only this particular individual, as if it came about after a recent act of misbehaviour, similar to an abuse of rights which his brought about a sanction in the distant past. Because of an obvious similarity between the disorders, the origins a are likewise regarded as being similar. In other words, a sanction of a reparation once evoked threatens to become a reality for any matrilineal descendant of the first offender, guilty of a misdemeanour. In fact, it is the similarity of meaning between the disorder in the distant past and that in the present which links the past to the present. And yet the oracle always puts the previous disorder and the reparation called for by it back into the past as the third or even the fourth ascendant matrilineal generation. This curse still weighs upon the matrilineal descendants and bears witness to the way the society's rules are still protected from abuse by this self-perpetuating system of reparation.

To summarize, we can say that life, rights and prohibitions together with the effect of the sanctions brought about by the curses, are all transmitted along the same matrilineal line. Often the oracle and especially the popular interpretations of it, sees the victim as being possessed by "a force" behind the transmission.

(c) The third approach deals with ritual institutions. Indeed, the different curses and different disorders which occur in the same matrilineal line, form an "institution" (*phoongu*) of the curse and of the reparation called for. The same institutions also deal with ways of intervening within this transmission. It is through reparation of the wrong, or of this abuse of an individual's rights and through ritual intervention of those who have responsibility for the matrilineal transmission of the individual's life, of his rights as well as his prohibitions, that the curse can be broken and its effect removed. There exist as many ritual therapeutic institutions (*phoongu*) as types of curse and types of affects. They number about twenty among the Northern Yaka. Of those institutions, *khita* as I have already mentioned, involves the greatest number of participants of patients. Ritual institutions are transmitted along the same matrilineal line as prohibitions and sanctions. The Northern Yaka refer to such a matrilineal transmission as a "hereditary transmission", called *yibutu-kulu*. In concrete terms, characteristic anomalies such as a twin, an albino, a dwarf and deformities, as well as all kinds of somatic and mental anomalies and disorders, caused by sanctions called for in a ritual institution, can also be passed on by this kind of matrilineal heredity.

Bearing these etiological principles in mind, I will show how the meaning of a gynaecological disorder is brought to light during the early interventions which combat the threat of a possible disorder and by the divinatory oracle.

Firstly, the present gynaecological disorder is seen above all as a state of social disorganization. This latter is seen in turn as arising from an abuse of rights and determines the position the woman has is her kin group and in relation to her in-laws. The present disorganization is understood to have been brought about through an analogy with a similar situation in the past involving the matrilineal ascendance, notably a disorganization resulting from a transgression of rights. This transgression is threatened with sanction and each of the matrilineal descendants belonging to the same line as the originator of the curse is open to its influence. Secondly, the disorder can be pointed out in the way people pay attention to the woman who is on the fringe of the community. Finally, they see the disorder as somatic, and not as being specifically organic and not in terms of genetic inheritance.

The nature of the ritual intervention depends on how the oracle has interpreted the origin of the disorder. Are we to suppose that because the etiology exists on three levels, that the ritual intervention will be carried out also on three levels, namely on the level of the family, of the residential group and on one physically affecting the patient?

4.2. Ritual *khita* intervention

In order to analyse a ritual intervention dealing with a gynaecological disorder, we have to understand in which way the disorder is considered as a social problem, and how they manage to point out its origin. By analysis, the distinction between the articulation of meaning in a predominant metaphoric form and a predominant metonymic form, will be of great heuristic value.

The ritual intervention has the effect of neutralizing the

origin of the disorder or getting to the root of the disorder in order to create conditions for successful fertilization which echoes the way in which the social disorder has been pointed out. On the level of interaction, we see how the main representatives of the alliance compromised by the disorder—the wife, her uncle and occasionally her father, her husband and sometimes the head of his family—,assemble again, and together with the ritual officer, become the protagonists of the ritual intervention for certain of the principal scenes during the performance. These are first the scenes of ritual compensation for the wrong committed in the distant past which calls for reparation in the form of a disorder each time a matrilineal descendant misbehaves in similar way. The scene of the removal of the curse follows, and then the scene which concentrates on the ritualization of the fertilization, i.e. where fertilization becomes the central figure. During the same process by which the alliance is restored, the woman is ritually led to go through the motions of fertilization and is reintegrated into the whole network of positions and kin relations which were thrown out by the disorder.

If we interpret this whole ritual operation in terms of a process of articulation of meaning, it is seen how transmutation of meaning converts "signifiers" of a past and present social disorganization into "signifiers" of a restored social network where renewed fertilization takes up a central position. This transmutation of meaning in ritual interaction echoes the levels of interpretation set up by the divinatory oracle: the matrilineal transmission and the curse become the levers for the transmutation of meaning, i.e. which help to pass on the meaning or to link the meaning of the past disorder, the present disorder and its reparation.

The healing effect of ritual intervention can be calculated by looking at the distinction between the two forms of articulation of meaning we have established. So, we can ask if a *khita* rite consists in "inducing" a new state of fertilization: this means that the wife is confronted with "signifiers" of fertilization which substitute metonymically the "signifiers" of the disorder. In other words, this means that the ritual treatment consists in repairing the wrong which was the origin of the disorder in order to get to the root of the disorder and to signify the different stage in the fertilization process, and so represent its coming into effect on a physical level. Or can we assume that the ritual operation is a predominantly metaphoric one and that the "signifiers" of the successful fertilization come to light in such a way that this ritual articulation of meaning comes about in spite of any similarity or analogy between the "signifiers" which are replaced and those which replace them? We have to consider if the representatives of the alliance are actually involved in the ritual process, not only to come together to renew the alliance for purposes of procreation, but also to bring about the renewal of this alliance in the same process by which the woman is symbolically made fertile.

The reply to these assumptions is as complex as is the *khita* rite itself, and we will only be able in this study to point out a few aspect of a single part of the whole process of articulation of meaning and then only to show the heuristic value of our form of analysis.

The part to be analyzed deals with the renewal of alliance relations in so far as they signify successful fertilization and lead the woman to take up her role child-bearer in the alliance. Before coming to the question of the exegetic, contextual, metaphoric and metonymic forms of articulation of meaning, I will outline the main aspects of the rite and to place it in the wider context of the sequence preceding the patient's confinement.

The ritual intervention deals in the main with the confinement of the patient or the medium within the house in which the rite takes place. The latter was built on the edge of the village generally near to the patient's uncle's house. On the night which heralds the start of the period of confinement, the husband or the head of his family brings gifts to the medium's uncle. These gifts—12 to 20 yds of rough white cloth—are symbolic compensation for the wrong suffered by the matrilineal ascendant, this wrong having demanded reparation in all other similar cases. The uncle takes up again the matrilineal ties with the patient for which he is responsible, lifts, the curse, and offers her gifts as compensation for the wrong caused by the gynaecological disorder. The "signifiers" of the disorder are transmuted metaphorically into "signifiers" of healing as a result of the whole ritual process and the way in which the participants come to assume their special role.

After this renewal of matrilineal ties, now seen as the line along which life, and no longer the curse passed on, is transmitted, the patient is handed over to the care of the ritual officer. In the context of the ritual institution, as ritual officer, he assumes the role of uncle to the patient. He curses anyone who might wish to harm the patient or prevent her from being cured. The medium then comes to take up her new role of child-bearer within the alliance. There follow some descriptions of this rite in progress.

The husband places one end of the trunk of a "parasol tree" (*n-seenga*: Musanga cecropioides, Moraceae) on his shoulder, the other end facing the entrance to the house in which the rite takes place; he then raises the trunk until it comes to rest on the roof of the house. The medium then hangs from the trunk by her arms, wrapping her legs around the part of the trunk supported by her husband, her head remaining close to the entrance. The patient's uncle and the ritual officer stand one on either side of her, and rock her from side to side.

The popular exegesis and that of the ritual officers explain the significance of this moment in the rite: "the wife hangs from the tree like a bat so that she may be restored to health."

In their representations of an "insectivorous bat" (*ngeembu*), the Yaka manage to capture its ambivalent nature: it is described as a "small bird-like mammal" (*phuku mubununi*). As the bat hangs upside down from the branch, they say it takes in food at the place where man passes it out, and vice versa. The bat is well-known as a nocturnal animal which moves and eats at night. The fact that only offspring results from each pregnancy makes it in this respect almost human. The bat is "forbidden fruit" to those initiated in the local ritual institutions, to young people becoming adults, and to pregnant women.

In this ritual context, the bat's ambivalent nature is used as a metonymic "signifier" of the transition of one state of life to another. Also the ability of the bat to remain hanging by means of the nails on its ten toes is in itself a metonymic "signifier" of a powerful liaison between the individual and what has been given to him. In this context, the way the powerful liaison between the patient and her cure becomes articulated, is brought out through analogy to other contexts or through the exegesis given concerning the bat's nails. As in other initiation rites, this moment of hanging from the parasol tree trunk corresponds to a similar moment in other initiation rites where the medium, prior to confinement, physically emerges from the group to become the central figure of the rite, emphasizing the nature of her disorder. Attention is brought upon her in order to reinstate her into the group this time as a person who suffers from a disorder which is no longer a reason to move her out to the fringe of society.

Only through the chanting and the way the participants come to assume their specific role, and only as the rite intensifies and becomes more complex, is the wife led to assume her child-bearing role and be reinstated in the alliance. The uncle and the husband actively participate in the rite, this being the husband's first appearance in the performance, and they both act out the reinstatement of the woman in the alliance. This interpretation of the rite in terms of procreation "signifiers" concentrates on the contexts or the structure of the rite; to my knowledge, it makes no reference to any specific exegesis given at this level of general interpretation. By looking at the ritual process in terms of its context and its structure, we arrive at the following interpretation of the significance of the parasol tree in the *khita* rite. The parasol tree is the first to grow in the fertile soil of fallow land and reaches its full size in three years; it can easily multiply and easily transplanted. The yellowish "bract" or the "grog-blossom" (*phwan-seenga*) sprouts leaves which form umbrella-shaped clusters; the trunk bears no branches. Here is a chant which accompanies the rocking of the woman as she hangs from the free.

Yeezeemba Kumbatyatsoombu	I am hanging from the
ye mebuundi elele.	palm whichhas one nut
	with little pulp and one rich in pulp[17]

It is possible to assume that the trunk of the parasol tree formerly signified fertilization, and because of the position taken up by the woman and of her husband's presence also formerly signified the male organ. This would mean that the rite metonymically represents a replacement of the conjugal act based on a similarity between its "signifiers".

What evidence have we to support the validity of this interpretation not found in any exegesis?

Is it then reasonable to suppose that the articulation of meaning is based on a similarity between "signifieds", or that the woman, by hanging from the parasol tree is having intercourse with her husband, which implies that the fertility of the tree represents the fertilization of the woman? But this replacement is neither given by any exegesis nor based on any former semantic connections capable of bringing about the replacement. The fertility of the parasol tree in itself has no actual former connection with human fertilization; why should this rite be interpreted only in terms of a metonymic articulation of meaning and why should we suppose this rite substitutes one reality for another by replacing the "signifier" of a desired fertilization by something which is by nature manifestly fertile? Is it not possible to see the rite as a process of generating meaning and of articulating meaning in a predominantly metaphoric way? In other words the rite brings meaning to light which did not exist before in any from whatsoever. Could it not be that because the rite signifies fertilization that the tree becomes in that specific context a "signifier" of fertility and that the position taken up by the woman signifies her desire to become fertile? It is not because the parasol tree has any striking characteristics of fertility that the rite signifies fertilization or that it comes about through the ritual process itself, no doubt retaining some link with the example of abundant fertility given by the parasol tree which still appears as a "signifier" component in the rite. Fertilization can then be seen as the only "signified" of several different "signifiers", such as "parasol tree", "woman hanging from the tree", "husband bearing the tree", "the presence of the uncle", "the palm tree in the chant", which are brought together to make up the rite.

It is impossible to see fertilization in terms of the effect of meaning brought about by the ritual process and to understand this process as being founded on similarities between the fertility of the parasol tree and the new significance its fertility assumes in the context of the rite, or indeed to see these similarities as existing before the rite. Why have we to assume that links between "signifiers" and "signifieds" still existed before the rite or outside the context of the rite? If the rite specifically chose the parasol tree to signify the male member, we can no longer talk in terms of symbols, but only in terms of signs and the situation appears thus as totally embarrassing and undignified for the woman. The more the articulation of meaning brings a meaning to light which only comes about through this process itself, the more this articulation is a predominantly metaphoric form, the more impossible it is to define this meaning in specific terms. Moreover, it is impossible to define this meaning in specific terms. Moreover, it is impossible to define the "signified" of a specific "signifier" in a metaphoric articulation of meaning; the metaphoric "signifier" establishes a totally new connection with its "signified". This connection is not based, structurally speaking, on other connections in former semantic contexts.

We come to understand the ritual meaning of fertilization through the analysis of the metaphoric articulation of meaning and of the way matrimonial or alliance relations are established and "signifiers" of fertilization are introduced into this ritual sequence which fits into the wider context of the whole ritual drama. Indeed, after the rite of rocking from the parasol tree, there follows another rite which transmutes "signifiers" of the disorder into "signifiers" of healing. And afterwards, the woman is led into the house of the rite to being her period of confinement. Then the trunk of the parasol tree is again planted at the entrance. Further analysis bring to light that the confinement is the "signifier" of the foetus waiting to be born; the house of the rite being the womb and the entrance to the house of the rite being a metonymic "signifier" of the entrance to the vagina. During this period of confinement, most of the attention is concentrated on therapeutical intervention, on a physical level. The introductions of herb-based potions into the anus are also frequent during this period. Everything being capable of being a "signifier" of a constitutional or gynecological disorder i.e. abortion, albino, dwarf, deformity, is treated in such a way that it comes to signify the opposite. In other words the cause of the deformity now becomes the victim of his own wrongdoing; i.e. witch might find himself on the receiving end of his own spell. The process of being released from confinement involves the reintegration of the patient in her group and in its social activities, and she assumes her status following her initation or her return to fertility.

The main question which arises from this analysis is that of the therapeutic effect of this intervention. The incidence of successful pregnancies following a *khita* intervention is not sufficient evidence to constitute a satisfactory answer to the question which is of a ritual of symbolic nature. It is in terms of the metaphoric or metonymic forms of articulation of meaning that we arrive at the question of the therapeutic effect of ritual intervention. Can we assume then that the therapeutic effect on the woman is brought about through the metaphoric or generating process of articulation of meaning of through the fact that this meaning is structurally new and leads to renewed fertility by transmuting "signifiers" of; the disorder? This question becomes all the more significant as the woman is the principal figure along with her husband and her uncle, and her involvement in the ritual process is so intense that she falls into a state of trance. In order to go deeper into the question of the physical effect of the rite on the patient, a multi-disciplinary approach is needed[18].

5. Hidden meaning and ritual articulation of meaning

This semiological approach is not only valuable for heuristic purposes in the study of ritual articulation of meaning, or in understanding the healing process in these rites. This approach also shows in which way ritual articulation of meaning can be said to be symbolic when we study meaning at the point of its articulation, at the point where it is brought out hiding. Its relevance to the study of symbolism validates the semiological approach, which goes a long way to answering D. Sperbers's question on the hidden meaning in symbolism and on the semiological approach itself.

Adopting some aspects of linguistic philosophy,Sperbers (1974; 1975) brings to light the autonomous, implicit and unconscious cognitive mechanism involved in symbolism, articulating conceptual representations. As the author says, these conceptual representations might be seen as forming an innate mental equipment that makes experience possible; they are stored in our memory, they are not yet relevant descriptions or understandings of things, acts or utterances, neither do they represent "reality" nor do they stand for something else (1974: 10-11, 16-46,119-125; XI-XII, 4-34, 107-113).

The semiological approaches which Sperbers questions, follow the Saussurean tradition by defining a linguistic sing as a paired unit of a "signifier" and a "signified". The conception[19] of a unique relationship between "signifier" and "signified" leads to the mis-conception of a similar or fixed relationship within a symbolic unit. The "signifier" is taken as the explicit part of the implicit "signified" or of a hidden meaning.

Sperber (1974:63-96; 1975:51-84) shows how Levi-Strauss' analysis of rite and myth, although it claims to deal with semiology as an approach, only point out the structure and transformation of ritual and mythical forms. On the other hand, Turner and Freud who made no attempt at the analysis of symbols using linguistic concepts, nevertheless developed different kinds to semiological approach. Concerning TURNER's approach to the study to the study of ritual symbolism, SPERBERS claims (1974:24-45; 1975:12-34) that the exegetical meaning and the operational meaning of the rite are to be considered not as an explanation of its meaning, but as an extension of it. In other words, interpretation resulting from an exegesis or from the ritual operation have to be taken symbolically and not literally. According to SPERBERS (1974:58-62, 94-97; 1975:47-50, 83-85), it is impossible to come to the real meaning of the symbolic phenomena through an interpretation of them, because it is impossible to define the connections between the "signifier" and the "signified" within the symbol and thus a symbol can no longer be understood as a constitutive unit of meaning. It implies that if symbols have anything to do with meaning at all, that this meaning would not be articulated in the same way as it would be through signs. On the one hand the author claims that the conceptual representations which go to make up meaning by the use of *sings* can be identified through the "encyclopaedic references" to the "world" and analyzed in terms of links within semantic categories. On the other hand, SPERBERS argues that *symbolic* activity comes about through conceptual representations which are as incomplete and inadequate as they are irrelevant and incapable of being analyzed in terms of references to the "world" or of links within semantic categories (1974:97f; 1975:85f.).

I contend that criticisms leveled at the semiological approach of LEVI-STRAUSS and TURNER have nor real bearing on this present study. This means, I did not use the dual concept of a sign as a paired unit as a basis of analysis for symbols. I made a distinction between symbols and signs. Not the sign but the ritual operation has been taken a the unit of analysis. I looked at symbolism and meaning brought to light by symbols in terms of a generating process, and not in terms of meaning through already established signs. This generating process precedes its representation in exegesis, in ritúal vocabulary, in commentaries, etc. In trying to fully understand the specific characteristics of ritual symbolism, the linguistic concepts of metonym and metaphor opened the way to an understanding of articulation of meaning in its metonymic and metaphoric form,. as well as to a definition of the specific characteristics of the symbol. The *symbol* is an agent which generates meaning through its articulation brought about before the distinction between "signifier" and "signified" is made, which is however one of the principal characteristics of a sign. However, infrequently used, the area of meaning of a symbol can be reduced to express single standardized association of meaning: the "signified" becomes predominant and the symbol takes on the main characteristics of a sign. In the same process, a symbol generates meaning and brings it to light. However, as soon as we define a symbol in terms of its meaning, it is preferable to use the term "signifier of" to the term "symbol". The more the articulation of meaning is predominantly metaphoric, the more the articulation is brought about through the transmutation of the structure of the elements and the more truly symbolic the meaning is. This means that this process of articulation of meaning is brought about through the interaction of participants, their gestures and of the intervening objects involved in such a way that the woman afflicted by a gynecological disorder is reintegrated in her alliance and in her residential group and reinstated in her role of child-bearer and that she is surrounded again by a propitious human and phenomenal environment. This effect of meaning which comes to light can be understood as the result of the transmutation of the semantic links "signifiers" of gynecological disorder and of fertility had in former semantic contexts.

By analyzing this process of articulation of meaning, we arrive at an understanding of some fundamental elements of symbolism or how symbols come about prior to an explanation of their meaning. To a certain degree, SPERBER deals with these cognitive aspects of symbolism and goes someway to defining them in terms of conceptual representations. On the other hand, a symbolic or ritual articulation of meaning seen as a process which generates meaning and brings it to light before this meaning is conceptually represented constitutes an approach which is fully distinguishable from a cognitive one. The present approach, which I have called semiological, analyses symbolism at the point preceding the distinction between a sign and its associated meaning, an idea and its conceptual representation, between what can be represented and its expression.

6. Summary

In order to study how meaning comes to light during rites and to understand the therapeutic effects on the participants in healing rites, certain, linguistic concepts helped me to build up my own approach which I have termed semiological.

Taking into account the attempts of R. Jakobson, C. Levi-Strauss and R. Barthes in using linguistic concepts in their approaches to non-verbal systems of signs i.e. a language, and what recent semiotics have to say of the generating process of meaning at the level of sentence or of a "text", following concepts have been devised for the study of ritual symbolism. The articulation of meaning in a predominant *metaphoric* form gives significance-which is predominantly symbolic-to meaning by bringing together alien significant elements; removed from their usual semantic context, those elements take on a new form and thus create a new meaning. Ant yet the articulation of meaning in a predominantly *metonymic* form achieves a new effect of meaning which it combines alien significant elements in a way pointed out by previous significant connections, which the significant elements might have had in former semantic contexts.

Those and other concepts are proving useful and of great heuristic value for the study of the ritual *khita* institution among the Northern Yaka in Kwaango Region (Republic of Zaire). This institution concerns the origin, the transmission and the ritual treatment of gynecological and constitutional disease or disorders. This present approach emphasizes the process of how the *khita* rites carry on by building up the etiology of the disorder, reintegrating the woman afflicted by a gynaecological disorder into the alliance as a child-bearer and into her residential group and bringing her back into her normal living environment.

This approach to the articulation of meaning reveals the

generating process at the point preceding the distinction between what can be represented and its expression, and also puts forward an analysis of symbolism which throws a different light on the subject already treated in other ways by TURNER and SPERBER.

BIBLIOGRAPHY

BARTHES,R.

[2]1970 Mythologies. (Coll. Points.) Paris: Seuil. [1975]

[2]1971 Elements de semiologie. In: Le degre zero de I' ecriture. Paris: Ed. Gonthier [1964] 77-176.

1967 Systeme de la mode. Paris: Seuil.

BEIR, L. DE

1975a Religion et magie des Bayaka. (Collectanea Instituti Anthropos, 4.) St. Angustin: Anthropose-Institut.

1975b Les Bayaka de M'Nene N'toombo Lenge-lenge. (Collectanea Instituti Anthropose, 5.) St. Augustin: Anthropos-Institut.

CARONTIN, E. et D. PERAYA

1975 Le projet semiotique. Paris: Editions Universitaires.

CORIN, E. et G. BIBEAU

1975 De la forme culturelle au vecu des troubles psychiques en Afrique. Propositions methodogiques pour une etude interculturelle du champ des maladies mentales. *Africa* 45/3: 280-315.

FIRTH, R.

1973 Symbols, Public and Private. London: George Allen & Unwin Ltd.

GREIMAS A.-J.

1966 Semantique structurale. Recharche de methode. (Coll. Langue et Langage.) Paris: Librairie Larousse.

1970 Du sens. Essais semiotiques. Paris: Seuil.

1976 Semiotique et sciences sociales: Paris: Seuil.

JAKOBSON, R.

1963 Essais de linguistique generale. Paris: Ed. de Minuit.

KRISTEVA, J.

1969 Semiotika, recherches pour une semanalyse. Paris: Seuil.

LEVI-STRAUSS, C.

1958 Anthropologie structurale. Paris: Plon.

LYONS, J.

1973 Structuralsim and Linguistics. In: D. ROBEY [edit.], Structuralsim: An Introduction. Oxford: Clarendon Press: 5-19.

MARTINET, A.

1965 La linguistique synchronique. (Coll. "Le Linguists".) Paris: P.U.F.

MUNN, N.D.
1973 Symbolism in a Ritual Context. Aspects of Symbolic Action. In: J.J. HONIGMANN [edit.], Handbook of Social and Cultural Anthropology. Chicago: Rand McNally and Company: 569-612.

PLANCQUAERT, M.
1932 Les Jaga et les Bayaka du Kwango; Contribution historico-ethnographique. Bruxelles: Institut Colonial Belge.
1971 Les Yaka. Essai d'histoire. (Annales du Musee Royal de I'Afrique Centrale, Sc. hum. 71.) Tervuren.

RICCEUR, P.
1975 La metaphore vive. Paris:Seuil.

ROOSEN'S, E.
1963 Monde yaka et developpement economique communautaire. *Cahiers economiques et sociaux* 1/5-6: 5-23.
1971 Socio-culturele verandering in Midden-afrika. Een geval-studie: de Yaka van Kwaango. (Studia Anthropologica.) Antwerpen: Standaard Weteschappelijke uitgeverij.

SPERBER, D.
1974 Le symbolisme en general. (Coll. Savoir.) Pairs:Hermann.
1975 Rethinking Symbolism. (Cambridge Studies in Social Anthrology.) Cambridge: Cambridge University Press. [Translation of: 1974. Le symbolisme en general.]

TURNER, V.W.
1968 The Drums of Affliction; A Study of Religious Processes among the Ndembu of Zambia. London: Clarendon Press.
1972 The Forest of Symbols: Aspects of Ndembu Ritual. (Conrell Paperbacks.)
[1967] Ithaca; Conrell University Press.

UCO, U.
1973 Social Life as a sign System. In: D. ROBEY [edit.], Structuralsim: an Introduction. Oxford: Clarendon Press: 57-72.

REFERENCES

1. From this viewpoint, an analogy an be drawn between the ritual *khita* institution and the *nkula* institution among the Ndembu described by V. TURNER (1968:52-88).

2. However the term "semiotics" covers several slightly different approaches, here it refers to the type of linguistic approach that studies the conditions under which and the way in which meaning comes to light. These types of approach follow two main traditions;

the first points out how the primary articulation of the minimal units of meaning in a specific language comes about; the second deals with the study of the process by which a "text" or a "speech" produces or builds up its own meaning (e.g. see GREIMAS 1970).

3. Anthropological fieldwork was carried out from January 1972 until May 1973 and from January 1974 until October 1974, principally by participant observation, among the Yaka population in the rural and traditional group or group of Yitaanda settlements. This group of settlements has a population of about 1500 people living in 13 village or settlements and headed by chief Taanda. Chief Taanda is himself a subordinate of N-Saka and N-Nene who are each heads of an important region; N-Saka is a "vassal" of *kyaambvu* from Kasongwa Luunda and N-Nene is a junior classificatory brother of the *kyaambvu*; this latter heads the political and traditional hierarchy in the Kwaango region. The Yitaanda group is situated in the South-West corner of the administrative partition, called "Zone de Kenge" , in the Bandundu Region.

4. We became aware of the Yaka population of Middle Kwaango and their culture as a result of studies carried out by E. ROOSENS (1963; 1971) who passed on the results of the anthropological field research he had carried out in the Middle Kwaango and among the Yaka who had migrated from the area to Kinshasa, from 1962 until 1965. Unique ethnohistorical data concerning Upper and Middle Kwaango is a result of the wok of M. PLANCQUAEAT (1932; 1971). The ethnographical data concerning the field of magic, witchcraft and religion was gathered by L.DE BEIR in Northern Kwaango from 1939 until 1945 and has recently been published (1975a;b). Anthropos 72.1977

5. The history of the successive waves of immigration migration in the Kwaango region still being investigated, and the existence of-called people of the substratum and of historically distinct strata dividing the indigenous population is by no means confirmed. Dealing with this hypothesis, M. PLANCQUAEAT (1971) divides up the history of the Yaka population by making extrapolations from data mainly concerning lineage segment names and devices.

6. During the course of my field research, I witnessed eighteen cases of ritual *khita* treatments within the Yitaanda group of settlements. In four cases. I witnessed almost all the confine-

ment rites and once the funeral rites of a twin. Additional information was supplied to me by twelve ritual officers of the *khita* institution, some of them belonging to neighboring settlement groups. Twenty-five out of more than two hundred divinatory oracles that I studies, deal with a gynaecological or a constitution disorder and of these, twenty-one concern the *khita* institution.

7. KRISTEVA gave a psychoanalytical approach to his concept of "semanalysis" ("semanalyse"). This concept refers to the study of a language ("langue") seen as a self-generating phenomenon which gives significance to meaning, and it has to be considered on the level of a "text".

8. Recent accounts of semiotic studies have been given for example, by E. CARONTINI and D.PERAYA (1975) and by J. LYONS and U.UCO in a work edited by D.ROBEY (1973).

9. A. MARTINET (1965: Chap. I) studies the second articulation or the articulation of the relevant differential traits which are meaningless by themselves as criteria in order to define human language. According to this definition, any significant system lacking this second articulation should not be considered as a "language". Other concepts of language might have grounds for justification, but these will have adopted another approach away from the semiological concept of language, and from the Saussurean tradition.

10. It was an abuse of terms to call BARATHES' older studies, collected in "Mythologies" (1957) "semiological". In these studies, the links between linguistic concepts put forward for analysis, and the way he carries out his analyses as well as the conclusions he draw, are obscure. The models and concepts for semiotic analysis worked out by GREIMAS (1966; 1970) are many and varied. His approaches to the study of unite of meaning, sequences and "dramatis personae" in tales and narrative accounts, and the way he tried to put these models into practice in the field of social communications and legal language (1976) could possibly be very useful for the study of ritual forms in the articulation of meaning.

11. This outline will be amplified in paragraph 4.2.

12. After having dealt with the problem of how a metaphoric sentence can be reduced to its simplest elements and how it differs from these elements, P. RICCEUR (1975: 221-272) considers metaphor

as the semantic "process" or as the "generating" process that excels all others. It will be remembered that this study is an inquiry into how significance gives light to meaning in order to examine how meaning comes about by itself, namely before meaning is conceptualized, or given an interpretation by comparison with an analogous situation. As will be shown, the process of articulation of meaning in rites, as a generating activity can be seen a metaphorical form or articulation; interpretation, exegesis, commentaries are predominantly metonymic forms of articulation of meaning.

13. The differences in exegesis according to the categories of informants can be shown as having two opposite tendencies. The more skilled or talented the informant is, after undergoing a process of ritual initiation, the more his information livens up the metaphoric processes in the rite by translating them or expresing them by means of other metaphors. On the other hand, the outsider or the uninitiated, easily transformed the symbolic elements into living things like "forces" or sources of extrahuman power.

14. The Yaka concept of hereditary transmission will be explained in paragraph 4.1.c.

15. Among the Northern Yaka, the major prohibitions consist of those which forbid stealing, "bewitching" and damaging in any way the ability of a woman to become fertile, in so far as those acts can be judged harmful or illicit by the elders of the community.

16. A separate study will deal with the wide area of chanting, cursing and sanction among the Northern Yaka.

17. *Tsaamba* or *mbati* is the palm famous for its oil (Elaeisguineensis, Palmae): one variety (var. tenera) bears nuts which have small core and a thick fleshy cover of pulp; another variety (var.dura) has a larger core and a thin fleshy cover of pulp. In some therapeutic rites for sterile men, this palm, famous also for the wine made from its fermented whitish sap which is tapped from the male inflorescence and collected in a calabash, appears as a metonymic "signifier" of the penis. Anthropos 72,1977

18. This approach is taken up by E. Corin and G. Bibeau (1975) when they outlined the way to carry out an interdisciplinary-anthropological, ethnopsychological and ethnopsychiatric—study, in an urban African, of the way in which psychic disorders experienced

by the patient as such and also defined by the group as such and what they are attributed to, and how interventions are carried out or what form interventions should take.

19. Attention must be drawn to the fact that SPERBER levels his criticism at a type of semiological approach which has partially been abandoned. He does not take into account the fact that the linguistic model used for the study of systems of signs in his approach, which follows the Saussurean tradition, has been invalidated. As already said, post-Saussurean semiotics are taking the "signifier" and "signified" components of signs as elements which fit together to give shape to meaning, and are inquiring into how meaning comes about as a generating process, and are treating it on the level of a whole. "speech" or "text" and no longer on the level of a sign.

---

* *Anthropos* 1977. vol. 72

Chapter-9

The Ancestors and Illness among the Zulu

By Harriet Ngubane

Chapter-9

Before looking into the activities of the ancestors, I want to consider the other "Beings" in the "Other world" and inquire to what extent they come into the picture of health and disease Zulu say that in the beginning there was *uNomkuhbulwane* (the first Being). At some point there was also *uNomkubhulwane* or *Inkosazane* (the Princes). At another, a reed growing on a river bank burgeoned and gave birth to a man. (No mention is made of a woman in relation to that man.) The people multiplied. *uMvelingangi* sent a chameleon (*unwabu)* to tell them that "they will not die". After some time *uMvelingangi* sent a lizard (*intulo*) to tell them that "they will die." The lizard overtook the chameleon, which had stopped on the way to feed on *ubukhwebezane*, wild mauve berries. When the chameleon at last arrived with the message that "people will not die," they refused to accept it, and decided to stick to the message already delivered by the lizard (*Sibambelentulo).* Meanwhile the *Inkosazane* promoted every fertility of the land, the people and the animals. Ideally every year in spring certain rites should be performed by married women and maidens to ensure good crops, more cattle and more healthy babies. These rites are directed to *inkosazane*. *uMvelingangi* is approached only in situations of catastrophe or impending disaster such as extreme drought, in which case both men and women participate. Although *uMvelingangi* is thought of as living "above" and does not normally affect the health or the life of an individual in day-to-day situations, there is nevertheless "mystical force" which is closely associated with him, as we shall see in the next chapter.

In considering the relationship between people and their ancestral spirits, I shall begin by relating briefly four cases of Illness associated with the ancestors.

Case 1 Thuli, who belonged to the Phewa lineage, was made pregnant by a man who was not prepared to marry her, but only paid damages (i.e. an ox for Thuli's father, a cow for her mother, a goat for girls of her age group, another goat to cleanse them of defilement, and £5 as a fine to the chief for committing a wrong in the community). After the baby's birth, Thuli's father slaughtered a goat *(imbeleko)* to thank the ancestors for the safe delivery, and also to ask them to protect the baby (a boy named Mandla). The baby was in this way adopted by Thuli's parents. He grew up calling them "father" and "mother" and regarding Thuli as a sister. Thuli later go married to someone else. Mandla grew up and in due course also married. Soon after wards he established his own home and took his genitor's name, Mvubu. This he did against the advice of all his relatives,who pointed out that one does not simply change a name without implicating the ancestors in the process. he soon experienced misfortunes. Hisfirst child died. His second child, a boy of 8 years, suffers from a disease that makes him unable to use his lower limbs; he is partially paralysed and spends most of the time as a patient in hospital,Mandla himself after 9 years of marriage became ill with swollen feet, and died early in 1970 at the age of 32. His illness was said to be a result of harmful substances smeared on the tools he used at work. Although he is believed to have died of sorcery, his death and his child's illness are associated with the lack of ancestral protection. His mother (his genitrix) concluding the account said: "Mandla was stubborn unto death. If he had heeded our advice he would still be alive."

Case 2 MaDladla was married in May 1968. Her parents had performed the nubility rites *(ukwemula)* for her two elder sisters before they married. But in her case the rites were not performed,as her father had suffered a financial set back and his cattle had diminished in number. After two years of marriage she had not yet conceived. her husband went to a diviner to ascertain the cause. He was told that MaDladla's ancestors were annoyed by the omission of the nubility rites,and when she got married, came along with her, and their presence around her created a "heaviness" *(bayesinda)* which stopped her from conceiving.

This was reported to MaDladla's father, who arranged to fetch the ancestors from his daughter's affinal home. He slaughtered a goat to propitiate the ancestors for the commission.he took the gallbladder of the goat and an old stick that had been used by his late father. He also provided himself with a green branch of *umlahlankosi* (a tre whose branches are used to place on a chief's grave). With these three objects he went to his daughter's affinal home, went to her own hut, told the ancestors that he had come to fetch them and lightly struck the thatch with the stick. He sprinkled the gall on the *umlahlankosi* branch, all the time addressing his ancestors. He then pulled the branch behind him while returning home. On arriving, he entered the main hut and placed the branch, the stick and the gall bladder at the upper part of the hut *(umsamo)* where the sacrificial goat's meat was hanging.

Later MaDladla was invited by her parents to come home, and a goat known as *eyezinkobe,* which usually replaces the elaborate nubility rites, was sacrificed to enable her to conceive by fulfilling the fertility rites demanded by her ancestors.

Case 3 Gwala, whose wife had given birth to twins, a boy and a girl, consulted a diviner because of the suddenillness of the baby boy The diviner said that the baby was sick because Gwala's ancestors were angry and had withheld their protection of the baby. She emphasized that it was not the baby's maternal ancestors who were angry, as they were satisfied with that procedure that had been followed concerning them. Gwala, who had not scarified to his ancestors when his wife came to his family, had sacrificed only when the twins were born. The baby was ill because the ancestors were asking Gwala who the mother of the twins was. The diviner stressed that the medicines she was giving him to cure the illness would have no effect unless Gwala made peace with the ancestors by admitting guilt and promising to put matters right as soon as he possibly could.

The following is Gwala's background story. He was the eldest son and head of his family,a s his father had died. His mother had a stroke and was paralysed. When this happened he was already half way with his marriage payments. Since there was o adult female in the house to nurse his mother, the girls's family was persuaded to allow her to live at this home while he collected enough money to cover the final wedding arrangements. The girl's father appreciated the difficult situation in which Gwala found himself and agreed. But before she left home, her father sacrificed and reported to the ancestors the circumstances surrounding her departure. This is what the diviner meant when she emphasized that the baby's maternal ancestors were satisfied because they had been given the respect which they considered their due. Gwala had missed out on this when he failed to report the circumstances surrounding the arrival of his future wife before the wedding ceremony.

Case 4 This case is concerned with a difficult birth. The woman in labour had her own home, near that of her parents. Her mother-in-law, who lived a distance way, had come to be with her during her delivery. When she was in labour her chief midwives were her mother-in-law and her own mother. When the labour became protracted, there was concern for the lives of both mother and baby. At this point the two chief midwives armed themselves with sticks, went outside the hut, and beat the thatched roof with the sticks, calling upon the ancestral midwives to do their duty: "Do you want this baby to die?Why are you sitting there doing nothing?" The ancestral midwives so addressed were said to be the paternal grandmother of the confined woman and of her husband. After the baby had been born, two house lizards *(izibankwa)* showed their heads between the mud wall and the thatched roof. One of the midwives in the house said, "there they are, look at them, now they are rejoicing and are looking at the baby". The ancestral midwives were believed to have materialized as house lizards.

To understand the thought patterns behind these cases it is necessary to look into how the ancestral cult operates.

There are many words to denote the dead. *Amathongo* is a collective term for all the departed spirits. *Izithutha* means in particular spirits that have materialized as snakes or house lizards. (Usually male ancestors materialize as snakes, while female ancestors, particularly old women, materialize as hose lizards.) *Izithunzi (isithunzi,* sing.) means "shadows." A shadow is believed to depart from the body when a person dies. A dead body is believed to cast no shadow. A shadow in this sense can be seen as synonymous with a soul, in that it is believed to depart from the body in the form of the body, although invisible. A dead person is initially an *isithunzi* until a sacrifice is performed after a period of mourning. The sacrifice intergrates him with the body of the ancestors and also brings him back home as an *idlozi. Amadlozi (idlozi,* sing.) are the ancestral spirits responsible for protecting or disciplining the descendants. The term refers in particular to the spirits with jural powers over the descendants. *Abaphasi* mans simply those who are down below, for the dead are believed to live "down below"—beneath the earth. It is synonymous with *amathongo,* as it refers to all the dead who belong to the family. The terms most commonly used by Nyuswa in everyday speech are *abaphansi* and *amadlozi.*

The ancestors are said to be primarily concerned with the welfare of their descendants. Whengood things of life are realized people say, "The ancestors are with us" *(Abaphansi banathi).* When misfortunes happen they say, "The ancestors are facing away from us" *(Abaphansi basifulathele,),* for the ancestors are believed to withdraw their protection and gifts of good fortune from erring descendants. Without their protection the descendant's become vulnerable to all sorts of misfortune and disease.

People distinguish between ancestors that can punish or reward and ancestors that are powerless to do this. A man's mother, father, father's mother, and father's father are the most important ancestors. His father's brothers are next in importance, as they are believed to share in the sacrifice offered to parents and grandparents. Btu they do not act independently of the latter. These are patristical ancestors to whom a man sacrifices as a homestead head *(umnumzane).*

The non-effective ancestors, who do not punish or reward as they have no jural powers over the living are those three generations or more removed from the homestead head. They nevertheless participate freely as guests of the effective ancestors. They are regarded as having a wide range of descendants, and they are free to be present at sacrifices by any one of them. Although they have no jural rights, such ancestors may possess a diviner, usually not as a leading spirit but as a supporting one. The spirits of people who die as minors, e.g. children and the unmarried, live with their elders in the spirit would and accompany them on sacrificial occasions.

Each child is placed under the protection of the ancestors by a sacrifice of a goat known as *imbeleko (beleka,* vb., to carry on the back. The skin of the goat is usually prepared to be used to wrap the baby on its mother's back). Sometimes the goat is referred to as *eyeziphandla (isiphandla* is the wrist skn-band). This goat provides the first wrist skin-band for the baby. By this sacrifice the ancestors are thanked for, and also requested to protect the baby. It is a form of "baptism" which puts the baby under the protection of a definite range of ancestors. Ideally the *imbelekao* sacrifice is performed as soon as possible,within the first year of the baby's life. It is through an *imbeleko* sacrifice that social parenthood is established. CASE I exemplifies this. mandla was adopted by his mother's parents through an *imbeleko* sacrifice and was given the same range of ancestors as his mother, who then became his sibling. When he got married he decided to change his name and assume that of his geniotor (Mvubu). In doing this he overlooked the importance of the *imbeleko* sacrifice. Mvubu's ancestors did not know him and therefore could not protect him, even if he called upon them when he sacrificed. This could have been rectified if Mvubu in addition to damages had paid anox to get custody of the baby. He would then have put the baby under the protection of his ancestors even though not married to its mother. Mandla as an adult could still have rectified the situation by paying the extra ox to his mother's brother or social brother), as hi smother's father (or social father) was then dead. If his mother's brother accepted the ox, Mandla could then have asked Mvubu to introduce him to the ancestors by an *imbeleko* sacrifice.

Normally the children of a homestead head marry before he dies. When his son's baby has an *imbeleko* sacrifice performed, it is placed under the protection of this grandfather's ancestors, because the grandfather is the homestead head and performs the sacrifice. These ancestors protect the homestead head and all his dependents. When, however, the baby attains the status of sacrificing to the ancestors as a homestead head, he will be sacrificing to his own father and grandfather, his mother and father's mother, people who, under normal conditions, would all have been alive during his infancy and his youth.

A baby is protected in the patristical line by its paternal grand-father's ancestors. The protection it receives from the maternal ancestors is not identical in nature.

A firl's father is responsible for ensuring that her fertility rites are carried out. A married couple's first baby is given an *imbeleko* sacrifice (first sacrifice) by both groups: first by its father's group, and then by its mother's, when she takes it to her own parents, who sacrifice to thank the ancestors for having made their daughter fertile. Later babies are given an *imbeleko* sacrifice by their father's people only, and not also by their mother's. In other words the ancestor of the baby's mother are thanked at the first birth, and not again subsequently, for demonstrating that she is reproductive and had been worthy of marriage.

The baby's maternal ancestors are more interested in its mother, their daughter. But since the baby is the product of he fertility, for which they are responsible, they are also interested in the baby, and can cause harm to demonstrate that they control the mother's fertility. This explains Case 2 where a woman whose nubility rites had not been performed could not conceive.

This case is of particular interest as demonstrating that the maternal ancestor do not only interfere with woman's fertility in order to exert pressure on the affinal group and coerce them into fulfilling matrriage-exchange obligations,but that they also exert such pressure to ensure fulfilment of what is due to them from their own descendants. For how could they be expected to make the woman fertile without have been requited to do so through a sacrifice?

The case also demonstrates that the place of a wife's ancestors is at her parental home, and not at her marital home. There canbe no equal range of ancestors in one home (except in the case of diviners who achieve this by certain sacrifices.

CASE 2 stands in contrast to CASE 3, where the paternal ancestors, angered by their descendants over marriage obligations, manifested their anger through the illness of the bay. The ancestors wanted to know who the mother of the twins was. I must mention here that sperm is likened to the seed sown in a woman's womb. The fruits of the seed belong to the sower.hence, while a woman's ancestors are interested in her as a daughter and in her ability to reproduce, her husband's ancestors are interested in her as their wife and in hat she reproduces as a mother. In this case Gwala had never introduced his wife to his ancestors, but had only presented them with the twins; accordingly they made one of the twins ill, to remind him to observed first things first. How could he expect them to protect the twins when he had failed to place under their protection the womb from which the children came?

CASES3 and 4 highlight the position of a married woman in relation to the ancestors in her life. She stands astride—as a daughter to one group, and as a wife and mother to the other.

As a daughter she takes her first child to be given an *imbeleko* sacrifice by her parents. When she is bereaved by losing either a child or a husband, she is ceremoniously cleansed by her daffiness and then goes home to be cleansed by her own people. If she had contracted an illness before her marriage, she goes home to get it cured when it recurs. If she misbehaves, say by committing adultery, she is sent home to her parents to be taught once again how to behave, and she is expected to return with live goat from them which her affines sacrifice to apearse their ancestors. If her parents (r brothers) slaughter a beast that was given for her *lobolo (amabheka)* she is entitled to a flank *umbhlubulo)* of the meat, which she takes back to share with her affines. (Her son is entitled to this portion if she is no longer alive.) When her daughter's nubility rites are performed, her brother (or there, if still alive) contributes a live goat. this is presented by her husband to his ancestors as a gift front he celebrant's mother's people *(omalume)* to help to promote her fertility. The gall is sprinkled on the girl, and she wears the inflated gal bladder on her head as an indication of her maternal uncle's good wishes. When a youth begins marriage negotiations the ideal negotiator is his mother's brother, who also plays a leading role in the ritual on the wedding day.

As a wife to her husband's people, a woman shares sacrifices with them. She is equally affected by lineage sorcery directed against her husband's group. If she falls ill as a married woman, it is the duty of her affines to gie her the necessary treatment; this may even mean a sacrifice to the ancestors to procure her recovery. As she grows older, she becomes progressively more identified with her affinal group and less with her own people. After her menopause she is not expected to observe the avoidance *(hlonppha)* laws. She may, for instant, pronounce word that are similar to the names of her senior male affines, or even use the names themselves. But the most significant token of her acceptance is that she may eat the special portion of meat (*inanzi*)—the third stomach (*caecum*)—of the sacrificial animal set aside for the ancestors. After her death she is brought back by a sacrifice as a mother, never as a daguther to her own people. By this time the transfer from her group of ancestors to that of her affines is complete.

This leads us to examine the degree of harshness shown by certain ancestors towards their descendants.

Every person who dies has a sacrifice performed after the period of mourning, in order to integrate him with the rest of the ancestors. The deceased is believed to live alone away from the other dead spirits *(amathongo)* and away from home. A person who becomes an effective ancestor, i.e. who has jural rights to punish or reward, is the one who had such jural rights while alive. To such person a sacrifice known as *vkubuyisa* is performed (*buya,* vb., come back; *buying,* bring back). If the deceased was a man a goat and an ox are sacrificed, if a woman a goat suffices, and the sacrifice is not referred to as *unkubuyisa,* calculated to bring the deceased home as such; it is calculated rather to integrate him with the body of the ancestors, in which case he comes home in their company. The ancestors concerned are particularly annoyed if the performance of this sacrifice is overdue. If a parent, he is said to come home in anger and bring choas and a series of misfortunes. Such an ancestor is said to be the harshest. Harshness is not necessarily associated with the sex of the ancestor, but it is associated with the gravity of the wrong.

I must point out here that the ancestors are thought of as withdrawing their protection if they are angered as a group. Without their protection a person is exposed to all dangers. In this sense they are not directly responsible for a death that may be brought about by other factors, because in the absence of their protection a person is vulnerable to sorcery and other environmental dangers as well as being prone to accidents.

Krige writes: "The spirits of old women and infants are often specially invited to come and eat a sacrificial meal, because the spirit of an old woman is supposed to be spiteful and malicious and capable of all sorts of harm, while that of an infant is pure and beneficent" (1950, p. 95). the Nyuswa in reply to this suggestion pointed out that the old woman is usually malicious in the context of an overdue *buyisa* ceremony. As a parent she cane afford to be harsher to her children and even to her husband, but the children's spirits cannot do this outside the context of the ancestors who are their seniors.

The *buyisa* or integration ceremony is closely related to the first sacrifice, the *imbeleko.* The two are held for every person whether young or old, married or single. The *imbeleko* sacrifice identifies him as an individual, gives him a place as a member of a particular lineage, and also puts him under the protection of a sacrifice integrates the spirit with its ancestors and other spirits of the lineage segment, and gives it a right to come home again as a spirit. The most significant point is that if a baby dies before the *imbeleko* sacrifice has been performed it cannot be integrated with the ancestral sprites through an *ukubuyisa* sacrifice. This was forcefully brought home to me by a woman two had lost her twins as infants. The first died soon after brother, and the second seven months later owing to burns. Explaining the because of death she said of the first twin: "It traveled in long journey back to where it came from." (In Zulu this is rendered in one word: *lenda.)* When twins die very young they are said to *end* (travel); this term is reserved for twins only. Usually the death of a twin is not associated with any of the other causes. But when one twin has *end, or endile,* the other is expected to live, particularly if it has outgrown the infancy stage. In this parti ocularly if it has outgrown the infancy stage. In this particular case the twin that lived had not yet been given the e*imbeleko* sacrifice. To explain the cause of death (obviously due in fact to being burned by boiling water), his mother said. He has notbeen given the *imbeleko* goat. His sister who *enda* was lonely and she fetched him so that she would have company. This happened easily because he was not a full person *9wengakabi umuntu,* not yet a person) as he had no *imbeleko."* There was no sacrifice to integrate both twins with their ancestors. I subsequently found that this was a widely held notion. it means that an infant is "made a person" by an *imbeleko* sacrifice, and being a person can then be integrated with the rest of the dead. No explanation is given regarding the whereabouts of those who die before *imbeleko.* It is usually said: "They return where they came from."

This leads to the question: Where are the ancestors supposed to be? I have already mentioned that, as a body of *amalthongo,* they reside "down below", underneath the earth. This is their base, and from, there they come to earth and live as an invisible section of the society.

During sacrifices the paternal ancestors, their guests (i.e. the spirits of the sacrificer's father's brothers and their wives), and the deceased minors of the family, congregate in the main but. This hut belongs to the most senior woman of the group, who may be the widowed mother or the senior wife of the homestead head. It is the hut in which the belongings of the ancestors are kept, goats are sacrificed, and guests are received, and it is generally the center of social life in the homestead. It is usually referred to as the "great hut" (*indlu enkulu*). The upper part of the floor is marked off by an inch-high ridge forming a semicircle known as *umsamo*. No stranger may go beyond the ridge into the burning incense: the beer set aside for ancestors is kept here and the sacrificial meat hangs here overnight—the beer is to be sipped and the meat licked or eaten by the ancestors.

The ancestors are also believed to rest on the rafters. This is well demonstrated by cases 2 and 4. It so further exemplified at divination sessions in cases of diviners possessed by the whistling ancestors (the great ancestors, *amakhosi amalkhulu*). They whistle and converse direct with their clients from the rafters, particularly above the *umsamo* area.

The cattle byre is another place frequented by the ancestors, and sacrifices of oxen are always performed within it.

Besides these particular areas, the ancestors are believed to go about like all other people within the homestead. Outside the sacrifice situation, only the dead who particularly belong to the home are believed to be within. They are also believed to be simultaneously at different places. For instance, a deceased man with many married sons has a *buyisa* ceremony performed by all of them, and is expected to be at each home after each son has performed it. The same notion prevails with regard to possession. While a married diviner is possessed by her ancestors, they are at the same time believed to be at her parental home.

This leads us to examine the different modes of interaction between ancestors and their descendants. The ancestors that possess a diviner are essentially her own paternal ancestors. If her maternal ancestors, such as her mother's after or mother's mother, appear to her at all in dreams, they are usually on the frings. The principal ones are always her paternal ancestors. There are not conceived of as taking possession of her and talking through her; they are though of as sitting on her shoulders and whispering into her ears.

The problem arises when the possessed girl gets married or when she becomes possessed while she is married. There then arises a clash in the range of ancestors within the homestead. To resolve it the husband sacrifices a goat of his ancestors and requests them to allow and diviner's ancestors to operate within the homestead. If this is not done she never divines there.

If the husband wants to from the proceeds of her divination, he shoulders the expense of her tanning as a diviner. (There are a series of goat sacrifices culminating with an ox sacrifice when her training is completed. But is when she marries him she is already a diviner, and had had her expenses paid by her father, she gives her earnings to the latter. To redeem the situation the husband pays her father an ox. I know of one diviner whose husband refused to observe this procedure. She always went back to her come, which was close by, to meet her clients. She gave her earnings to her widowed mother, who was also diviner. The mother reserved the right to dispose of the money as she wished; she occasionally gave it to her daughter as a present. She also provided her daughter with the goats necessary for the constant sacrifices made by diviners. Since sacrifice is a means of establishing closer contact with the ancestors, a diviner sacrifices much more often to promote and maintain her special contact with the ancestral spirits.

Incidentally, this notion also operates in the case of lineage sorcery. If a man destroys all or most of his agnates, the ancestors will focus on him, and their constant presence would put him in the same position as the diviner, in that he would have to sacrifice oftener to recognize their presence. For this reason,v lineage sorcery if practised indiscriminately may boomerang, in that illness may result from the heaviness caused by the excessive spiritual contact. Such heaviness may only be allayed by constant sacrifice.

The question that arises is: Do the ancestors ever show their positive behaviour? To arrive at an answer it is important to look once more at the notion of "balanced" relationships. The world is thought of as basically good with the people an ecology blending together in harmony, and all things being equal the people get the necessary blessings from the ancestors to enable them to maintain the balance in their lives. As long as a man has a relatively successful life, i.e. had gold relations within his family and with his fellow men, and a satisfactory economic situation, he considers himself as enjoying adequate protection and blessings from his ancestors. That is to say the ancestors normally bestow blessings, and withdraw them in exceptional instances only.

The ancestors are thanked from time to time by a sacrifice known as *ukubonga*, thanks giving.

The following is a list of the different types of sacrifices, some of which have already been mentioned, that usually mark definite occasions.

1. *Imbeleko* A goat, which is the first sacrifice offered for a baby and which places it under the protection of lineage ancestors.
2. *Ukubuyisa* A goat and an ox if the deceased was a married man, a goat and a cow if the deceased was a married woman, a goat only if the deceased was a minor. The sacrifices integrate the deceased with the rest of the body of ancestral spirits.
3. *Ukabonga* A goat or an ox, to thank the ancestors for good things of life, e.g. a good win at the races, or a good job, or a generally satisfactory life.
4. *Ukucela izinhkanhla* A goat, to ask for the blessings of the ancestors before undertaking any major or risky, e.g. before going out to major cities to seek employment.
5. *Ukushweleza* A goat, to appease the ancestors if there is evidence that they had been annoyed.

6. *Ukuthetha* A goat sacrificed to "scold" the ancestors if misfortunes continue to happen in spite of all efforts made to put things right.
7. *Ukukhomba inxiwa* A goat to show the ancestors "the new home" if the descendants move house.

These are the usual types of sacrifice which a homested head (*umnumzane*) is likely to have performed during his lifetime.

There are, however, some occasions when a man slaughters a goat or an ox not for purposes of sacrifice but for general feasting.

The question that arises is how does an onlooker decide whether the killing is sacrificial or just for feasting? Since each sacrifice has particular rituals appropriate to its nature, it would not help to suggest that an onlooker should watch out for such rites, excepting one in particular that runs through all sacrifices. This is the use of the gal. The ancestral spirits are said to have a particular liking for the taste of gall. It is therefore always used specifically in order to achieve a special contact with them. It is always sprinkled on, certain people to single them out for spiritual contact. I shall look more closely into the importance and significance of the bile later on.

Of those illness and deaths which are attributed to the anger of the ancestors nearly all are in connection with failure to fulfil marriage obligations. For this reason I am going to give a rather detailed account of the animals killed for wedding purposes, in order to establish the degree of their importance and also to distinguish those killed for sacrifices and those killed as a form of gift exchange. This is the account of animals killed at a traditional wedding I witnessed on the 15the May, 1971.

The progress of marriage arrangements is marked by sacrifices and exchange of gifts. And each sacrifice or gift takes the arrangements a step forward. I shall concern myself only with animals killed as sacrifices or as gifts, and not with the other forms of gifts.

a. The bride's father at his home killed a goat "to accept the negotiator of marriage" (*eyokuvuma umkhongi*). His brother sprinkled the gall on the negotiator's right-hand index finger.

b. On a later occasion, the negotiator with a party from the groom's people brought a variety of gifts for the bride's people. The bulk of the gifts (*izibizo* from *biza*, vb., to name or to call for. In this context he bride's mother lists or names the presents or gifts she wants for herself) were for the bride's mother. On this occasion the bride's father slaughtered a goat to honour the groom's mother. Such a goat is referred to as *uhudo* (*huda,* vb., to suffer from diarrhoea), because of the nursing care the woman gave to her son, the groom, as a baby.

The negotiator presented the bride's mother. Such a goat is referred to as *uhudo (huda,* vb., to suffer from diarrhoea), because of the nursing care the woman gave to her son, the groom, stomach after giving birth to her child.

The negotiator's wife on the same occasion also presented a goat to the bride, to signify that she should dress up he rhair in the special style *(inkehli)* worn by married women.

The bride in turn presented a goat to the negotiator's wife, in appreciation of the latter's gift to her, which marked her new status.

All the goats exchanged on this day were slaughtered and eastern. the groom's people took a portion of their meat back home.

c. Later on the bride and he rage-mates took food gifts (*umbondo)* to the groom's home. Two goats known as *indlakudla* were slaughtered—one for the bride and the other for her companion. The goats enabled both the bride and her bridesmaid[3] to eat the food of the groom's people, which was otherwise taboo to them. The gall of the two goats was sprinkled on the index finger of the bride's companion.

d On a later occasion the groom paid a special ceremonial visit in the company of his age-mates and girls of his locality. A goat was slaughtered to enable him to eat the food of the bride's home. The gall was sprinkled on the negotiator. The goat is known as *indlakudla*.

e. At some other occasion the bride's father performed a nubility ceremony for her . He killed an ox and a goat, as well as another goat from her mother's brother. The gall of the three animals was sprinkled on her, and the gall bladders were inflated and worn on the head by her during the ceremony. When the ceremony was over the inflated bladders were carefully kept to be worn again on her wedding day. The gall bladder of the ox was pierced and worn by her as a wristlet. The ceremony is known as *unkwemula*.

f. A few days before the wedding the bride's father and his brothers went to the groom's home to "see" the *lobolo* cattle before they were transferred to the bride's home. The groom's father slaughtered a goat for the bride's father. The gall was sprinkled on her father's brother. The goat is known as *ilongwe,* i.e. the dry cake of cattle dung.

g. On the eve of the bride's leaving home to be married, her father slaughtered a goat known as *eyokunama. (Ncama,* vb., to eat before commencing a lognjourney). This goat was intended to report her departture to the ancestors, and also to provide her with something to eat during her wedding ceremonies, as she was not supposed to eat any of the meat slaughtered on that occasion.

h. When the bridal party arrived, the groom's people gave them a goat called *eyokucola. (Ukucola* means "to give a feast in honour of the bride.") The gall was sprinkled on her companion, who also wore on her head the inflated baldder.

i. On the first day of the wedding a cow was presented by the groom to the bridal party. It is known as *eyesihlahla,* "the beast of the trees," because during the nearly part of the day the party sat outside the home under a tree where they cooked and ate the meat.

J. On the second day a cow provided by the brid's father to

the groom's mother was slaughtered. The beast is known as *eyezibhoma,* which merely means "chunks" of meat.

k. On the same day the bride's people killed a goat and placed it in a large basin after piercing it to remove the gall, which was sprinkled on her by her father. She carried it unskinned and unopened in the basin, and presented it to her mother-in-law. The latter removed the basin from the bride's head and in return gave her a string of white beads. this action is known as *isethulo,* "to pay tribute, to make a present of respect". The carcase of such a goat is known as *isinyikan yika,* translated by Doke and Vilakazi as "complicated fair, matter difficult of solution, something requiring disentangling."

1. The most important beast of all was also killed on the second day. It was cow known sometimes as *eyesikhumba,* "the beast of the skin", as its skin is used to make a skirt for the bride. Another, more appropriate, name is *eyokwendisa (-enda,* vb., to undertake a long journey), since when a woman marries she is said to *ukwenda,* "to go on a long journey." This beast was —as it the custom—provided by the bride's father. I was slaughtered in the groom's battled byre by the negotiator, who used a special ancestral spear belonging to the groom's people. (He himself was the groom's mother's brother.) the groom's mother sprinkled the gall on the bride's index finger and big toe, and herself wore the pierced and empty gall bladder as a wristlet. There ear several other rituals surrounding this beast, which I cannot recount here. The carcase is bisected, and one half is given to the groom's people, the other being retained by the bride's. It is this beast the is said to "render the woman married."

m. Later in the day, i.e., on the second day, the bride's father went to the negotiator's home, where the groom's father had provided a goat knows as *uthuli lomkhongi,* "the dust of negotiator" (because during the period iof negotkiations he walked to and fro, between the two families). This goat is said to thank both the negotiations to a happy conclusion.

n. On the third day, only the bridge age-mates remained. They were given a goat to kill, skin, cook, and eat to mark the consummation of the marriage. The goat is Known as *umeke,* to split open, i.e. to deflower.

Tabel 1 shows more clearly how these exchanges of animal figts and sacrifices are balanced.

I have mentioned the animals slaughtered in connection with this particular wedding. There may be differences elsewhere, but most of the Nyuswa people thought this wedding illustrated almost the whole range of Zulu wedding rites.

The purpose of listing here the animals killed for the wedding is to demonstrate that they are not always killed for purposes of sacrifice. The basic criterion is the gall. It is significant that only the gall of sacrificial animals from the bride's people was sprinkled on her. (These are numbers 5,6,9,10 in Table. 1.) In other cases where the gall features, such as numbers 1,4,8, it is sprinkled on people who represent a particular group. In each case the animal is provided by one group and the gall is sprinkled on a member of the other. The first group (i.e. the providers of the animal) sprinkle the second group (i.e. the receivers of the animal) with the gall, on order to introduce them to the provider's ancestors. The animals in numbers 2,3,7,11 and 12 are not sacrifices. but just gifts, in which the gall does not feature.

These differences are important for the understanding for changes in the traditional wedding rites. In less elaborate wedding rituals, the animals slaughtered as gifts are fewer in number, and they tend to be converted into currency. The is understandable, because the gifts are subject to exchange. If the first party has not given a gift to start with, the second one has nothing to reciprocate. A good example of this is number 7, the ox, which is a present from the groom to the bridal party, and the cow, which is a present from the bride's father to the groom's mother. In this case, the initiator of the gift is the bride's father, who must indicate the beast that he is presenting. If the groom's family cannot afford a speciāl beast to be given to the bridal party, his mother passes on to him her gift from the bride's father; he then gives it to the brideal party. In other words, for the bridal party to receive this particular gift from the groom the bride's father must have given it first.

Sacrifies given by one group for the other are easily converted to money instead of a slaughtered animal—provided that the recipients are prepared to accept the money. But where the sacrifice is for a member of the group, giving money would be tantamount to giving it to oneself. So, if people are unable to provide the necessary sacrifice, they offer incense to the ancestors, tell them the reasons for omitting the sacrifice, and express willings to put the matter right at some future time.

Vilakazi has this to say:

> Throughout the negotiations, these gifts are anticipated because they are institutinalized, and each gift or goat begets another gift or goat begets another gift or goat. It s not uncommon to find that one of the parties requests that certain gifts should be cut out altogether. the request is often granted because in any case none of the figts are unilateral.

TABLE 1.

The balancing of beasts given for slaughter by the two groups in marriage presentations and sacrifice

	Beasts given by the bride's family	Gift or sacrifice	purpose of slaughter
Killed During the Period of negotiations			
1.	*Imuuma* goat killed for the negotiator on his second visit to the bride's home	Sacrifice	To report to the ancestors of the bride the beginning of marriage negotiations and point out the future affinal relationship represented by the negotiator
2.	*Uhundo* goat slaughtered for the groom's mother on her ceremonial visit to the	Gift	A recognition and appreciation of her period of nursing and bringing up the groom

	bride'shome		
3.	A goat slaughtered for the negotiator's wife who visits the bride's home on the same occasionas in (2) above	Gift	To thank her for her gift of a goat to the bride
4.	*Indlakudla* goat for the groom on the occasion of the occasion of this ceremonial visit to the bride's home	Sacrifice	To enable the groom to eat the food (excepting milk) at food (excepting milk) at the to the bride's home and also tc point him out to the bride's ancestors
5.	*Ukwemula* ox and goat slaughtered for the bride at her home	Sacrifice	The bubility beasts calculated to persuade the ancestors to make the bride reproductive
KIlled During the Wedding as Part of the Ceremony			
6.	Umnecamo goat for the on the eve of her departure	Sacrifice	To report to the ancestors her departure fromher home to that of the affines
7.	*Eyezibhoma* cow from the bride's father to the groom's mother, slaughtered at the groom's home during the wedding ceremony	Gift	To honour the groom'smother
8.			
9.	*Eyesikhumba* ox. The most important beast surrounded by numerous rituals	Sacrifice	To surrender the bride to her affines, unite the two lineages in affinal relationship
10.	*Isinyikanyika* goat given by the bride to her mother-in-law	Sacrifice	To pay respects to the mother-in-law and surrender herself to her as an understudy
11.			
12.			

	Beasts given by the groom's family	Gift or sacrifice	Purpose of slaughter
1.	*Ilongwe* goat slaughtered	Sacrifice	To report to the groom's

	for the bride's father when a few days before the wedding he visits the groom's home to "see" the *lobolo* callte		ancestors the transference of the *lobolo* cattle and also to point out the bride's father who represents the new affinal relationship
2.	*Ubikibiki* goat brought by the groom's people as part of the gifts to the bride's mother ©	Gift	An appreciation of there period of nursing and bringing up the bride
3.	*Eyokukhehla* goat given by the negotiator's wife to the bride	Gift	The goat indicates that the bride should dress up her hair in special way appropriate to married
4.	Two *indlakudla* goats for the bride and her companion on the occasion of their visit to present food gifts to the groom's house (*umbondo)*	Sacrifice	To enable the bride and her companionto eat the food
5.			
6.			
7.	*Eyesihlahla* ox given by the groom to the bridal party slaughtered at the groom's home on the first day o the wedding	Gift	To honour the bridal pary
8.	*Eyekucola* goat slaughtered for the bride and given by the groom	sacrifice	To welcome the bride and report her arrival to the ancestors. It was the first beast killed on the arrival of the bridal party.
9.			
10			
11.	*Uthuli* goat given by the by the groom's faher and the bride's father and slaughtered at the negotiator's home	Gift	To thank both the negotiator and the bride's faher for having carried out negotiations which successfully led to marriage
12.	*Umeke* goat from the groom to the bride's age-mates after the marriage has been consummated	Gift	To mark the end of the bride's virginity and her separation from her age-mates

It may seem peculiar that the leborate wedding rituals seem to be primarily concerned with the bride and her mother-in-law.

The wedding beast is sacrificed to integrate the bride into the ilineage. The mother-in-law wears the gall bladder as a wristlet. Also, she receives the unique tribute of the unopened carcase of a goat. This becomes more understandable if we examine the meanign of the word *enda* used for marriage in Zulu. Literally, it means "to go on a long journey", the journey in this cas ebeing the transference of the bride from her home to the groom's home. The main beast "weds" her *(eyamendisa)* and links her with her groom's people. The link is symbolized by the gall that is sprinkled on her and the gall bladder worn by her mother-in-law. Since it is the bride who is transferred and who is expected to be fertile, it is not surprisign that she is surrounded by many rituals to effect her transfer and her fertility at a mystical level. The groom is said to "take her" *(uyathatha)*, whereas she "travels" to him *(uyenda)*.

The bride and her mother-in-law are the two peopel who have "travelled a long journey" to perpetuate the lineage of their affines. The bride has come to continue where the mother-in-law has stopped; she has come to furthe rth ereproduction. The *isinyikaryika* goat, which the bride presents to her mother-in-law, suggests that she is giving herself as an understudy to the latter, who will orientate her in the routine and practices of the family.

I must also mention her etha ta married woman has the status more of a mother than a wife. In English culture, for instance, if Miss Jones marries Mr. Smith, she becomes Mrs Smith, his wife. In Zulu culture she would become "Mother Jones" (Ma Jones). She retains her clan name, and in this sense she is someone who has come to her affinal lineage to be a mother. It is therefore not surprising that marriage rites are focused on the bride and her mother-in-law. They are the mothers of the lineage, on whom th econtinuity of the lineage is dependent.

Meanwhile I must mention that marriage rituals with regard to their emphasis on motherhood can bring about social maternity.

A good instane is provided by the case of a man who had two

wives. The first wife had three girls only, and the second had a boy and a girl. When the son of second wife got married he used the *lobolo* cattle of the first wife's daughters, on the understanding that his bride would be placed into the house of th efirst wife to perpetuate it (*aveuse indlu,* to raise the house), as she had no boys. Although the family was by now Lutheran, the son married according to traditional Zulu custom (i.e. not according to Christian marriage), in order to be free to take a second wife and place her in his own mother's house. His bride performed all the wedding rites in relation to the first wife as her mother-in-law. She later had seven children, three of whom are boys. Her husband had married three other women, who all belonged to the house of the second wife (his biological mother). But none of them bore him any children. His father and his two "mothers are now dead, and he is the head of the homestead. Whenever he sacrifices for the benefit of his children (for instance, performs an *imbeleko* sacrifice), he calls upon his father and his father's senior wife to protect them, since they belong to her through the marriage rites. But when he sacrifices for his own benefit he calls upon his father and his own mother (his father's second wife). The problem now facign the family is that his own mother's house will not be perpetuated, since none of the there women belonging to it have children. This could be solved if the eldest son of his first wife, who is already married, would marry another woman and place her in the hose of the second wife. Alternatively, a younger son could marry and place his wife in that house. But the mother of these sons does not get on well with her co-wives, and she refuses to accede to this suggestion, which cannot be adopted without her consent.

This case is a good illustration of the meaning behind the rites surrounding a bride and her mother-in-law.

I have dwelt on the ritual of marriage to emphasize the point that the illnesses and misfortunes believed to be caused by ancestral wrath are mainly associated with the non-fulfilment of marriage obligations. The following figures are indicative of this.

Information was collected on the married couples within one

hundred homesteads. I am interested here in sacrifice, particularly the one believed to make the woman wedded, i.e. "the ox of the skin" *(eyesikhumba,* No. 9 in Table 1). There were 258 married women. Of thse, 166 (63 per cent) had had the "ox of the skin" sacrifice, 45 (18 per cent) had only a goat slaughtered by the groom's people on arrival (to report the circumstances and a hope of having a wedding ceremony some time in the future) and 47 (19 per cent) had no sacrifice at all. Except for 5 cases in the last category, all the women had had marriage negotiations started and some marriage exchanges made. In almost all cases where there was no sacrifice or where only a goat was sacrificed, marriage negotiations had dragged on for a long time (3 to 10 years); the woman got pregnant, and on taking the baby to the groom's people for its first sacrifice *(imbeleko)* she usually stayed on and never returned home. Some women claimed that they had come only temporarily to bring the baby for an *imbeleko* sacrifice or because it was ill, that they would return home as soon as possible. It was difficult to discriminate between those who would return home and those who would remain permanently, particularly because the history of most units where no sacrifice was performed, or ultimately one of a goat, started in this way. This group consisted mainly of younger women, at most in their early thirties. They included cases such as that of case 3, as well as some in which a woman's father wanted all the *lobolo* paid before he would consider letting her get married, or in which the father had died and the heir was unwilling to shoulder the wedding expenses. Without exception, such women regarded themselves as not properly married, even in cases where the marriage had been registered at the magistrate's court.

The kind of misfortune usually suffered by women for whom son sacrifice at all had been performed to report their presence was attributed to the husband's ancestors wanting to know "who they were" by making their children ill, or else such women experience "heaviness" at night and heard voices saying: "Who are you? What do you want here?" Those who had only goats slaughtered to report their presence within the homestead tended to experience misfortunes of "no peace" in the family (i.e.

quarelling over trivial matters between spouses). Their children were also sickly. Properly wedded women suffered such misfortunes as sterility, miscarriage, or delayed conception owing to non-fulfilment either of nubility rites or gift exchange on the wedding day or anger of the woman's ancestors because *lobolo* cattle were still owing.

Associated with the ancestral anger, 11 cases of deat, 14 of illness and 19 of other misfortunes were reported.

Of the deaths, 9 were of children deprived of ancestral protection owing to non-fulfilment of marriage duties. The other 2 were due to the anger of ancestors owning to neglect of other duties (cf, case I, p. 48).

The illnesses included 3 cases of women who experienced sleeplessness at night because of "heaviness in the house" and voices whispering into their ears and asking who they were. In 7 cases children became ill, either because the ancestors wanted to know who their mothers were or because they were dissatisfied with the delay of marriage rites. The 4 other cases were attributed to non-fulfilment of duties unconnected with marriage rites; for instance, a woman kept quarrrelling with her mother-in-law, and as a result her children became ill.

The 19 miscellaneous case of misfortune included 4 of sterility, 2 of delayed conception, 2 of children being either few in number or all of the the female sex, 6 of discord between spouses, and 5 of desertion by one of the spouses.

Alghouth these figures merely reflect tendencies, I believe they justify the attention I have given in this chapter to carriage sacrifices, as they indicate the main cause of ancestral anger.

However, I must mention here that in reply to the question: "What type of action annoy the ancestors most?" *(Yiziphi izenzo ezibacasula kakhulu abaphansi?),* the answer was usually: "Quarreling within the homestead" (*umsindo ekhaya,* the noise within the home). Yet according to the case ancestral anger is most often aroused by non-fulfilment of marriage duties. If anything, lack of "peace in the home" is, in the cases reported, an indication rather than the cause, of misfortunes owing to anger of the ancestors. I believe the answer to the question above was often an abstraction based on the assumption that the marriage duties and other duties towards the ancestors should have been performed.

I want now to comment on some sociological interpretations of ancestral behaviour, more particularly the analysis suggested by J.D. McKnight.

McKnight has written an interesting paper on "Extra-Descent Group Cults in African Societies" (*Africa,* 1967, pp. 1-21). In it he questions Radcliffe-Brown's observation: "The father punishes his children, and so may the ancestors on the father's side. On the other hand, the mother is tender and indulgent to her child, and her relatives are expected to be the same, and so also the maternal spirits." (1952, p. 28) In other words, in partrilineal societies the maternal ancestors are believed to be benevolent because the maternal ancestors are believed to be benevolent because the maternal relatives, who are without jural authority, are benevolent.

McKnight, in questioning this "extension" theory, cities the LoDagaba situation as described by Goody and the Tallensi as described by Fortes. Among the LoDagaba the relationship with the mother's brother is often one of considerable conflict, yet the mother's brother's spirit is not aggressive (Goody, 1962, pp. 20, 282, 430). Fortes (1959, p. 235) writes: "But the spirites of female ancestors are believed to be specially hard, cruel and capricious. This is remarkable when we consider the love and devotion a mother shows her child throughout his life." McKnight further argues that in most patristical societies (such as the Tsonga, Bhaca and Mpondo of Southern Africa) the maternal ancestors may be regarded as a cause misfortune. He then proceeds to demonstrate that among matrilineal societies the extra-descent ancestors (i.e. the paternal ancestors) may also be a cause of illness, although they have no jural responsibility over their descendants.

He points out that the infant is both kin through blood ties to his extra descent group and also an affinal relative when he represents his descent group.

He concludes by observing that it is in the role of an affinal relationship that the extra-descent group ancestors make the infant ill. They use him to bargain for their rights in the affinal relationship, as he is the only one they can reach in his descent group. He writes:

> It is therefore not surprising that the sister's son may be used as a vehicle of revenge by the bride wealth-receiving groups to enforce their rights...If we view the power attributed to the extra-descent group ancestors as a means of enforcing rights over members of an affinally related descent group, then, to some degree, the punitive aspect of the extra-descent group ancestors becomes understandable.
>
> 1967, pp. 16-17

In support of this view, he cites Middleton who, on the Lugbhara, has this to say:

> The hostility felt by the mother's brother's group against the sister's son is directored against him not as sister's son, a relative by "blood", but as a representative of the potentially hostile affinal lineage. He is the victim merely because being connected by "blood" it is only he who is liable to be affected in this way.
>
> 1960, p.57

In Table 1 it is indicated how the bride's father has to provide a number of sacrificial animals which are intended to render the bride fertile. By these sacrifices he guarantees her fertility. Should he omit them he is likely to be responsible if his daughter does not conceive, or miscarries, or if her babies die or sicken. In such a case it is his ancestors who interfere with her fertility because the relevant rites that would enable them to promote it have not been performed.

Case 2 demonstrates this. MaDladla, whose nubility rites

(*ukwemula)* had not been performed, could not conceive, because of the "heavy presence" of the spirits of her ancestors at her affinal home. Annoyed over the omission of the nubility rites, they had accompanied her there. To correct this they had to be fetched by her father, who later invited her back home to perform her belated nubility rites. In this case the ancestors were angry with her father, their own descendant, for failing to fulfil his duties.

Reader says of the Makhanya-Zulu:

> An important part of the wedding preparations by the girl's group at this stage is the assembly of these cattle. The *ukwendisa* (giving in marriage) consist essentially of two beasts: the *inkabi yezinkomo,* an ox sometimes known as the *impandla kayise* (father's bald head), a thank-offering to the father of the boy for the *lobolo* cattle, and the *isikhumba,* a beast nominally to make the bride a skirt, but in reality having a ritual significance in joining the ancestors of the tow descent groups...The beasts bear the ancestral sanction that if they are not provided the bride will eventually fail or miscarry in childbirth...
>
> 1966, p. 194

Although Reader does no tell us which ancestors are particularly annoyed by the omission, he does confirm that the girl's father has to provide the cattle which are sacrificed to promote her reproductivity. However, the woman's ancestors can only be expected to promote her fertility if the husband's people have fulfilled their part of the marriage obligations in terms of *lobolo* and other rexchages. If such exchanges are omitted the maternal ancestors may interfere with the conception or make the baby ill as an expression of their anger against the affinal relations.

It is not only the maternal ancestors who may express their displeasure in this way. The paternal ancestors also disapprove if marriage obligations towards them or towards their descendants have not been fulfilled.

CASE 3 is a good example of ancestors beign annoyed by

nonfulfilment of the obligations by their own deswcendants towards them. Because they had not been requested to protect the womb from which the baby came, they declined to protect the baby when requested to do so, as they considered this as putting the cart before the horse,

Vilakazi gives another example of the case where paternal ancestors were angry with their affinal relations. He writes:

> A case of failure to give the requisite gifts which resulted in illness was quoted from a Goba family amonng the Qadi. The *umakoti* (bride) did nto give any *umabo* gifts to the decased grandfather of the boy. A younger "father" drew the attention of the lineage to this omisson, but he was told that since the family was Christian, they were not going to give to the dead as that would constitute worshipping ancestral spirits.
>
> A few days after marriage, however, the *umakoti* fell ill and, as she was already pregnant, miscarried. This was explained by the old people as beign due to the anger of the gods and the girl's father was asked to provide a beast to apease the ancestral spirits, which was done.
>
> 1962, pp. 68-69

This suggests that ancestral wrath over marriage obligations can be reduced to four variables:

a. When the women's ancestors are annoyed by thier own descendants.

b. When her ancestors are annoyed by her husband's people.

c. When the husband's ancestors are angry with their own descendants.

d. When his ancestors are angry with his wife's people.

To appreciate the variables let us remind ourselves that the expectation is that a man will marry during his parents' lifetime. If the proper marriage observances are not performed, the ancestors may, for instance, hold responsible the groom's father, whose duty it is to see to those obligations. The crucial point here is that such ancestors are in fact the baby's father's father's and partly its father's effective ancestors. When the baby reaches manhood and sacrifices in his own right, he will be sacrificing to his father and his father's father. This means that the ancestors who protect the baby do so on behalf of its grandfather and father, as these are the people who stand to lose if there are no progeny to sacrifice to them. Thus, if the ancestors allow the baby to become ill, they could well be treatening to cut off the progeny of its grandfather and father, as they themselves would not lose anything by that. They may well use this as pressure to get recognition and appreciation of their protection. In the case of the twins mentioned above, the diviner harped on the fact that the ancestors wanted to know who was the mother of the twins, which in fact is another way of sayng: "You cannot take us for granted and expect us to protect the womb from which the seed germinates."

The question that arises is: To what extent can the descent interpretatin hold true for maternal ancestors?

To be childless is considered a great ffliction by a married woman and her own people. She cannot form a uterine (*kwethu)* unit that constitutes an economic unit and assures her of a comfortable middle or old age when her daughter-in-law takes care of her. Child-bearing also ensures the perpetuation of her name as an ancestress of her own sons and grandsons. It is therefore in the insterest of her people that she gets children who grow up to maturity, as this would not only make her later life confortable, but in the life hereafter she would be an ancestress.

The descent principle can thus explain all four variables of ancestral anger over marrige obligations: it is in the interest of the living to satisfy the ancestors by fulfilling the marriage obligations, as this ensures that the ancestors will protect the issue of the marriage, who in turn will perpetuate the names of the living generations as ancestors.

This may seem to suggest that female children have no place in the descent scheme; since descent is from male to male, female children would not be used as a lever to exert pressure. In answer to this it must be noted that girls make it possible to "raise the house", since *lobolo* accruing from a daughter's marriage may enable an agnatic relation to marry a woman to perpetuate a descent line which has no male issue.

The expectation is that one dies in old age, leaving married sons who perform rituals that integrate the spirit with the body of ancestors and enable it to come home and operate as an ancestor or ancestress. This is the type of "heaven" in the context of ancestral cult. Any spirit which is not integrated with the others wanders about and leads a lonely and miserable life. It is in some sort of "limbo" or hell for the spirit and this is the most undersirable situation.

McKnight has also used the descent principle to explain the extradescent ancestor cult behaviour and sees it as a means of pressurising the affinal group to fulfil their obligations. This approach does not adequately explain the four variables. It cannot, for instance, be used to explain the cases where maternal ancestors among the Zulu interfere with fertility to register their disapproval of their own descendants.

We can now examine McKnight's main thesis that, contrary to Radcliffe-Brown's extension principle, maternal ancestors are not as benevolent as living maternal relations, in that such ancestors may be regarded as a cause of illness.

While the Zulu material confirms McKnight's observation that maternal ancestors sometimes do cause illnets, it does not necessarily validate the rejection of Radcliffe-Brown's assertion. Among the the Zulu, all things being equal (e.g. marriage obligations duly fulfilled), maternal ancestors would have no reason to interfere with fertility. In general, people try hard to fulfil the marriage obligations, and the expectation is that the obligations will be fulfilled, or an agreement is reached that will satisfy both groups. "Malevolent" behaviour by maternal ancestors is an exception rather than a rule. Accordingy, it may well be said that these ancestors are benevolent save in exceptional cases.

This is confirmed by Wilson's material on the Nyakyusa (1957, p.181). McKnight quotes her as saying:

> In all the cases we traced, in which a woman's ancestors were believed to have made her, or her child, ill, there was dispute between her father (or his heir) and her husband over marriage cattle or the bull of puberty; and we were told that her father's shades are angry only if marriage cattle have not been paid and for no other reason.

In pointing out that the Zulu material does not necessarily invalidate Radcliffe-Brown's theory, I do not claim that he had that material in mind when he made the statements related to maternal ancestors. For instance, he writes:

> But though, according to the statements made to me, the maternal ancestors will not punish their descendant with sickness, they can be appealed to for help. When therefore, a child is sick the parents may go to the mother's brother of the child, or to the mother's father if he is still living , and ask that a sacrifice shall be offered, and an appeal for help made to the child's maternal ancestors. This, at any rate, is stated as a practice in the Sotho tribes, and one of the purposes of the *ditsoa* cattle that go from remarriage payment to the mother's brother of the bride is said to be to make provision for such sacrifices if they should be needed.
>
> 1952, p.27

I find the last sentence somewhat confusing in that the recipient of the *ditsoa* called is the child's mother's mother's brother, not its own mother's brother..

The passage above gives the impression that Radcliffe-Brown was not aware of the fact that maternal ancestors are sometimes believed to cause illness. McKnight thus had reason to question the assertion that "the maternal ancestors will not punish their descendants with sickness". The greatest weakness of Radcliffe-Brown's extension theory is that he bases his argument on emotional sentiment—which cannot be measured. In addition, I believe, it is open to question whether in causing the illness the maternal ancestors are really malevolent against the baby. The living maternal relations are benevolent on a person-to-person basis, between mother's father and daughter's children, or between mother's brother and sister's children. In cases of any maternal ancestral anger over the marriage obligations, that anger is directed against the baby's father's father (or its father), whose responsibility it is to fulfil the marriage obligations. The relationship of dispute is between the maternal ancestors and the baby's paternal grandfather, and the dispute is whether such a grandfather is entitled to have a grandchild. I would therefore argue that the children are the center of dispute, and the question of benevolence or malevolence towards them does not arise.

There is yet another point which must be considered in an analysis of this kind. This is the importance of the time factor in the development cycle.

If all the marriage obligations have been fulfilled, the maternal ancestors are not expected to interfere with the reproductivity. This suggests that their displeasure can be related to a definite time in that they signal their displeasure during the early stages of marriage. Once whatever annoys them is put right, subsequent illness of the children would be attributed to something else.

If we take into account the time factor we can more readily understand how the relationship of the individual to the ancestors changes during the different stages of his life.

I have already mentioned how the maternal ancestors are interested in the baby as evidence of their daughter's fertility, which they had guaranteed on marriage. They extend a tacit protection over the baby even though they have no jural powers over it. As it grows into an adult its mother becomes more and more identified with her affines, and when she dies her spirit is integrated with the sprites of her affines, not with those of her own people. She becomes a "patristical" rather than a maternal ancestor in that she is identified with the patristical ancestors of there children.

I make this point here to draw attention to the possible differences in permutations of the ancestral structure in patristical societies.

For instance, the Zulu and the Tallensi are in sharp contrast with regard to maternal ancestorship. On the Tallensi, Fortes has this to say:

> Nevertheless it is a basic assumption that a wife never ceases entirely to be a "stranger" in her husband's clan. For she never, as we have learnt, loses the social identity conferred on her by birth as a member of a different clan. She does not adopt her husband's totemic taboos, and though her health and fertility, begin essential for the satisfactory performance of her wifely role, come under the guardianship of his ancestors, she does not participate in the cult of his lineage ancestors.
>
> 1949, pp. 98-99

It is important to consider notional differences in different partilineal societies when discussing maternal ancestors. In the case of the Zulu, for instance, on cannot discuss fruitfully the role of the maternal ancestors without establishing the point in time one is concerned with in particular context.

In concluding this chapter I want to point out that perhaps one of the Zulu, exogamy rules are very stringent, in that a man avoids marrying not only women of his own clan, but all who belong to his mother's clan, or to a grandmother's clan (on either side), or even a great grandmother's clan, or who have relationship with any of these clans. So the women that are married are strangers, upon whose fecundity the husband is dependent for the perpetuation of his descent group. Given the system of belief that a wife's fertility is essentially depended on the fulfilment of marriage obligations by both parties (i.e. her family and he husband's), she depends entirely on the sense of responsibility of these two groups. She may miscarry, fail to conceive, or have chronically sick children, as a result of ancestral wrath over unfulfilled marriage duties; but she is helpless, as she cannot in there own right appease the ancestors or correct what is wrong.

What is further ironical is that even when marriage duties have been duly fulfilled, her motherhood (reproductive period) makes her an outsider, hemmed in on all sides by various rules of over respect and avoidance (*ukuhlonipha*) from which she is only released by menopause. It is this logic that determines her roles as a mother and wife, a daughter and sister.

---

* Excerpted from *Body and Mind in Zulu Medicine:* An Ethnography of health and disease in Nyusma-Zulu thought and practice. 1977